INTRODUCTION TO SPECIAL EDUCATION ASSESSMENT:
PRINCIPLES AND PRACTICES

P9-DFC-698

Carol Gearheart
Bill Gearheart
University of Northern Colorado

LOVE PUBLISHING COMPANY®
Denver, Colorado 80222

Contents

Preface 1

Chapter 1
The Nature and Role of Assessment 3
    Type of Assessment 4
    Purposes of Assessment 5
    Approaches to Assessment 6
    Origins of Present-Day Assessment Practices 8
    Single-Purpose versus Ongoing, Multifaceted Assessment 10
    Factors Influencing the Nature of Assessment 11
    Who is Involved in The Assessment Process? 15

Chapter 2
Assessment-Related Concepts and Terminology 19
    Tests 19
    Measurement Scales (Preciseness of Measurement) 21
    The Normal Curve 23
    Measures of Central Tendency 24
    Measures of Variability 25
    Item Analysis 29
    Population, Sampling, Parameters 30
    Statistical Significance 30
    Correlation 31
    Grade Equivalent (GE) 32
    Validity 33
    Reliability 34
    Standard Error of Measurement 35
    Standard Error of Difference 35

Chapter 3

The Assessment Process 37
    Prereferral Intervention 38
    Steps in the Assessment Sequence 39

Chapter 4

Potential Problems in Conducting Assessment and in Using Assessment Data . 49
    Ethical Principles in Assessment 50
    Cultural Diversity and Assessment 51
    Sociocultural Factors That Influence Assessment Results 54
    Qualifications of Assessment Personnel 57
    Multidisciplinary Team Deliberations 59
    Shortcomings in Continuing Assessment 59
    Litigation Relating to Assessment 60

Introduction to Chapters 5 Through 15 61

Chapter 5

Measures of Cognitive Ability and Adaptive Behavior 63
    Cognitive Ability/Intelligence/Academic Aptitude 64
    Adaptive Behavior 75

Chapter 6

Informal Assessment 81
    Curriculum-Based Assessment 82
    Systematic (Direct) Observation 84
    Checklists 86
    Error Analysis 87
    Task Analysis 89
    Work Sample Analysis 90
    Interviews 90
    Questionnaires 91
    Inventories 91
    Modified Assessment Techniques 92
    Diagnostic Probes and Diagnostic Teaching 92

Chapter 7

Assessment in Early Childhood 95
    Assessment of the Family 97
    Instruments for Family Assessment 99
    Screening and Assessment Processes for Children 106
    Instruments for Assessment of Infants and Toddlers 108
    Instruments for the Assessment of Preschool Children 114

Chapter 8

Tests of Academic Achievement 127
Group Achievement Tests 128
Major Individually Administered Achievement Tests 130
Other Individually Administered Tests of Academic Achievement ... 133
Criterion-Referenced Achievement Tests 135

Chapter 9

Reading Assessment Instruments 137
The Focus of Reading Assessment 137
Standardized, Criterion-Referenced, and Informal Reading Inventories . 138

Chapter 10

Mathematics Assessment Instruments 149
Concepts in Mathematics 150
Instruments Used in Mathematics and Computational Assessment .. 151

Chapter 11

Oral and Written Language Assessment Instruments 159
Components of Language and Communication 159
Language Assessment Instruments 161

Chapter 12

Assessment of Behavior Problems 177
Informal Observation 178
Instruments for Assessing Behavior 179

Chapter 13

Assessment of Sensory Abilities, Perceptual Abilities, and Motor Skills 195
Assessment of Auditory Abilities 196
Assessment of Visual Abilities 196
Assessment of Perception and Perceptual-Motor Skills 198
Perceptual-Motor Tests 198
Motor Tests 203

Chapter 14

Career, Vocational, and Transition-Related Assessment 205
Measures of Vocational Aptitude 206
Interest Inventories 208
Social and Daily Living Skills 211
Work Samples 213
Informal (Self-Developed) Work Sample Assessment 215

Chapter 15

Special Areas of Concern in Assessment 219
   Assessment Relating to Giftedness, Talent, and Creativity 219
   Tests of Creativity 221
   Computer Applications in Assessment 224
   Assessment Relating to Transition from Special to Regular Classes .. 225
   Other Assessment Instruments 225
   Assessment of the "Difficult" Child 228
   Assesment Reports 229

References 233

Appendix A: Rules and Regulations Regarding Least Restrictive Environment,
Public Law 94-142 255
   General 255
   Continuum of alternative placements 256
   Placements 256

   Appendix B: Test Publishers in This Text 257

   Test Index 261

   Subject Index 267

Preface

This text is about assessment principles and practices; it also is about assessment instruments and techniques. It was written primarily for teachers, or students in teacher-education programs. Most individual assessment is initiated as a result of apparent educational, developmental, or social problems; therefore, most assessment instruments and techniques focus on ability to learn, achievement (what has already been learned), specific learning problems, areas of giftedness or creativity, social/behavioral adjustment, interests, or specific skill areas such as motor skills. In most cases, assessment of a given student involves assessment in more than one of these areas.

We have not attempted to duplicate comprehensive assessment reference works. Rather, we have described assessment instruments and techniques that are representative of the various assessment arenas (e.g., achievement, aptitude, behavior), and some that have unusual significance because of the manner in which they illustrate a particular type of assessment. *The practitioner must carefully consider the reasons for administering a test and analyze available tests to determine which one(s) provide valid and reliable measures.*

Although the content of the total text is important to understanding assessment principles and practices, our chapters on Preschool and Early Childhood, Informal Assessment, and Career, Vocational, and Transition Assessment may be of particular interest. These areas often are underrepresented in assessment texts and deserve special attention. We hope our efforts have resulted in an understandable description of the assessment tools and techniques that may be used to gain more information about students so that educators may more effectively plan to maximize their educational success.

Carol J. Gearheart
Bill R. Gearheart

1

The Nature and Role
of Assessment

"Assessment" has different meanings to different individuals and to different professional groups. A parent might first think of formal testing; educators know that much more than formal testing is involved. Some may think of a one-time process; others may acknowledge the critical need for ongoing assessment. Educators who work with young children may focus on assessment of readiness or development of basic skills; secondary-level educators may be more interested in what has been learned through the use of basic skills. Early childhood educators may be more concerned with the assessment of social interactions, motor skills, or the quality of the home environment and child-parent interactions. Educators of the mentally retarded may have great concern with the development of adaptive behavior.

Whatever the orientation of those involved, assessment often is initiated to determine whether some specific student is eligible for special educational services (classification) and which educational techniques and approaches are most appropriate (intervention). It also may be used to (for example) determine the special needs of gifted or creative students, to assist in secondary school level vocational planning with nonhandicapped students, to determine which mathematics program is most appropriate for some student who is neither gifted nor handicapped, and for other similar purposes. With varying understandings and interpretations of assessment, a working definition of assessment, as conceptualized in this book, must be provided. That definition is:

Assessment is a process that involves the systematic collection and interpretation of a wide variety of information on which to base instructional/intervention decisions

3

and, when appropriate, classification or placement decisions. Assessment is primarily a problem-solving process.

Much of the information in this book relates more directly to assessment of students who are under consideration for special education services, or who are receiving such services. But some of the tests, and many of the other, informal strategies discussed apply to many other students. The principles of information gathering and objective problem solving that are essential to effective assessment have value in application to any student.

Types of Assessment

Assessment is commonly classified according to two broad types: *formal* (tests, procedures, strategies) and *informal*. In discussions of assessment, formal procedures and strategies, especially standardized tests, traditionally receive the most attention, but in most situations informal strategies also must be included to acquire all relevant information. Both are essential in the broad spectrum of assessment that takes place in schools. For any individual student, however, emphasizing one or the other may be appropriate.

Formal assessment involves the use of individual assessment instruments such as tests of intellectual ability (learning aptitude), achievement tests, measures of specific abilities (motor abilities, auditory discrimination, discrimination of color, adaptive behavior, various language abilities, and others), and behavior or social adjustment. Informal assessment includes procedures or techniques such as systematic observation, work sample analysis, task analysis, error analysis, inventories, diagnostic teaching, checklists, interviews, questionnaires, analysis of records, and others.

These are *tools* that may be used in a process—not the process itself. Further, assessment is not justifiable unless it has some specific purpose(s). No matter how comprehensive, assessment cannot always solve a problem or answer a question, but it can become part of an eventual solution, or answer to a question.

A somewhat different way of viewing assessment (Campione, 1989; Feuerstein, 1979, 1980) is based on classifications of static and dynamic assessment. In this system *static assessment* is product-based assessment (traditional assessment), in which the emphasis is on what the student can do, what he or she knows, or what he or she can produce, not how the student develops the product. *Dynamic assessment* is a term sometimes used to characterize assessment approaches that also have been called mediated assessment, learning potential assessment, or some similar terminology. Here the emphasis is on "evaluating the psychological processes involved in learning and change" (Campione, 1989, p. 157).

4

Whatever the system for classification of types of assessment, the focus in this text is assessment *as it relates to an individual student,* whether it be for instructional or for classification purposes. Another level of assessment in the schools relates to decisions regarding curriculum content in general. For example, large groups of students may be tested to determine how well they are performing in the major academic areas; reading, mathematics, social studies, and so forth. Based on the results of such testing, the mathematics or social studies curriculum may be modified and teachers may be formally admonished to teach more effectively. Such general, large-group testing is formal testing, and although the results of such testing may be of interest when planning for some individual student, it will not be addressed in any detail in this text.

Purposes of Assessment

The purpose of assessment is to gain additional information, which in most cases will be used in some type of decision making. But beyond this general purpose, there are certain identifiable classifications of purpose. *Placement-related assessment* is the focus of much of the testing, data gathering, and other related activities that are so much a part of special education. The questions are many, but include:

- Should the student receive special services or be placed in a special program?
- For which services or programs is the student eligible, under existing state regulations?
- If eligible, which services and programs will be of greatest benefit?

A wide variety of relevant tests and assessment techniques should be used in placement-related evaluation.

Readiness-related assessment is utilized to determine whether a student is ready to move into a new unit or a new area of study. Either standardized or teacher-made tests may be effective in this type of assessment.

Diagnostic assessment is well known to most educators. Its purpose is to provide information about strengths and weaknesses in some given subject or skill area and to offer guidance on what to do next. Diagnostic assessment may involve the use of published diagnostic tests, or a variety of informal assessment procedures (outlined in chapter 6).

Formative assessment is ongoing assessment intended to provide information to both the teacher and the student regarding progress and immediate needs. Teachers use a variety of types of formative assessment to evaluate smaller segments of the curriculum than are typically measured by tests used at the end of the semester or at the conclusion of a major unit. Formative assessment may include diagnostic components or implications, but *the major focus is what students know,* or what skills they have—not why they do not know or where their skill development is deficient. Formative tests might be tests provided by textbook publishers, system-wide tests developed by committees of teachers and curriculum consultants, or various informal assessment techniques or measures developed by the individual teacher.

Summative assessment typically takes place at the end of a major instructional unit, at the end of a semester, or at the end of the school year. Norm-referenced achievement tests are most commonly used for this purpose, although other tests might be employed, depending on the type of achievement or skills targeted and local motivation or practice.

The same test may be used for more than one of the foregoing purposes. Also, a test initially given for one purpose may have implications for other purposes. This multiple-use possibility, however, entails caution so as to avoid over-projecting meaning with respect to any given test or assessment technique.

Approaches to Assessment

Some authors advocate various alternatives to the more traditional formal versus informal classification of assessment. For example, Witt, Elliott, Gresham, and Kramer (1988) outline four general approaches to assessment: norm-referenced, criterion-referenced, ecological, and informal. We will consider norm-referenced and criterion-referenced through a direct comparison of these two approaches. Ecological approaches will comprise a separate topic. Because informal approaches will be considered in more detail in chapter 6, they will not be discussed further here.

The concept of "approaches" of assessment, as different from "types" of assessment, may be illustrated by the following statement about ecological assessment by Witt et al.:

> Ecological assessment is not a category of tests or even a theory of assessment. Instead it is more of a viewpoint of assessment. Virtually any type of criterion-referenced, norm-referenced, or informal test could be used in an ecological approach. (p.53)

Norm-referenced assessment involves the use of tests in which a large representative sample of the general population has been tested and becomes the "norm group." Many norm-referenced tests have been studied extensively with respect to application for predictive purposes, and results from these studies represent "known quantities"—especially if individuals being assessed are from populations similar to those in the representative sample. Norm-referenced tests provide comparisons that may lead to information such as grade equivalents, mental age estimates, and so on. The results of norm-referenced tests are more likely to be of value in research and in determining eligibility for special education services. They were the first products of the modern testing/assessment movement to receive significant recognition from scientists in other disciplines.

Criterion-referenced assessment involves measurements that lead to information regarding whether a given student has mastered specific objectives under consideration. Though comparisons with other students might be drawn, this is not the purpose of criterion-referenced measurement. Criterion-referenced assessment should lead to information such as which skills should be taught next. Thus, it may be described as *instructional program-based*. Table 1.1 provides a further comparison of the advantages and disadvantages of norm-referenced and criterion-referenced tests.

Ecological assessment, as indicated previously, represents a viewpoint on assessment. Its focus is the student's total environment at school. (In some instances, this environmental perspective is expanded to include home and neighborhood environment.) It is a process of analyzing interrelationships between the student and other students, the student and his or her teacher(s), social mores, parent expectations, room temperature and furniture arrangement, noise level, what is (or may be) happening that may be seen through the windows, and other, similar environmental variables.

Teachers who espouse this concept must carefully reassess their own expectations, how they respond to student behaviors, alternative instructional techniques, and other, similar teacher practices. This point of view assumes that the problem under consideration more likely relates to interactions between the environment and the student than to a problem within the student.

Ecological assessment has many advantages, including the likelihood that teachers will become more sensitive to environmental factors as they influence the academic and personal behavior of *all* students, not just the one(s) under direct consideration. It reduces the likelihood that teachers will try to "diagnose" a student's problem based on the results of one or two standardized tests.

But ecological assessment has certain, definite disadvantages. First, it is complex and may be highly subjective. One reason for using standardized tests is that teachers' subjective evaluations may be influenced by affective considerations, resulting in serious misjudgments that may be made and acted upon to the student's detriment. Second, few teachers have been trained to do ecological assessment, so there is some uncertainty as to how such training should be accomplished.

Ecological assessment appears to be most often advocated for use in data gathering and planning interventions for students with behavioral problems. Nevertheless, its potential as a general assessment approach certainly is not

7

Table 1.1

Comparison of Norm-Referenced and Criterion-Referenced Tests

	Norm-Referenced Tests	Criterion-Referenced Tests
ADVANTAGES	• Are valuable for verification of legal eligibility for special education services. • May help determine if a student is achieving up to expectations. • Provide a comparison of achievement gains to gains of other students. • Provide for program comparisons, on a "national" basis.	• Are valuable to verify specific skills; provide direct guidance for instruction. • Analysis of test items indicates where individual pupil program is effective or ineffective. • Provide a vehicle for more meaningful communication and accountability. • Are especially appropriate for determining program progress of handicapped children.
DISADVANTAGES	• Results are often too general to provide specific instructional guidance. • Are directly "keyed" to instructional sequence of program. • Cannot modify to relate to learner's background. • Are of minimal value in indicating *how much* very low or very high achieving students learned.	• May be difficult to establish suitable criterion. • Many teachers are not well informed about how to construct. • Are of little value in identification of atypical children. • Are ineffective for measuring level of achievement or achievement gains as compared to other children.

---

limited to this arena. As a "viewpoint" on assessment, it can overlap and be used effectively in conjunction with other assessment approaches.

Origins of Present-Day Assessment Practices

Assessment practices are an outgrowth of a variety of efforts commencing in the mid-19th century. Earlier efforts to better understand, and provide some type of training for, persons with mental retardation led to establishment of formal efforts by pioneers such as *Wilhelm Wundt*. In 1879 Wundt and his coworkers established a research laboratory in Leipzig, attempting to formulate theories or "laws" of learning that would better explain the behavior of the human species. Thus was born the field of experimental psychology.

At about the same time *Sir Francis Galton,* an English biologist, stimulated a parallel thread of interest through his efforts related to human heredity. And just a few years later *James Cattell,* an American who studied at Leipzig, became highly involved with the measurement of individual differences, stimulated by his contacts with both Wundt and Galton. Cattell subsequently had a great deal of influence on the establishment of experimental psychology research laboratories in the United States.

Cattell appears to have been the first to formally use the term "mental test," and, along with others, he worked to develop this concept during the last decade of the 19th century. In addition to being skilled experimental psychologists, he and his coworkers recognized the potential practical applications of "mental testing" in the schools and in industry. They worked on a wide variety of projects, but their major concern seemed to be that of discovering a way to measure general intelligence.

One of the problems with the early attempts to assess general intelligence stemmed from a number of preconceived notions about correlates of intelligence. The reasoning was that some type of summation of performance on these tasks might provide a measure of intelligence if relative weighting for each characteristic could be determined. After a wide variety of attempts to pursue this avenue, in the U.S. and in various parts of Europe, the final conclusion was that the "sum of the scores of positive characteristics" approach was of little value. As a result, the results of much of the work accomplished thus far were abandoned.

In 1904 educational authorities in Paris, attempting to sort out children for whom the existing educational programs were of little value, appointed a commission to accomplish this task. What they wanted was a quantitative way to measure intelligence, a yardstick to apply to children so as to predict success or failure in advance, and to save time and money. A French psychologist, *Alfred Binet,* was among members appointed to this commission. Fortunately, he was well aware of earlier, unsuccessful efforts to measure intelligence. He based his efforts on the premise that intellectual ability was a complex characteristic rather than a simple mathematical summation of discrete traits.

With support provided by Parisian educational authorities and with the help of a coworker, *Theophile Simon,* he published the first test of intelligence that effectively tapped intellectual ability. The Binet-Simon scale won rapid acceptance in most of the Western nations and was the forerunner of modern tests. In the United States, *Lewis Terman* developed an American version of the Binet test, called the Stanford-Binet—a test that still is widely used. (The Stanford-Binet is discussed in chapter 5.)

Since the 1920s, the testing movement has grown by leaps and bounds.

Though earlier efforts often were directed toward individual testing, group tests soon became a great commercial success because of cost factors and because testing was soon to be prescribed for all students in the schools and for large groups of individuals in industry. Tests have been used to predict who will succeed at various specialized tasks, who should enter college, or some specialized educational arena such as law school or the armed forces. They have been used to determine aptitudes, to ascertain whether an individual was responsible for his or her actions after (admittedly) killing another person, and whether students in the fourth grade are up to national standards in some academic area.

Thus we might say that tests have been used to predict, to project, or to estimate qualities, aptitudes, or abilities. They have been used to evaluate teaching approaches, to compare the effectiveness of various curriculum sequences, and for other, similar purposes. They *have* been used in these various ways, but serious questions arise as to whether they have always been valid in all of these usages.

More recently, some sociologists, educators, civil rights advocates, and others have questioned whether standardized tests should be used at all—especially with some populations. Judicial orders following litigation have forced drastic changes in the use of tests and other assessment procedures in certain situations. Informal measures have replaced formal, standardized measures for some purposes, but they too may be misused or overused. These and other potential problems inherent in the assessment process will be discussed further in chapter 4.

Today there is a wider variety of standardized tests, more valid and reliable tests, and more knowledgeable assessment personnel than at any time in the history of the testing/assessment movement. But there is also more awareness of, and information about, the potential misuse of tests. The continuing challenge is to use tests and other assessment instruments and techniques appropriately, protecting the interests and rights of all involved.

Single-Purpose versus Ongoing, Multifaceted Assessment

At times single-purpose assessment is called for, but this is the exception to the rule. More often assessment is ongoing and involves many facets. For example, perhaps a child may seem to have visual problems, leading to a referral to assess both far-distance and near-point vision (normal reading distance). In addition, color discrimination, depth perception, and other abilities related to visual acuity may be tested. If another problem is discovered, referral to an eye specialist may end the matter. In most cases, however, certain educational problems will have triggered the original concern—in which case follow-up assessment will be done to determine where visual corrections, once made, are helping educationally. The very nature of the educational process, and the concerns that lead to the perceived need for assessment, dictate that someone should follow up to determine if remedial/corrective procedures are having the desired effect.

Much of the assessment that will take place in relation to special educational services consists of (a) initial assessment, to determine eligibility for special program provisions; (b) additional assessment to assist in developing an individualized education program (IEP) and in making meaningful program placement decisions; (c) regular, ongoing assessment to monitor program effectiveness and provide a basis for program modifications, if needed; and (d) assessment required by IEP review regulations, to determine whether the program is meeting the student's needs, and whether continued special education services are warranted. This sequence and the types of assessment that may be required are outlined in Table 1.2.

Certain single-purpose testing may take place with relation to very specific goals. Such assessment may relate to areas such as interest inventories, high school graduation/competency tests, tests related to college entry, or specific skill tests in areas such as manual dexterity, speed with work processing equipment, and the like. These are important for these specific purposes, and in such cases single-purpose assessment is appropriate.

Factors Influencing the Nature of Assessment

A variety of factors influence the nature of assessment in any given educational setting. Assessment practices in, say, New York and Texas have many similarities, but certain differences also prevail. The same could be said about assessment practices in New York City and a small community in upstate New York, or Dallas and a community in rural Texas. What are the major determinants of these similarities and differences? Factors that are most likely to determine local assessment practices are summarized in Figure 1.1.

Perhaps the greatest single force encouraging more similarity in assessment practices has been the Education for All Handicapped Children Act (PL 94-142) regulations relating to evaluation and placement in programs for students with handicapping conditions. Though these regulations do not dictate the nature of all assessment in the schools, they regulate such a major part of such assessment that in effect they regulate most individual assessment. These regulations were, at least in part, a result of various litigation regarding assessment and placement in programs for the handicapped. The influence of court rulings plus federal regulations and guidelines have led the various state governments to a considerable degree of similarity in assessment practices. Because

---

Table 1.2
Assessment in Special Education

Initial Assessment

Purposes
- To identify, clarify
- To determine eligibility for program placement

Formal measures; standardized tests
- Intelligence measures
- Visual acuity
- Auditory acuity
- Emotional status or stability
- Achievement tests
- Language development or abilities
- Diagnostic tests
- Visual discrimination
- Auditory discrimination
- Motor abilities

Informal measures, histories
- Developmental history
- Educational history
- Criterion-referenced measures
- Rating scales
- Checklists
- Work sample analyses
- Diagnostic teaching
- Interviews
- Records of direct, systematic observation
- Sociocultural data
- Information from other community agencies
- Health history/status

Physical examination

Program Entry Assessment

Purposes
- To assist in developing IEP
- To assist in program placement decisions

All of the initial assessment information will be reviewed.

(continued)

(continued)

In some instances, additional information may be required to develop the IEP.
In most cases curriculum-based assessment (CBA) will assist in answering the
questions of what to teach, how to teach it, or where to provide instruction.

Regular, Ongoing Assessment

Purposes
- To monitor program effectiveness
- To provide basis for program modifications

Most of this assessment will be informal, conducted by the teacher. For some
special purposes the teacher may call in outside specialists.

IEP Review-Related Assessment

Purposes
- To determine where program is "on target"
- To suggest possible program modifications
- To determine whether student requires continued special
  education services

This assessment could include any of the assessment procedures outlined
previously and will focus on improvement/growth in areas specifically mentioned
in the IEP.

Adapted from B. Gearheart & C. Gearheart, (1989), *Learning Disabilities: Educational Strategies* (5th ed.),
Columbus: OH: Charles E Merrill. Used by permission.

of their impact on assessment practices, these regulations are included here.

In addition to the Regulations for PL 94-142, other factors influencing the
manner in which assessment is carried out in any local school district are
indicated in Figure 1.1. These account for the majority of similarities and
differences found throughout the United States. As noted in the figure, factors/
influences outlined on the left side tend to lead to similarities; those on the
right more often lead to differences.

Federal government guidelines, including those provided through PL 94-
142, lead to similarities in assessment practices. A less obvious federal influence
is that resulting from approval of state plans (related to receiving federal
funding for programs for the handicapped) and through grants to universities,
which provide an indirect influence on the training of future special educators.

A second major influence on assessment practices is that of court decisions
resulting from litigation directed against various public school educational

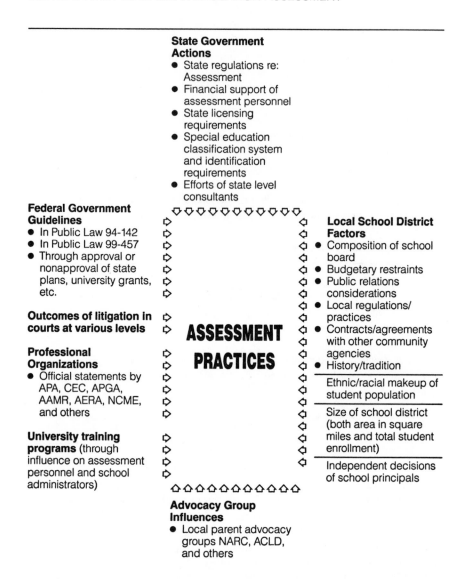

State Government Actions
- State regulations re: Assessment
- Financial support of assessment personnel
- State licensing requirements
- Special education classification system and identification requirements
- Efforts of state level consultants

Federal Government Guidelines
- In Public Law 94-142
- In Public Law 99-457
- Through approval or nonapproval of state plans, university grants, etc.

Outcomes of litigation in courts at various levels

Professional Organizations
- Official statements by APA, CEC, APGA, AAMR, AERA, NCME, and others

University training programs (through influence on assessment personnel and school administrators)

ASSESSMENT PRACTICES

Local School District Factors
- Composition of school board
- Budgetary restraints
- Public relations considerations
- Local regulations/practices
- Contracts/agreements with other community agencies
- History/tradition

Ethnic/racial makeup of student population

Size of school district (both area in square miles and total student enrollment)

Independent decisions of school principals

Advocacy Group Influences
- Local parent advocacy groups NARC, ACLD, and others

Note. The factors indicated above operate to provide both a degree of similarity in national assessment practices and also differences in practices. In general, factors outlined on the left side of the chart dictate similarities; those on the right may lead to differences.

Figure 1.1
Factors Influencing Assessment Practices

programs and practices. Such litigation had a major influence on the passage of PL 94-142 and has continuing influence through ongoing litigation. This influence promotes similarity in practices.

Two additional influences, which are related, are those of statements and actions of various professional organizations (such as the Council for Exceptional Children, the American Psychological Association, the American Association on Mental Deficiency, and others) and university training programs. Professional organizations influence university training programs, and training programs influence assessment personnel, school administrators, and special education teachers. These influences promote similar assessment practices.

Actions of legislatures and government officials in the various states promote both similarities and differences. Many of the similarities promoted by state level actions are direct results of federal actions and the states' attempts at compliance. Differences are promoted as a result of variables such as state-promulgated assessment standards, licensing requirements for assessment personnel, and requirements for eligibility for financial reimbursement for special education programs or personnel.

Advocacy groups (primarily parent groups) have some direct influence on assessment practices. Their greater influence, however, may be through their continued contact with state and federal educational agencies or through the support of litigation.

A number of factors shown on the right side of the figure may lead to *differences* in assessment practices. These include local history/tradition, the educational/socioeconomic level of the community and the school board, or the ethnic/racial makeup of the student population. In addition, size of the district, budget considerations, availability of services through other community agencies, and, of course, local interpretations of state regulations, as evidenced by local regulations and practices, may lead to differences.

Finally, decisions at the local school level by the building principal may lead to differences. Although state and local regulations apparently may be clear and unambiguous, experience indicates that two different school principals in the same school district may interpret them quite differently.

Who is Involved in The Assessment Process?

Assessment, once thought to be the province of a limited number of highly specialized personnel, is now recognized as the responsibility of all who have direct contact with the student, in addition to those who may be asked for assistance related to their special training and qualifications. Who orchestrates and coordinates the assessment process depends on the purposes of assessment and guidelines established by state or federal regulations. If the purpose of

15

PL 94-142 Regulations Regarding Evaluation and Placement

(With respect to evaluation procedures, the Rules and Regulations for Implementation of PL 94-142 state:)

State and local educational agencies shall insure, at a minimum, that

(a) Tests and other evaluation materials:

  (1) Are provided and administered in the child's native language or other mode of communication, unless it is clearly not feasible to do so;

  (2) Have been validated for the specific purpose for which they are used; and

  (3) Are administered by trained personnel in conformance with the instructions provided by their producer.

(b) Tests and other evaluation materials include those tailored to assess specific areas of educational need and not merely those which are designed to provide a single general intelligence quotient.

(c) Tests are selected and administered so as best to ensure that when a test is administered to a child with impaired sensory, manual, or speaking skills, the test results accurately reflect the child's aptitude or achievement level or whatever other factors the test purports to measure, rather than reflecting the child's impaired sensory, manual, or speaking skills (except where those skills are the factors which the test purports to measure).

(d) No single procedure is used as the sole criterion for determining an appropriate educational program for a child; and

(e) The evaluation is made by a multidisciplinary team or group of persons, including at least one teacher or other specialist with knowledge in the area of suspected disability.

(f) The child is assessed in all areas related to the suspected disability, including where appropriate, health, vision, hearing, social and emotional status,

(continued)

---

assessment is to establish eligibility for special education programming and is carried out in the schools, regulations provided by the various states will be the determining factor.

On the other hand, some assessment in infancy and very early childhood is carried out primarily by the physician and related medical staff members, following their own guidelines. Assessment related to evaluation of the results of educational programming may be carried out primarily by the teacher. Other assessment may be accomplished jointly by the teacher and the school counselor. Vision screening and some individual vision testing may be done by the school nurse. Still other specialized assessment may be carried out by

(continued)

general intelligence, academic performance, communicative status, and motor abilities. . . .

Comment. Children who have a speech impairment as their primary handicap may not need a complete battery of assessments (eg., psychological, physical, or adaptive behavior). However, a qualified speech-language pathologist would (1) evaluate each speech impaired child using procedures that are appropriate for the diagnosis and appraisal of speech and language disorders, and (2) where necessary, make referrals for additional assessments needed to make an appropriate placement decision. *(Federal Register,* 1977, pp. 42496-42497)

(With respect to placement procedures, PL 94-142 states:)

(a) In interpreting evaluation data and in making placement decisions, each public agency shall:

   (1) Draw upon information from a variety of sources, including aptitude and achievement tests, teacher recommendations, physical condition, social or cultural background, and adaptive behavior;

   (2) Insure that information obtained from all of these sources is documented and carefully considered;

   (3) Insure that the placement decision is made by a group of persons, including persons knowledgeable about the child, the meaning of the evaluation data, and the placement options; and

   (4) Insure that the placement decision is made in conformity with the least restrictive environment rules.

(b) If a determination is made that a child is handicapped and needs special education and related services, an individualized education program must be developed for the child.

From *(Federal Register,* 1977, p42497.)

the rehabilitation counselor or by testing personnel from some private company. In some states, certain assessment related to personality/psychological problems must be done by a psychiatrist. The same testing may be done by a clinical psychologist in other states, and in still others it may be done by a school psychologist.

We may summarize, then, by indicating that who is involved in the assessment process depends on:

1. Federal regulations.
2. The state in which assessment takes place.
3. The purpose of the assessment.

4. The nature of the assessment (tests used and other types of information to be gathered).
5. The age of the subject.
6. To some extent, geographical considerations that dictate availability of certain specialized assessment personnel.

We also may generalize that assessment is recognized as a team effort, and community resource persons in addition to school personnel are widely involved. Further, parents are involved, both through providing permission for the assessment to take place and through their direct, invited input—prior to any group meeting to weigh and evaluate all available data, and during such a meeting.

If persons involved in the assessment process include those who refer for possible assessment, we must recognize that at times students may refer some other student or refer themselves because they believe they need help. If it is to be an effective information-gathering and problem-solving process, assessment must gather information from all sources that might be able to provide information of value to the process.

Assessment-Related Concepts
and Terminology

Certain concepts and terminology are basic to an understanding of the assessment process. Some describe tests, and most are statistical in nature, because statistics form the foundation of the measurement process involved in tests. We will begin this consideration of assessment-related concepts and terminology with a discussion of tests.

Tests

Some confusion exists regarding use of the word "tests." However, in its Standards for Educational and Psychological Testing, a joint committee established by the American Educational Research Association, the American Psychological Association, and the National Council on Measurement in Education (1985) provided the following guidance.

> The term "test" usually refers to measures of either the constructed performance or structured behavior sample type, in which test takers are expected or instructed to try their best. Instruments for identifying interests and personality characteristics through self-report are typically and properly entitled "inventories," "questionnaires," or "checklists" rather than tests. (p.4)

In their formal statement of standards, writers from these three prestigious groups often refer to such self-report instruments as tests, "to simplify language" (1985, p. 4), and we will follow the same approach.

Anastasi (1982) provided a rather simple definition of a psychological test. She indicated that it is "essentially an objective and standardized measure of a sample of behavior" (p. 22). In her further discussion of the nature and use of psychological tests, Anastasi made two critically important points:

1. A psychological test can do no more than measure behavior.
2. Whether such behavior can predict other behavior must be determined through empirical tryout.

Standardization of any test involves a number of factors, all critically important to its potential value. It must be administered to a large group of individuals who are representative of the type of persons for whom the test is being developed. It must be administered in precisely the same way to each of these individuals. Then norms (normal or average performance) must be determined to establish a yardstick for future reference. After this has been done, the same test can be administered to other individuals, and their position or standing with respect to the standardization sample can be designated. Other questions, such as *reliability* (Is it consistent?) and *validity* (Does it measure what it was designed to measure?), also must be addressed. (These concepts are discussed later in the chapter.)

The difference between psychological tests and educational tests is subject to different interpretations. Some would suggest that a psychological test is administered individually, by a trained test-giver (e.g., psychologist, psychometrist, counselor). In contrast, an educational test might be administered to individuals or groups to measure educational achievement or to predict future achievement. This distinction, however, is not really clear-cut and may be further confused by the existence of tests called "psychoeducational batteries." Further potential confusion is generated by the fact that the Standards for Educational and Psychological Testing publication mentioned earlier, seems to indicate some differences between educational and psychological testing, but does not clarify such differences.

Perhaps we may only conclude that these terms will be used differently by individuals from different disciplines and, in many cases, by individuals from the same discipline. A majority of standardized tests utilized in the field of education might possibly be called psychological tests. In common practice, however, those whose primary function is to provide information about academic achievement may more often be called educational tests.

Some assessment techniques psychologists use are mislabeled psychological tests. Prominent among them are projective procedures such as the Rorschach inkblot technique. These will be discussed briefly in a later chapter. Suffice it to say that, because of minimal standardization and a very unstructured format, such techniques and procedures are not properly called "tests."

Criterion-Referenced Tests; Norm-Referenced Tests

Tests are often referred to as *criterion-referenced* or *norm-referenced*. This important distinction was addressed in chapter 1.

Measurement Scales (Preciseness of Measurement)

Assessment usually involves some type of measurement. In education, measurement usually means some type of statistical treatment. Purposes of measurement vary, but in general we may categorize it into a four-level hierarchy according to the degree of preciseness of measurement. These four scales, from the lowest (simplest) level to the highest are nominal, ordinal, interval, and ratio scales. Many authorities suggest that the use of interval or ratio scales is much to be preferred when they can be used appropriately. A brief description of these four scales should reveal why interval or ratio scales are preferred, and also why this sometimes is not possible, given the data and purposes of evaluation.

Nominal Scales

This is the lowest, simplest level of measurement. Some statisticians even question whether it is measurement at all. This level is used to classify or identify. For example, students may be classified as male and female, leading to the information that a given class has 13 males and 15 females. *Nominal scales use names rather than numbers,* and there is no inherent relationship (e.g., no rank order, no relative value) between the names. Another example might be that of classifying members of a football team as offensive or defensive linemen, or members of the starting team or reserves. In this case, a given individual might have two different classifications. Nominal scales provide a way to report data, and for some purposes this kind of classification is meaningful.

Ordinal Scales

Ordinal scales are "ranking" scales. They are used to evaluate according to some characteristic that cannot be measured in a manner that indicates the exact amount of difference between those ranked number 1, number 2, number 3, and so on. There may be considerable differences between the amount or degree of the characteristic observed—for example, between number 1 and number 2, or between number 7 and number 8.

Ordinal measurement may be useful when evaluating students with respect to things such as cooperativeness, class participation, and other, similar characteristics. Meaningful statistical procedures are available for use with ordinal (ranking) scale measurement, but, unfortunately, too often we find that interval scale or ratio scale statistics are applied to ordinal scale data. The result may be inaccurate conclusions, and those misusing such statistics may never realize their error.

Interval Scales

The third level of measurement is the interval scale. It requires equal intervals, or distances, between each number and the next higher or lower number, but no known zero point. Most tests used in education involve measurements at this level. For example, two boys, Tom and Jimmy, may score 30 and 60 (30 questions right and 60 questions right), respectively, on a given test. We *can* say that one boy got 30 more questions right than the other boy, but *we cannot say the person knows twice as much about the subject or the content area allegedly measured by the test.* Why? There is no known zero point; that is, if one of the boys had missed *all* the questions, this would not necessarily mean that he knew nothing about the subject. It would mean only that he could not answer the questions the teacher or test-maker elected to ask.

Looking at the preceding example in another way, the test-maker possibly could have asked an additional 30 very simple questions that both boys would have gotten right. Then the scores would have been 60 and 90, and with the same amount of knowledge of the subject under consideration, one boy would appear (inaccurately) to know 50% more than the other, rather than twice as much as the other (also inaccurate).

In terms of statistical procedures permissible for use with interval data, one cannot presume, as in the above example, to interpret scores as being some multiple of each other. Rather, by assuming that each question is of equal value,[1] such scores can be added and subtracted and an average derived. The mathematical manipulations relating to the conversion of raw scores to any of several types of derived scores depend on the assumption of interval level data. Thus, most teachers learn to think of statistical procedures that depend on the existence of measurement at the interval level—or higher. Serious difficulties may arise if educators use interpretations based on an assumption of interval data when the measurements are actually ordinal or nominal in nature.

---

[1]The assumption that one question is of equal value to any other is debatable, but this is generally accepted practice in psychological and educational measurement.

Ratio Scales

The highest level of measurement is the ratio scale. Ratio scale measurement is like interval scale measurement, but in addition the ratio scale has a true zero point. In measuring weight, length, or reaction time, there is an absolute zero; thus, these are ratio scales. This level of measurement permits the use of addition, subtraction, multiplication, and division, but quite often the purposes of analysis of ratio-level data suggest use of the same statistical procedures used at one of the lower levels.

A word of caution should be interjected here—following a description that might seem to rather specifically divide measurement into four discrete categories. In practice, to determine with certainty into which of these levels a certain set of measurements fits is sometimes difficult. This is particularly true regarding interval versus ordinal scales. Therefore, if in doubt, the higher level often is assumed, and the results checked against subjective reasonability. If results do *not* lead to reasonable conclusions, the lower level is used. Controversy about whether certain data represent interval or ratio data is not so often a problem in education because, for most purposes, assuming interval data is quite sufficient for required or desired analysis.

If we remember that using all of the mathematical operations with all data that may be available for any given student is not legitimate, some misinterpretations may be avoided. IQs, percentile ranks, grade equivalents, and measurements of height and weight, although all indicated as numerical values in a pupil folder, must be treated as different kinds of numbers.

The Normal Curve

The *normal curve* is a theoretical representation of the manner in which an infinite number of scores will vary by chance. It is sometimes called the *bell-shaped curve*; and it has been found, in psychology and education, that repeated sets of measurement *with a normal population* often closely approach this curve. The normal curve, illustrated in Figure 2.1, is closely related to the *standard deviation* (SD) (discussed next), but the theoretical considerations involved are quite advanced. Practical use of the normal curve relates to the approximate number of scores that might be expected within each standard deviation from the mean.

In most cases, for a distribution of measurements to be similar to the theoretical normal curve, we must have a normal (not atypical) population and a large number of subjects or a large number of measurements on a smaller number of subjects. The normal curve, and the theoretical construct it represents, is important in developing standardized tests and in interpreting

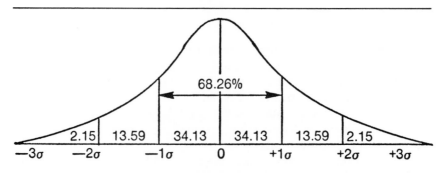

Figure 2.1
Percent of Cases Falling Between Standard Deviations In the Normal Curve

certain types of test data, but it may have limited application in everyday use for most teachers.

Measures of Central Tendency

Among the more commonly used descriptive terms applied to a set of scores are those relating to central tendency. The most commonly used of these in education is the *mean* (M); it is also the most useful in most situations. *The mean is simply the arithmetic average*, and its value is enhanced by the fact that it is involved in the computation of various other, more complex statistical computation.

A second measure of central tendency, the *median* (Md) is also of considerable value. *The median is the point at which the number of scores above it and below it in the distribution are the same*. It may be a point, not an actual score, but it often is a score. For example, in the distribution 22, 20, 19, 18, 14, 13, 10, 10, and 9, the median is 14. (The mean is 15—the sum of the scores divided by 9.)

The *mode (Mo) is the score, within a set of scores, that occurs most often*. In the preceding distribution, the mode is 10.

Often the mean and the median are both of interest and value in describing a distribution of scores. If a distribution is such that many scores occur somewhere other than at the approximate midpoint, the median is likely to be a more meaningful indicator of central tendency than is the mean. If the distribution of scores fit the normal curve, the mean, median, and mode will all be the same.

Measures of Variability

Because a distribution of scores for a small group of individuals seldom conforms to the distribution represented by the normal curve, more information than the mean, median, and mode is important. For example, two fifth grade classes might each have 30 students, and each class might have the same mean performance on a given achievement test. But the "spread" of scores around this central measure might be very different. The range of scores in one class might be from 65 to 95, while in the other the range might be from 72 to 89. In many situations the variability (spread) of scores may be a much more useful characteristic of the distribution than measures of central tendency. *Measures indicating how scores are distributed around the central measure* are called measures of variability.

Range, the most basic measure of variability, is simply *the difference between the highest and lowest scores.* In the first hypothetical class, above, the range was 95 minus 65, or 30. In the second class, it was 89 minus 72, or 17.

A second measure of variability, the *standard deviation*, is the most commonly used when reporting the results of educational testing. Whereas the range indicates only the distance between the lowest and highest scores in a distribution, *the standard deviation reflects the variability of every score in the distribution.* The formula for computing the standard deviation is:

$$\sqrt{\frac{\Sigma\, X^2}{N}}$$

To determine the standard deviation, we first calculate the mean. Then we subtract each score from the mean. This difference between each score and the mean is the x in the SD formula. Next we square each x, which eliminates negative values, and add together all of these values. We now have the sum of the squared values of the extent to which each score in the distribution differs from the mean. This value is then divided by N, the number of scores in the distribution. Finally, to eliminate the effect of the fact that we squared each x, we take the square root of this result. The final result, the standard deviation thus reflects the variation of each score in the distribution and permits more meaningful comparisons of scores from various tests.

As a reference point in considering the meaning of the standard deviation, we might consider that in a normal distribution, about 68% of the scores lie between 1 SD below the mean and 1 SD above the mean (see Figure 2.1). Perhaps the most meaningful use of the concepts of normal curve and the standard deviation data that may be derived from a distribution of scores relates to comparison of any one student's scores to the scores of others, or to compare one person's score on two different tests. This is accomplished through use of *standard scores.*

Standard Scores

Standard scores may be highly useful for comparative purposes. *The standard score indicates the number of standard deviation units a given score is either above or below the mean.* The formula for converting raw scores to z-scores is:

$$\frac{X - M}{SD}$$

where X is the student's score, M is the mean of the distribution, and SD is the standard deviation of the distribution.

The standard score indicates how "extreme" a given score is, in terms of standard deviations. Through use of the standard score, we can meaningfully compare a student's performance on (for example) a test containing 260 items and one containing 85 items. By using standard scores, we can convert both tests to the same scale. Performance on the two tests then can be interpreted in terms of deviation from the mean, with the numerical values (representing such variation) directly comparable. Three common types of standard scores are: z scores, with a mean of 0 and a standard deviation of 1, T scores, with a mean of 50 and a standard deviation of 10, and the standard score most often used in special education, with a mean of 100 and a standard deviation of 15. These are illustrated in Figure 2.2.

Percentile Ranks

Although standard scores have a specific purpose, percentile ranks are more often used to indicate relative position in a distribution of scores. *A percentile rank indicates how any given student's score compares with scores of others who took the same test.* A score of, for example, 50 correct, which has a percentile rank of 65, means that those who got 50 right scored equal to or above 65% of the students who took the test. Another way to state this is that a percentile rank of 65 means that 65% of the students who took this test had a score of 50 or lower than 50. On another test, a student who got 50 correct might have a percentile rank of only 30, indicating that only 30% of those who took that test scored 50 or below.

The Normal Distribution

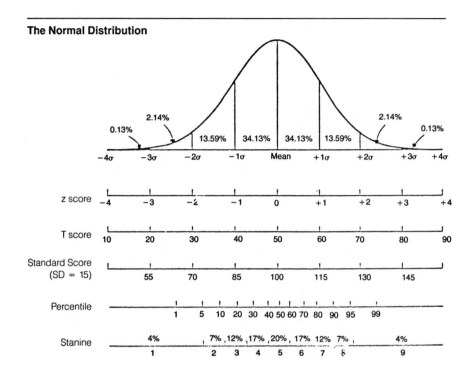

*Many norm-referenced tests have a mean of 100 and a standard deviation of 15.

Figure 2.2
Relationships Between the Normal Distribution and Various Types of Scores

The most common error in misinterpreting percentile ranks is to confuse this concept with "percent right"—the time-honored concept many teachers and parents use. For example, on a given test containing 50 questions, the top score may have been 40 right. This would be 80% correct. Or, some might say, it's a "score of 80." But the percentile rank of this score would actually be 99, indicating that 99% of the others who took the test scored equal to or lower than this score.

In addition to this potential for confusion with "percent right," percentiles on any standardized test may have limited interpretive value for various reasons. For example, if the group on which a test was standardized was quite different from the group with which it is now being used, percentile rank interpretations may have very limited value. Purposes in testing also are highly important.

27

Certain simple observations may be made to determine if percentile ranks for a given test are providing the kind of information desired.

For example, if the actual achievement test scores of more than half of the class are between the 85th and 95th percentiles, and an additional 20% of the scores lie above the 95th percentile, certain observations and decisions must be made. If this achievement test is to be used to determine year-to-year basic skills gains, the following steps might be taken:

1. Reevaluate the test to determine if it actually measures what you want it to measure. The following three steps may assist in this determination:
   a. Establish *in detail* what the school wants to measure. Do this with the input of school personnel and without, at the same time, looking at the test.
   b. Analyze what the test actually measures. First, consider what the test publisher indicates the test measures, and then go through the test, item by item. *Caution:* Two different groups should accomplish a. and b. to guard against any "self-fulfilling prophecy" effect, or a reverse self-fulfilling prophecy effect.
   c. Compare a. and b. to see how well they coincide.
2. If a. and b. coincide to a considerable degree, develop local percentile norms to allow the sensitivity of a full range (1st through 99th) of percentiles.

Percentiles are convenient, seem to be explicit and unlikely to be subject to misinterpretation, and are widely accepted by the general public. In addition to the cautions just stated, however, at least one more potential shortcoming must be considered in their interpretation. Because within a given group of students the tendency is for the majority to score near the average (see the normal curve), the likelihood is that a 10-percentile point difference near the middle scores (say, between the 40th and 50th percentile or between the 50th and 60th percentile) will represent a much smaller difference in the number of right answers on a test, as compared to a 10-percentile point difference near the extremes of the distribution (say, between the 15th and 25th percentile or between the 85th and 95th percentile). This may lead to misinterpretation of differences by both teachers and parents in these areas of the distribution.

If a test with percentiles based on national norms is used to indicate how a given school's students compare to those of other schools, the national percentiles may be of value and entirely appropriate. But caution must be exercised in comparing schools.

Deciles and Quartiles

Deciles and quartiles divide a distribution into larger units than do percentiles. *Each decile represents 10 units.* The 1st decile point coincides with the

10th percentile point; the 5th decile point is the same as the 50th percentile point. *Quartile points divide the scale of measurement into four equal units.* The 1st quartile point coincides with the 25th percentile point; the 2nd quartile point coincides with the 50th percentile point and the 5th decile point. Decile and quartile scores are interpreted in a manner similar to that outlined for percentiles.

Stanines

Stanine is a contraction of "standard nine," referring to the fact that stanine scores are standard scores and range from one to *nine. This weighted scale divides performance on a testing instrument into nine equal segments.* Some consider the stanine more valuable than percentile rank information because it is a "standard score." Therefore, differences between different points on the scale (for example, the difference between 8 and 6 and between 5 and 3 on the scale) are equal in terms of the number of correct test answers they represent. Percentile rank scores show the position of an individual (a score) among a ranked group of individuals (scores) in a distribution. Stanines are used with some regularity in reporting achievement and aptitude tests because of their standard score characteristics.

Item Analysis

Analysis of individual items on a test is called item analysis. Items may be analyzed in a number of different ways, for several different purposes. Generally speaking, the objective is to learn more about the *level of difficulty* of an item, or *how well it discriminates* between factors such as knowledge, ability, those who will more likely succeed and those who will not, or other factors related to the purpose(s) of the test in question. Some types of item analysis involve relatively complex statistical procedures, which will not be described here, but for the classroom teacher, concrete value often may be derived from simple inspection of items and further investigation of hunches or hypotheses resulting from this inspection. On many tests the major use of item analysis may relate to test revision, and may more often involve empirical analysis. The educator and others dealing with students can learn a great deal through inspecting answers to certain questions, determining patterns that exist with regard to types of questions missed, skills required to answer the questions, or common features of the questions. This, too, may be considered a type of item analysis.

Population, Sampling, Parameters

In educational research the term *population* describes or refers to an entire group—*the total or aggregate of entities from which samples are taken for any particular purpose.*

There are a number of methods of *sampling,* but most are designed *to obtain a relatively small sample of a much larger population,* which may be observed, tested, surveyed, or whatever is appropriate in a particular case. The hope is that the outcomes of such observation, testing, or surveying will closely resemble the results that would have been obtained if the entire population had been observed, tested, or surveyed. Generally, all efforts are directed toward the goal that the sample will be representative of the total group (population) from which it was drawn.

If we were actually to test an entire population and were able *to characterize or describe the population in terms of a particular property or properties,* these would be called *parameters.* When we sample a population and compute a particular statistic, the statistic is really an estimate of a parameter, based on sampling.

Statistical Significance

One major question which should be asked about any statistic derived from a sample is: How significant is this statistic? In simple language, this means: Does it truly indicate how a given population feels or how it will act? How closely does it approach the parameter it purports to represent?

The results would be of greater value (when we are interested in how a population thinks, what it wants, for whom it will vote) if we could measure the entire population, but usually this is not possible. Therefore, we attempt to determine the answer by using a sample from the population. But in taking the results of information gathered from a sample, we should know something about the value of the information derived.

A variety of statistical methods are available to the competent researcher; and a few general rules apply to all situations. One rule is that we should *always use the simplest appropriate statistical methodology.* Complicated statistics do not make up for other shortcomings. Another rule is to *use statistics only when the question is a statistical one.* For the classroom teacher, as a consumer of reports that might contain statistics, perhaps one of the most important understandings is also one of the simplest. Most statistical studies indicate findings and then indicate those findings as being significant at a particular "level." Generally, *if findings are significant at the .01 level or the .05 level, they are considered sufficiently significant to be labeled "meaningful"* or considered "true." Whatever the findings and whatever the statistical methods involved, the .05 level indicates that these results might be expected to have been obtained as many as 5 times in 100 *by chance*. Or it might be said that 95 times in 100 such results must be considered as real and meaningful. The .01 level provides a more rigorous test of significance than the .05 level.

To summarize—levels of significance indicate the likelihood that any result (often this is a difference between two groups or two methods) may be a chance happening, and *the smaller the number that represents the level of significance, the more significant are the findings.*

Correlation

Correlation is *a measure of the degree of relationship between two variables.* The *coefficient of correlation* is a numerical representation of any such relationship. In relation to assessment, we usually are considering a relationship between characteristics and scores, or sets of scores. The coefficient of correlation may range from a perfect positive relationship (+ 1.0) to a perfect negative relationship (-1.0).

One correlation that is often cited in education is that existing between letter grades and intelligence. If we assign point values to letter grades (e.g., 5 for an A, 4 for a B, 3 for a C, etc.), we find that, generally, the higher the score on measures of intelligence, the higher is the average of letter grade values. This is not *always* the case. Some students with high intelligence make lower letter grades, for any number of reasons, so the coefficient of correlation for any group of 100, randomly selected students would not be 1.0. But it likely may be between .70 and .90, which is a relatively high, positive correlation. In fact, ordinarily a correlation of +.70 or above, and -.70 or below is considered a high correlation.

In contrast, a negative correlation may exist between the number of days a student is absent from school and letter grades; the higher the absentee rate, the lower the grades. This relationship has exceptions, notably related to students who attend regularly but have much lower than average mental ability, and to others who attend regularly but are unmotivated.

If we randomly search through lists of scores or values of any sort, we likely may find correlation—a statistical relationship between data for which no logical, causal relationship is apparent. These are *chance correlations* and in most cases mean nothing more than the fact that someone took the time to do such a random search. *The coefficient of correlation describes a relationship, but it does* not *necessarily demonstrate a* causal *relationship.* In fact, this assumption of casuality, based on demonstrated correlation, is not a problem limited to the field of education. It has been a significant contributing factor in many

31

of the biases and prejudices of the past. Generalizations based on demonstrated correlations between (for example) certain minority groups and statistics on crime have sometimes ignored correlations with a third factor, poverty. Generalizations based on correlations between gender and (for example) mechanical ability have not taken into consideration the effect of a third factor, imposed societal roles.

Certain other cautions also should be mentioned with regard to the value and applicability of coefficients of correlation. Generally, in addition to the degree of correlation indicated by the number (.90 indicates much more correlation than .60), *the significance of any given coefficient of correlation depends greatly on the size of the sample and the representativeness of cases involved.* For example, we might select four students from a given class and find a perfect positive correlation between grades and IQ. We might select four other students and find no correlation.

For purposes of understanding assessment procedures and interpreting assessment results, we do not have to be able to calculate a correlation coefficient, but it is important to understand the concept of correlation. It is nothing more, or less, than a measure of the relationship between two variables or two sets of scores. It describes just one thing; the tendency for values of one variable to change systematically with changes in another variable.

Grade Equivalent (GE)

This apparently simple term is useful, but it sometimes is overused or misinterpreted. The school year is divided into 10ths, and GEs may be interpreted as follows: 4.5—equivalent to work expected of a "normal" youngster halfway through the fourth grade; or 6.1—equal to work expected of a sixth-grade child after one-tenth of the sixth grade has been completed. The major problem with the grade equivalency concept is its acceptance as an absolute level. If it is used as an indicator of general levels or as a tool in determining trends, it may be considered a useful evaluative aid.

Grade equivalents are less meaningful in practical application the further they vary from the pupils' actual grade placement. For example, in reporting results on an achievement test administered to fourth-grade children, a difference between the performance of child A with a GE of 4.9 and child B with a GE of 5.9 is probably more meaningful than an equal GE performance difference between child C and child D, if C's GE is 7.9 and D's GE is 8.9.

Another serious shortcoming inherent in the manner in which many teachers use grade equivalents is the tendency to accept the GE without further considerations. This may lead to serious misconceptions. For example, a GE of 4.3 in reading tells us almost nothing about the child's specific reading skills. It does not indicate whether the child is stronger in oral or in silent reading and says nothing about what strategies were used. *The GE is a very general score,* and in the case of unmotivated children tested in a group setting, it may show little more than the lack of motivation. As a general rule, the more atypical the child (in total educational performance), the less valuable is the concept of grade equivalent. For most special education teachers, the most important thing to know about the concept of grade equivalent is its general inapplicability in meaningful planning for the exceptional child.

Validity

According to the Standards for Educational and Psychological Testing (American Psychological Association, 1985), "Validity is the most important consideration in test evaluation" (p. 9). If we use a test for a purpose for which it is not valid, we may have done something worse than doing nothing. If it is not valid for our purposes, the results are not meaningful. But even worse is the possibility that someone may try to interpret the test results—to use them—as if they were valid.

Each test must be evaluated with respect to its validity *for the purposes for which it is being considered or used.* A given test may be highly valid for one purpose but useless for another. Validity-related evidence often is classified into four categories: content, predictive, concurrent, and construct; however, the predictive and concurrent categories sometimes are grouped together as criterion-related. Whatever the categorization, "Rigorous distinctions between the categories are not possible. Evidence identified usually with the criterion-related or content-related categories, for example, is relevant also to the construct-related category" (American Psychological Association, 1985, p. 9). For purposes of convenience in discussion, however, we will utilize these four categories.

Content validity is the extent to which a test includes a sufficiently representative sample of the skill, attribute, or trait under consideration. Content validation involves the test maker (or later evaluator) deciding or determining that items on the test represent the skill, attribute, or trait targeted by the test. All tests must be evaluated with respect to content validity, and achievement tests in particular must receive such consideration. Most achievement test makers utilize experts in the relevant subject areas to assist in validation, but individual schools (committees, consultants, etc.) and teachers also must consider content validity.

Predictive validity is established by comparing the results of a test against future performance in the areas the test purportedly measures. Aptitude tests in particular should be subject to this type of evaluation and determination.

They may be evaluated by following up on the future performance of individuals who have "high" or "low" predicted success on the test.

Concurrent validity involves comparing test performance with other (criterion) data that are available at the time of testing. Once established, concurrent validity is important in determining the value of a given test for purposes of diagnosing the existing status, but it does not necessarily indicate appropriateness for predicting future outcomes.

Construct validity reflects the extent to which a test is of value in measuring a given construct or hypothetical trait. In education, the construct more often targeted than perhaps any other is intelligence. Others might be self-concept, anxiety, and motivation. These constructs are not directly measurable, and construct validity must be determined in relation to the theory underlying the concept—a relatively complex process.

Reliability

With respect to assessment, reliability means *stability* or *consistency*. This terminology is used most often as it applies to the reliability of scores or measures obtained when successive measures are taken with the same instrument or with parallel or equivalent tests. The principle of reliability is equally important when applied to the use of informal measures, observations, or interviews. The following discussion relates primarily to reliability as it is determined for tests and reported in test manuals; this is the traditional concept of reliability. Nevertheless, educators must strive to increase the reliability of informal assessment, or its value may be greatly diminished.

Examples of attention to informal assessment reliability include the use of at least two different competent observers when drawing conclusions from observed classroom behavior. The questions might include whether each observer saw the same behavior and whether each saw about the same amounts of each behavior. If differences occur, is the observation of value in making determinations about a child's future? Other obvious examples relate to the use of teacher-made tests. Are they reliable? Do they measure consistently?

Standardized tests are, to a considerable extent, the result of a desire to be able to make more consistent, reliable determinations about behavior or performance. Various methods for determining test reliability are recognized and may be reflected in the literature related to tests under consideration for use, or tests that have been used already with a given student. The three most common methods are test-retest, equivalent-form, and split-half. The *test-retest* method involves readministering the same test and determining the correlation between the two sets of scores. This procedure may give rise to problems in any test in which practice leads to improvement. One way to avoid the practice effect result is to use the *equivalent-form* method. This is ordinarily considered to be better than the test-retest method, but it is possible only with equivalent or parallel forms. A third procedure, the *split-half* method, involves dividing the test into two comparable halves. Then the correlation between the two halves may represent the reliability. The major concern with this method is splitting the test into *comparable* halves.

Reliability can be determined, and, in general, major test makers have approached the reliability question with serious intent. Reliability data on most tests are meaningful. But test administrators can reduce reliability through improper administration, which may render scores from a "reliable" test nearly meaningless.

Standard Error of Measurement

The reliability discussion related to consistency in obtaining the same result when repeatedly measuring the same behavior, attribute, or ability. The standard error of measurement (SEM) of a test indicates *the extent to which chance errors may cause variations in the scores that might be obtained from the same individual if the same test were administered an infinite number of times.* Can we be confident in a score? Is it a "true" score? The standard error of measurement is just another way to indicate reliability.

Highly reliable tests have a lower standard error of measurement; the low SEM means less variability of the obtained scores around the "true" score. In simple terms, if the SEM is 5, this means that approximately 2 times out of 3 (68% of the time) the score of any given individual will fall within a range of 5 points above to 5 points below the "true" score.

Standard Error of the Difference

The importance of determining the extent of any discrepancy between a student's expected performance and actual performance increased in importance with the acceptance of a national definition of learning disabilities. The actuality of such a discrepancy is central to this definition, and thus to identification of learning disabilities.

Calculation of the standard error of the difference (Anastasi, 1982) determines if such differences are true differences or occurred by chance. The formula for the standard error of the difference is:

$$SE_{diff} = SD \sqrt{2 - r_1 - r_2}$$

35

In this formula, SD is the standard deviation of the two tests, r_1 is the reliability coefficient for test 1, and r_2 is the reliability coefficient for test 2. The standard error of the difference is multiplied by 1.64 to determine a 10% level of confidence (90% probability of a real difference), 1.96 for the 5% level (95% probability of a real difference), and 2.58 for the 1% level (99% probability of a real difference).

The Assessment Process

The assessment process has a number of variations, depending on the purpose(s) of assessment, the age of the individual involved, the setting, information already available, and others. Most of this chapter relates to the more comprehensive assessment involved when a student is experiencing educational difficulties (including academic as well as primarily behavioral difficulties) that lead the teacher to conclude that he or she needs additional assistance to assure that the student is receiving maximum benefit from the educational program.

This assessment ordinarily relates to (a) verification of the nature of the difficulty, and (b) specific interventions which may be of value in increasing the effectiveness of the educational program. Some assessment, however, relates to indications of a specific, verified difficulty (for example, for a blind student), in which case the assessment will focus almost exclusively on how to adjust or adapt the school environment to maximize the student's learning opportunities. This includes modifications in the school program and training to assist the student to fully utilize the adapted program. At the preschool level the process is considerably different from that usually implemented in the elementary or secondary schools. Additional insight into assessment at the preschool level is presented in chapter 7.

Normally, comprehensive assessment follows referral by some interested party, which sets into motion a series of requirements dictated by law or state or local regulations. But many educators have a growing conviction that pre-referral intervention should receive serious consideration.

Prereferral Intervention

Prereferral intervention is based on the same rationale as advice on "what to do before you call the doctor" or before you call the TV repair service. Prereferral intervention's strongest advocates are, of course, interested in helping the student, but they are at least equally interested in avoiding the likelihood that, following referral and assessment, students may be needlessly classified according to some handicapping condition and removed from the regular classroom for at least part of the day.

Prereferral intervention has a number of variations, but in most the process is:

1. The teacher formally requests assistance within the school.
2. A conference is held, and intervention strategies are suggested.
3. After implementation of suggested strategies, another conference is held to determine whether to continue the interventions, modify strategies, or consider other interventions.
4. If, after try-out of various suggested strategies, little improvement is realized, a formal referral will be made.

This process becomes, in effect, an intermediate step between the teacher's awareness that additional help is needed and the actual, formal referral that will trigger a specific process, usually guided by federal or state regulations and specified by local school district policies. In some descriptions of the prereferral intervention process, parents are not directly contacted and involved in the original conference but are later notified of the steps that have been taken. In other school districts, bypassing parents at this step is not permitted.

As part of the prereferral process, some informal assessment may take place after the first prereferral conference. Formal assessment should *not* be implemented during the prereferral process without obtaining specific parent permission, and extensive informal assessment might be interpreted as attempting to bypass the need for parent permission.

Reports of the success of existing prereferral systems are somewhat contradictory. In a study by Harrington and Gibson (1986), the results indicated that only about half of the teachers contacted (teachers involved in prereferral intervention) planned to continue using the system presently in place in their school. Further investigation of this concern gleaned the following impressions:

1. Administrators must be in favor of and support the process.
2. The preassessment process takes a lot of time.
3. More consistent home-school communication and parental support are required.
4. Teachers *do* need assistance in finding and trying out new intervention options.

Our conclusions in relation to preassessment intervention programs as they exist today are:

- The principle of preassessment intervention is important.
- The prereferral intervention process may provide an effective source of comprehensive assistance in discovering and implementing new intervention options.
- If prereferral intervention is avoiding parental involvement at the early stages (Graden, Casey, & Christenson, 1985), this practice requires reevaluation.
- Attempting to meet the complex needs of some students over a relatively long time, with only limited success, could be interpreted as denying them the appropriate educational program guaranteed by Public Law 94-142.

Steps in the Assessment Sequence

The assessment sequence normally proceeds as follows: prereferral considerations, referral, parent permission for assessment, multidisciplinary assessment, multidisciplinary meeting to evaluate assessment results, development of individualized education program (IEP), initiation of special programming, further assessment to determine program effectiveness and need for modifications or continued programming. Obviously, this is not all "assessment," but it all *relates* to assessment, starting with the perceived need for assessment and including assessment following prescribed interventions, to determine progress and see if modifications are needed.

This is the assessment sequence that evolved out of the regulations through which PL 94-142 was implemented, to provide services for handicapped students. Other assessment—for example, to determine if a high school student has manual dexterity and hand-eye coordination sufficient to successfully complete some specialized vocational program—would not follow this involved sequence. Also, if, following assessment, it is determined that a given student should not be classified as having a handicapping condition, the IEP may not be developed and the student will not be served through special education. He or she may be served through some other program such as remedial reading. Figure 3.1 presents this sequence. In the following sections each step in this assessment sequence is discussed.

Referral for Assessment

Referrals by the classroom teacher are the most common means whereby students come to the attention of assessment personnel. Referrals also may come from other members of the school staff, from parents, from physicians, or from community health or mental health workers. Teacher referrals usually are based on the fact that the teacher knows that a particular student is not achieving satisfactorily in the school setting, but believes that with special assistance his or her achievement could be improved. Some have observed that a referral means that a teacher is crying "help." This is, we believe, an accurate observation.

The referral process is specific, usually including completion of a referral form indicating the reason for the referral, what interventions have been tried already, and related information that assessment personnel find useful. The forms vary considerably from district to district but their intent is the same: to obtain all possible pertinent information so that the assessment efforts can be focused.

Sometimes the impetus for referral is the result of screening procedures. All teachers are familiar with screening for possible vision problems or hearing problems, and many of them are familiar with screening for speech problems. In addition to these areas, some schools use a screening procedure for the characteristics that might indicate learning disabilities. And, in some instances, sociograms completed by an entire class provide information regarding social acceptance, which may be of value. Readiness screening at the kindergarten/pre-first grade level also is common. The results of screening in the areas of vision and hearing may lead to referral for that one, potential problem.

Screening in most other areas should not be used as the basis for referral without a good deal of additional corroborative information. Screening may be of particular value in school districts in which the student population is highly mobile, for in such settings students may not be in one location long enough for teachers to have an opportunity to observe their needs. However the referral is accomplished, whatever the steps or the triggering mechanism, it is the means whereby many students who eventually are involved in the assessment process come to the attention of assessment personnel.

Parent Permission for Assessment

Before formal assessment can begin, parent permission is required. This does not include total class testing, as in testing hearing or vision, total class testing in academic areas, or giving a special, diagnostic reading or math test to learn more about how to teach a given student effectively. If individual assessment requires the use of specialized assessment personnel, however, parents must be informed of the need, and they must consent. At this same time they must be told of their rights, and due process must be explained to them in a language they understand. Federal and state regulations have provisions for the unusual situation in which the parent gives a flat "no" and school personnel think the matter is critically important to the student. We will not outline these provisions here because, in practice, they are seldom required.

Scope of Assessment

The scope and depth of assessment can vary greatly, depending on the apparent need as indicated in the referral, and after completion of initial assessment procedures. The areas of assessment included most often are outlined in Figure 3.1. The physical exam, health history, developmental history, social worker's report, and educational history (grades, attendance record, etc.) are usually a part of assessment. An individual test of mental ability is almost always included, and if there are indications of academic difficulties (the vast majority of cases), individual academic assessment is done, focusing on "trouble areas" indicated in the referral. The areas of personality, social adjustment, or behavior disorders are assessed, but the degree to which this assessment takes place varies. If the referral indicated primary concern in an area of behavior, this will be a major focus in the assessment.

In addition, if the student or the family has been seen by other community agencies (e.g., mental health, social services), information is gathered from these sources. The objective is to gain information that will provide the most complete picture of the student, his or her abilities and possible disabilities, motivations, self-perception, and past and present environment. Assessment should lead to information about the student as he or she is today, plus historical data that may provide insight as to why the student is as he or she is today.

When initiating assessment, school personnel must not assume that they "know" a given student is learning disabled, or mentally handicapped, or whatever. But assessment procedures must start somewhere, and they more often start on the basis of what *might be* the problem, given the referral information. For example, if the referral information indicates that the problem could be a learning disability, the assessment might proceed as follows:

1. Test for visual acuity and auditory acuity. Make certain that these are not primary causes of the observed academic problems.
2. Obtain a health history and results of a physical examination.
3. Gain sociocultural information—family information, background.
4. Obtain educational records, and develop an educational history. This may be a combination of information from the schools the student has attended, and from the parents.
5. Administer an individual test of intelligence. If the IQ is very low, learning disabilities cannot be the classification.
6. Complete individual achievement assessment with a focus on academic/ skill areas indicated in the referral as the major problem areas. This is

Referral/Assessment/

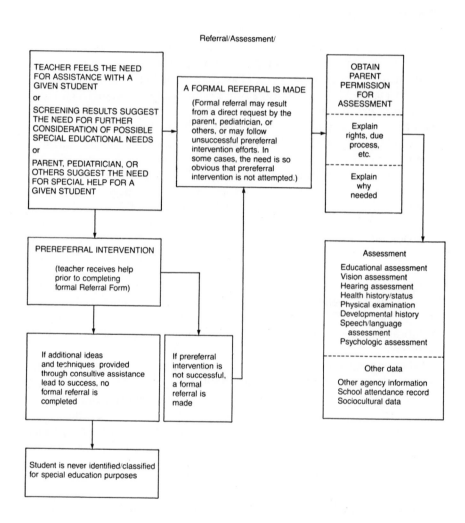

TEACHER FEELS THE NEED FOR ASSISTANCE WITH A GIVEN STUDENT

or

SCREENING RESULTS SUGGEST THE NEED FOR FURTHER CONSIDERATION OF POSSIBLE SPECIAL EDUCATIONAL NEEDS

or

PARENT, PEDIATRICIAN, OR OTHERS SUGGEST THE NEED FOR SPECIAL HELP FOR A GIVEN STUDENT

A FORMAL REFERRAL IS MADE

(Formal referral may result from a direct request by the parent, pediatrician, or others, or may follow unsuccessful prereferral intervention efforts. In some cases, the need is so obvious that prereferral intervention is not attempted.)

OBTAIN PARENT PERMISSION FOR ASSESSMENT

Explain rights, due process, etc.

Explain why needed

PREREFERRAL INTERVENTION

(teacher receives help prior to completing formal Referral Form)

If additional ideas and techniques provided through consultive assistance lead to success, no formal referral is completed

If prereferral intervention is not successful, a formal referral is made

Assessment

Educational assessment
Vision assessment
Hearing assessment
Health history/status
Physical examination
Developmental history
Speech/language assessment
Psychologic assessment

Other data

Other agency information
School attendance record
Sociocultural data

Student is never identified/classified for special education purposes

From B. R. Gearheart & C. J. Gearheart, (1989), "The Referral Assessment Staffing IEP Placement Process," (Figure 4.1) *Learning Disabilities: Educational Strategies*, Columbus, OH: Charles E. Merrill. Used by permission.

Figure 3.1

Steps in the Assessment Process

Staffing/IEP Placement

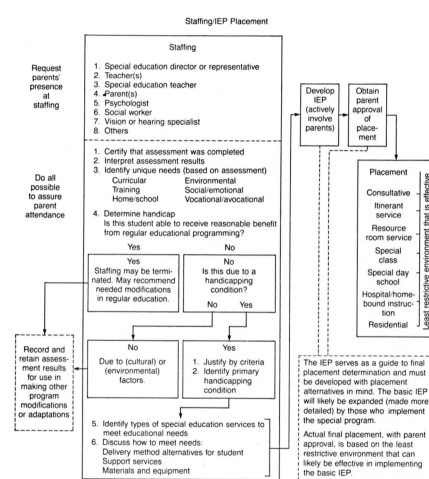

Staffing

Request parents' presence at staffing

1. Special education director or representative
2. Teacher(s)
3. Special education teacher
4. Parent(s)
5. Psychologist
6. Social worker
7. Vision or hearing specialist
8. Others

Develop IEP (actively involve parents)

Obtain parent approval of placement

1. Certify that assessment was completed
2. Interpret assessment results
3. Identify unique needs (based on assessment)

Curricular	Environmental
Training	Social/emotional
Home/school	Vocational/avocational

Do all possible to assure parent attendance

4. Determine handicap
   Is this student able to receive reasonable benefit from regular educational programming?

Yes / No

Yes
Staffing may be terminated. May recommend needed modifications in regular education.

No
Is this due to a handicapping condition?

No   Yes

Record and retain assessment results for use in making other program modifications or adaptations

No
Due to (cultural) or (environmental) factors.

Yes
1. Justify by criteria
2. Identify primary handicapping condition

5. Identify types of special education services to meet educational needs
6. Discuss how to meet needs:
   Delivery method alternatives for student
   Support services
   Materials and equipment

Placement

Consultative

Itinerant service

Resource room service

Special class

Special day school

Hospital/home-bound instruction

Residential

Least restrictive environment that is effective

The IEP serves as a guide to final placement determination and must be developed with placement alternatives in mind. The basic IEP will likely be expanded (made more detailed) by those who implement the special program.

Actual final placement, with parent approval, is based on the least restrictive environment that can likely be effective in implementing the basic IEP.

43

required as part of the classification procedure and is also part of an attempt to learn more about the type of problem the student is experiencing, not just that he is "behind" in a given area.

7. Have at least one member of the interdisciplinary team other than the student's regular teacher observe the student's academic performance in the normal class environment. Dictated by federal regulations, this requirement must be met if it appears the student might be classified as having a learning disability.

Each area of potential handicap (behavior disorders, disability in hearing or vision, etc.) has its own unique assessment needs; the preceding was provided as an example of an area that has an unusual number of assessment requirements, dictated by federal regulations. The scope of the assessment varies, and results at one juncture of the assessment process may change the procedures at that point.

For example, in the preceding example, if the individual test of intelligence indicated an IQ of 61, and other measures of intelligence seemed to verify this considerably lower-than-average level, learning disabilities would be ruled out as the primary disability. But then a test of adaptive behavior would be needed to determine if adaptive behavior test results would confirm a classification as mentally handicapped (or whatever terminology is used in the state in question). Another change would have been dictated if tests of auditory acuity had indicated a moderate or severe hearing loss. Assessment teams in most school districts have a procedure for handling retracking of the assessment path, but the initial path and planned initial scope are determined by the information provided at the time of referral.

The Multidisciplinary Team Meeting

After gathering pertinent assessment information, a meeting of a multidisciplinary evaluation team and parents is convened to evaluate assessment results. This type of meeting is variably called a staffing, an IEP meeting, or a case conference. We might conceptualize each piece of information gathered as a piece of the total (assessment) puzzle. In the process of assessment, attempts are made to put these pieces together, to obtain as complete and meaningful a total picture as possible. A multidisciplinary team determination (as contrasted with a determination by one person, or by only two persons) is required for classification of most handicapping conditions.

One area of special educational services—speech/language disabilities—may be certified by a single professional, the speech/language pathologist, but this is an exception to the general rule. In practice, local school districts often require that the speech/language pathologist involve others in this decision, and if there is the likelihood of additional areas of handicap, the multidisciplinary team will be used.

Parents are key participants in this meeting. Federal regulations require that every effort be made to meet when parents can attend, and school districts may be asked to provide proof that these efforts are made, especially if the records show that meetings are often held with no parent present. Federal regulations require detailed records of all staffings, including who attended and the official capacity of each attendee. The requirement that serious efforts be made to ensure parental involvement in the meetings can be related to the assertion of parental rights, which in turn was related to a variety of litigation and the passage of PL 94-142. In fact, the parent is a highly important source of assessment information and, in every sense of the word, a team member. In some few cases, parents may be defensive, disagreeable, or disruptive, but this, too, constitutes important information when piecing together the assessment puzzle.

In general, the following persons (in addition to the parent(s)) may participate in the staffing.

1. The student's teacher, or when evaluating preschool children, a qualified preschool teacher, even if the child does not attend preschool.
2. A representative of the Public Agency, such as the Principal or Director of Special Education.
3. One or more persons qualified to conduct individual diagnostic evaluations (e.g., school psychologist, speech/language pathologist, reading diagnostician).
4. A specialist in the area of suspected handicap or disability.

In many instances the findings relating to the handicap are very evident to all members of the committee, including the parent (e.g., if the child is blind or hearing impaired). In other instances the situation is much less clear, and considerable discussion may result (e.g., learning disabilities or behavioral disorders). Depending on which handicapping condition (if any) is found, the team must file a written report, including certain specific minimum statements. If the team finds, for example, that the student has a specific learning disability, the following, at least, must be included in the written report:

1. Whether the child has a specific learning disability.
2. The basis for making this determination.
3. The relevant behavior noted during the observation.
4. The relationship of that behavior to the child's academic functioning.
5. The educationally relevant medical findings, if any.
6. Whether there is a severe discrepancy between achievement and ability that is not correctable without special education and related services.
7. The determination of the team concerning the effects of environmental,

cultural, or economic disadvantage, in relation to the discrepancy between achievement and apparent ability. (Federal Register, 1977, p. 65083)

These requirements for learning disabilities classification are more detailed than for other handicapping conditions, because of the perceived difficulties in accurately determining the existence of learning disabilities and the tendency to overdiagnose learning disabilities. Other handicapping conditions, however, may also have unique and specific requirements in various states.

The Individualized Education Program (IEP)

Some consider the IEP as part of the assessment process, and others consider it closely related to, but not a part of, assessment. We will take the point of view that it is a part of assessment, because (a) without the results of assessment and the staffing the IEP could not be completed, and (b) included in the IEP are guidelines for, and a requirement to continue, assessment. PL 94-142 required the IEP because prior to that time, only minimal assessment for classification purposes was included too often, and essentially no assessment to determine what should be taught, how it should be taught, in what setting(s) it should take place, and what future evaluation should be carried out.

According to federal regulations, the IEP must include at least the following:

a. A statement of the child's present levels of educational performance;
b. A statement of annual goals, including short-term instructional objectives;
c. A statement of the specific special education and related services to be provided to the child, and the extent to which the child will be able to participate in regular educational programs;
d. The projected dates for initiation of services and the anticipated duration of the services; and
e. Appropriate objective criteria and evaluation procedures and schedules for determining, on at least an annual basis, whether the short-term instructional objectives are being achieved. (*Federal Register,* 1977, p. 42491)

The format of IEPs varies within states and from state to state in relation to state or local guidelines. The content varies with respect to the type of handicapping condition, severity of the handicap, and other factors. Most, however, meet the minimum requirements outlined in the preceding paragraph. The information included in Table 3.1 provides additional information as to the major components of the typical IEP. A properly developed IEP provides

Table 3.1
Components of the Individualized Education Program (IEP)

1. *Identification and background information.* Student's name, parents' names, address, telephone numbers, gender, birthdate, primary language.

2. *Assessment Information.* All information obtained by school personnel through formal or informal assessment procedures including a definitive statement of present level of academic functioning in pertinent areas and information about nonacademic areas (e.g., social skills) if such information is pertinent to targeted learning problems or concerns.

3. *Other information.* May include medical information, health history information, information from other community agencies, and historical information about past school attendance and past academic performance; when this information is included, the source must be fully documented.

4. *Statement of annual goals.* A statement of academic and/or social performance goals to be attained by the 1-year IEP anniversary or by the close of the school year; also a statement regarding how they will be evaluated.

5. *Statement of short-term objectives.* Specific objectives consistent with each of the annual goals.

6. *Educational placement recommendations.* For example, occupational therapy or speech therapy services, consultative assistance, resource room instruction, or instruction in a special vocational setting. Also might include special provision such as "end of chapter" test given orally or taped reading assignments in content areas.

7. *Educational placement recommendations.* Setting (e.g., consultative assistance, resource room), time spent in each special placement, rationale for such placement(s), and time in the regular classroom, if any.

8. *Time frame for special services.* Significant dates, including at least (a) service initiation dates, (b) duration of services, (c) approximate dates for evaluations, and (d) approximate dates for additional conferences, if applicable. (Note that different services may be initiated at different times, and the duration of service may vary for different services.)

9. *Signatures.* IEP conference participants' signatures, indication of approval or nonapproval (including reasons for nonapproval plus alternate recommendations), and parents' signatures indicating program approval.

valuable guidelines for implementing the special program and for determining the effectiveness of that program.

Planned Reassessment (Including Ongoing Assessment)

The need for continuing assessment was mentioned previously, but it deserves reaffirmation in this discussion of the assessment process. Historically, assessment was viewed as important to determine the status of the subject under consideration, leading to classification (e.g., mentally retarded, emotionally disturbed), which theoretically led to intervention. Later, assessment was expanded to attempt to discover in detail how the subject was different from age peers, specific abilities or strengths, and disabilities and weaknesses. Such assessment was for the purpose of planning individualized programs of remediation or amelioration. This second level of assessment was a giant step forward.

A third step in the assessment process is equally important: the planned, ongoing assessment necessary to determine whether present interventions are effective. If we assume that we can assess and plan effectively for a student, we have a status report—a statement of present status, providing guidance for effective educational programming. But it is equally important to determine if change is taking place and the nature and amount of change. Especially when dealing with interventions intended to encourage more acceptable behavior, the change might be negative. Obviously this is essential information so that modifications can be made.

In the case of targeted change in some academic or skill area, reassessment is equally important. The student may be learning some skills the staffing team determined to be important but not learning others. At times, limited success in one arena may mask the lack of success in another. The teacher possibly may be so pleased with success in one arena that other areas are ignored. Planned daily and weekly assessment (usually informal) provides valuable, immediate information, and more comprehensive assessment (usually a mix of formal and informal assessment) at preestablished check-points (every 6 or 9 weeks) provides a more comprehensive picture.

The IEP (see Table 3.1) should include a description of the manner in which evaluation of annual goals will take place. Federal regulations require this assessment prior to the annual review to indicate to the parents and other team members the degree and type of progress. It provides a basis for decisions regarding program modifications or, in some cases, termination of special services. The IEP time frame statement should indicate approximate dates for shorter term evaluations and for additional conferences, if they are needed, following this evaluation.

Potential Problems in Conducting Assessment and in Using Assessment Data

In conducting assessment and in applying assessment data, a number of potential problems come to mind. Several of these will be reviewed in this chapter. This does not suggest that assessment should be discontinued but, rather, that we must assess with care and with full knowledge of the pitfalls that must be considered in the course of assessment.

Problems in assessment may be considered with respect to three overlapping areas: (a) problems inherent in the actual tests or assessment procedures, (b) problems relating to those who conduct the assessment, and (c) problems that arise when attempting to interpret the results of assessment. Consider, for example, the question of appropriateness of a particular measure for a specific purpose. The test may not be appropriate because of cultural considerations, the age of the student, or other reasons. If this is so, there is also a problem with those who conduct the assessment if they do not recognize this inappropriateness. Finally, if a marginally appropriate measure is used and the examiner voices serious concerns or cautions but those interpreting its results choose to ignore the cautions, the problem may rest with interpretation. We will discuss potential problems without specifically noting that they belong to one of these three groupings, but we suggest that readers may keep these groupings in mind while reading the remainder of this chapter.

Ethical Principles in Assessment

One of the first considerations for all professionals should be to establish an ethical frame of reference. Operating within such a frame of reference will not assure that one will never be questioned or criticized with respect to professional actions, but it will reduce the likelihood of serious errors when dealing with the lives of students. Therefore, reviewing the matter of ethical principles in assessment seems reasonable before continuing with our consideration of problem areas in assessment.

Ethical principles in assessment of children and youth are grounded in common sense and consideration of their personhood and rights as individuals. Various professional groups and authors of texts related to assessment have developed statements of ethical principles involving areas such as responsibility, competence, moral and legal standards, public statements, confidentiality, professional relationships, and assessment techniques. These are seven of the 10 areas outlined in the "Ethical Principles of Psychologists" (American Psychological Association, 1981). (The other three areas are not directly applicable to assessment practices as considered in this text.)

Many professional organizations have developed their own versions of ethical standards in assessment. For example, the Council for Exceptional Children (1983) adopted a Code of Ethics and Standards for Professional Practice, which addresses, among other factors, the appropriate assessment of exceptional individuals. The *Standards for Educational and Psychological Testing*, prepared by a joint committee representing the American Educational Research Association, the American Psychological Association, & the National Council on Measurement in Education (1985) provides a set of guidelines related to ethical considerations and "a basis for evaluating testing practices" (p. 2). Salvia and Ysseldyke (1988) emphasize five of the areas cited by the American Psychological Association's ethical standards:

1. Responsibility for the consequences of one's work.
2. Recognizing the boundaries of one's competence.
3. Confidentiality of information.
4. Adherence to professional standards on assessment.
5. Test security.

In their concluding statements relating to legal and ethical considerations in assessment, Salvia and Ysseldyke state: "As in all areas of testing and data maintenance, common sense and common decency are required" (p. 56).

Another way to view ethical considerations is to consider them in relation to (a) questions in which our actions are governed primarily by state or local regulations, and (b) those that are more personal in nature and less subject to monitoring and regulation. These "conscience-related" ethical concerns certainly are as important as those that are more visible and subject to regulation.

In the remainder of this chapter we will consider potential problems that may arise in various combinations as assessment is conducted and assessment data are used. Some of these problems can be controlled; others will remain as problems, as they are in part, beyond our control. As we consider these various problem areas we will be, in essence, expanding on the topic of ethics in assessment. A general statement that we believe encompasses the major ethical concerns and considerations in conducting assessment and using assessment data in the schools follows.

Assessment in the schools should be carried out in a manner consistent with both the letter and the spirit the Evaluation Procedures outlined in the Regulations of Public Law 94-142 (see chapter 1). Although the focus of PL 94-142 is "evaluation and placement"—that is, evaluation for possible classification, and thus placement in an appropriate, modified educational program—the major emphasis of assessment must be that of gaining more insight into how a student functions in various environments, how he or she learns, what factors impede the learning process, and how the learning process may be enhanced. In so doing, we must respect the rights of both student and parent and work cooperatively with other professionals.

School personnel must always be advocates for students. When school personnel complete assessment procedures or otherwise gather and record data, those data should be carefully verified, and all possible related information as to source(s), setting, time frame, purpose, and similarly relevant information recorded. Schools should not release such data (except under subpoena) without the written consent of parents, or of students who are over age 18. Finally, when other guidelines are unclear, the principles of relevancy, common sense, and protection of the rights of others should be basic in all decision making with regard to ethical principles in assessment.

Cultural Diversity and Assessment

One of the major, persistent problems in planning and carrying out meaningful assessment is the fact that many of our assessment tools are of questionable value with a culturally diverse student population. Some have maintained that many, perhaps most, of the accepted tests of intelligence have an "anglocentric" bias (Samuda, 1976). The disproportionate numbers of Black and Hispanic children in classes for students with mental retardation proved to be the triggering mechanism for much of the historic litigation relating to assessment and placement practices.

More recently, concerns about referral, assessment, and placement procedures for Black and Hispanic students placed in programs for the severely emotionally disturbed have caused concern. For example, in the *Lora v. Board of Education of the City of New York* case, involving Black and Hispanic students in New York's segregated special day schools for emotionally disturbed students, the court was convinced that the assessment and placement procedures "permitted knowledgeable parents and guardians with sufficient resources to obtain the placements they desired for their children, for example, remaining in the regular class or being placed in a private day school of the parents' choice at public expense." (Wood, Johnson, & Jenkins, 1986, p. 325).

In the *Lora* case, the court's opinion was that the bias began at the referral level and continued through assessment and placement. (Assessment and placement often have been targeted; in the *Lora* case, *referral* was prominently mentioned.) In this case, as in others, the findings emphasize the difficulty of completing nonbiased assessment and indicate that not enough was done to implement *what is known* about reducing the bias in assessment. This case related to identification as emotionally disturbed, which undoubtedly will always include some elements of subjectivity, but the proper standards and procedures certainly can reduce such subjectivity, if they are consciously followed. Selected Standards and Procedures from *Lora v. Board* (abbreviated and paraphrased) follow:

1. The school staff member who makes the initial referral shall briefly describe the problem, specifying its frequency, and also shall describe comparable behavior of other students in the same classroom.
2. The student must be interviewed and assessed in a language she can understand; determination of this language shall follow approved school district procedures. When possible, assessment shall be conducted by personnel fluent in this language, and when a translator must be used, this must be recorded.
3. At least one member of the assessment team shall complete a structured observation of the student in the setting where the problems are reported to occur. The assessment team is strongly encouraged to conduct observations in more than one setting, with observations by more than one person. Attention should be given to recording the frequency with which the targeted behavior occurs and the comparable behavior of other students in the same class.
4. Assessment procedures should be employed only for their stated, accepted purposes. If, for some supportable reason, nonstandard use is made of an assessment instrument, this usage must be fully explained

and justified in writing. If appropriate norms are not available, data collected shall be treated as only descriptive. If such nonstandard use of instruments is employed, or data are reported for which no appropriate norms are available, this shall be discussed in team meetings, and the substance of the discussion recorded.

5. If self-reports of the student's thoughts and feelings are collected, great care shall be exercised in their interpretation with attention to the student's linguistic, cultural, and ethnic background. When projective tests are used, the same cautions shall be observed. *The student shall not be classified as emotionally disturbed solely on the basis of her projective test performance.*

6. Assessment data and other information shall be provided the multidisciplinary team, which will permit it to rule out sensory or cognitive difficulties and linguistic, cultural, or ethnic differences as possible primary causes of the student's problem.

This abbreviated presentation of the *Lora v. Board* Nondiscriminatory Standards and Procedures does not include a number of standards that are essentially restatements of the assessment guidelines found in the regulations developed pursuant to PL 94-142 (see chapter 1), but apparently were not being followed with respect to assessment and placement in some segregated programs for students with emotional disturbance.

Assessment of students from culturally diverse populations is undoubtedly less inappropriate, less biased than it was 10 or 20 years ago, but it still represents a special challenge for assessment personnel. Awareness of, and sensitivity to, the difficulties inherent in assessment of this nature is essential if it is to provide meaningful information for educators. In a discussion of cultural diversity in special education, Heward and Orlansky (1988) have discussed the concerns of a number of specific culturally diverse groups: Blacks, Hispanics, American Indians and other Native Americans, Asian Americans, bilingual or language minority children, and migrant students. Assessment in each of these groups may require somewhat different testing instruments and approaches. The most common difference relates to language, but many other differences exist. One difference is illustrated by the following anecdote, related to the authors by a professional acquaintance.

Dr. Michael O., an Hispanic Language Consultant in a large school district (Dr. O. speaks and reads four languages fluently) tells the following story about his own childhood, and specifically about testing in the schools.

"Up through age 10, when I was in fifth grade, I always scored low on standardized tests given in school. I'm not sure what I would have done on an individual test of intelligence, because I wasn't given one, but on achievement tests and reading diagnostic tests, my achievement was low. My teacher would talk to me about it, as did my mother. Both felt I could do better. My behavior in the classroom and on the playground was very good, because I wanted to please my mother, but I had gotten the idea from somewhere—I think it was from my older brother—that I shouldn't let my teachers know all that I knew. I was "Mexican," and they were not. We had to keep some things to ourselves. Other young Hispanic boys did the same thing. I don't know about the girls.

I had taken this "don't let them know all you know" attitude for several years. Then, for some reason, in the sixth grade I simply decided on my own that I should let the teachers know all that I knew. I knew it would make my mother happy, and I didn't care any more about the teachers, or my brother. So from then on I did well on tests and was counted as a "bright" kid. I'm not sure how many other Hispanic boys had this same idea, or what would have happened if I had carried the idea on through school. Among other things, I was building horrible habits with regard to test taking. It was purely *attitude*, and in my case it had to do with my Hispanic origins."

We suspect that this is just one of thousands of stories that might be told about factors that can influence assessment results. Some children other than those from minority cultures may have similar influences at work in their lives. It is not just a matter of differences in language. It may be, as in the example, attitude. Or it may be differences in critical life experiences, differences in how children relate to peers, culturally-related differences in attitude toward multiple-choice situations or trial-and-error approaches, or any of a dozen other factors and influences. The bottom line is that assessment of students from culturally diverse populations must be approached with care and sensitivity.

Sociocultural Factors That Influence Assessment Results

A concensus can be derived from the results of the variety of decisions that have come out of litigation related to assessment of students from culturally diverse backgrounds, and certain sociocultural factors appear to influence such assessment. In her handbook, *Assessing Minority Students with Learning and Behavior Problems,* Collier (1988) has suggested that the "primary emphasis (must be) on the identification and assessment of sociocultural factors which permeate various learning or behavior problems of minority students" (p. v).

Collier further states that careful consideration of these sociocultural factors will help assessment personnel determine "whether the learning and behavior problems exhibited by the minority student are due to either sociocultural factors, some other problem or disability, or a combination of these" (p. 9). The five sociocultural factors Collier outlines are discussed in the following paragraphs.

Cultural and Linguistic Background

The student's cultural and linguistic background may be the most significant factor influencing assessment results. As Collier pointed out, our educational programs are based for the most part on culturally based assumptions about what should be learned, how and where it should be learned, and why it is important. Students from considerably different backgrounds come to school with different bodies of knowledge, which they will have learned differently. This influences how the students learn in the school setting but may have an even greater influence on how the students react to assessment procedures. This must be considered when assessment results are interpreted and probably can be most meaningfully interpreted by someone who is, or has been, part of the cultural and linguistic background from which the student comes.

The assessment team's complete understanding of this factor (actually several, overlapping factors) may be more important to the achievement of meaningful assessment results than, for example, the student's level of understanding of the English language. Assessment personnel must work just as hard to understand the student's cultural and linguistic background as they do to make sure the student understands the language, intent, and content of assessment instruments.

Experiential Background

Like cultural background, experiential background is a highly complex factor, and, of course, it overlaps cultural background. Both immigrant and migrant families very likely have not had educational experiences that place them on a par with the majority, Anglo population. Assumptions on which assessment tools are based are simply not valid for many of these children. Collier points out things such as use of inquiry techniques, practice in making cause-effect associations, discovery (versus rote) learning, and other commonly used instructional strategies. Any of these may lead to below-average achievement, and perhaps referral for assessment.

Some of these same skills and understandings may be required in relation to assessment. Thus, if assessment personnel are not very alert, serious underestimation of ability or achievement level may result. In some cases the student must adapt to both the general American culture and the culture of the school.

If students are from a culture that values indirectness and distance, they may not respond as we would expect to praise. Then, if we do not properly interpret their response, the result is misinformation and misunderstanding. Students may come from an experiential background in which primary reinforcement is given to contribution *by* the individual *to* the group and in which individual achievement may have been viewed as negative. As a result, they do not respond to efforts to encourage them to show on an individual basis how well they can achieve.

Acculturation

A third factor of importance, acculturation (adapting to a new cultural environment) is something that does happen, but it happens at different rates with different students. Various studies reveal a significant relationship between ethnic minority group membership and referral for special education services. As the percentage of minority students in the school increases, however, the referral and placement rate of minority students becomes more similar to that of non-minority students (Collier, 1985; Finn, 1982). This has been interpreted as being related to greater acculturation; however, it also may relate to more experience of school staff and assessment personnel with students who are "different" from the majority group.

Sociolinguistic Development

Sociolinguistic development usually means general development in knowledge and use of language. A student with a low level of sociolinguistic development is literally lacking language—unable to use language effectively to communicate within a social context. Collier believes that very few minority students actually have unusually low sociolinguistic development but that we often cannot adequately assess their sociolinguistic development if English is their second language. Her concern is that we evaluate both English and native language development during the assessment process and that we look beyond the school setting to achieve meaningful assessment results.

Cognitive Learning Styles

Collier's fifth factor, cognitive learning styles, might include (a) external versus internal locus of control, (b) impulsive versus reflective approach to learning, (c) analytic versus global frame of reference, (d) broad versus narrow categorizations, and (e) degree of tolerance for unusual or ambiguous stimuli.

These and other characteristics of how individuals organize environmental cues and data and how they approach the learning task are of considerable importance when attempting to learn more about any student. They are particularly important when assessing a minority student, in that minority students are more likely to be different from what teachers may expect.

Collier suggests that we may derive information about sociocultural factors through a number of recognized assessment techniques, including interviews, work sampling, analytic teaching, observations, and, of course, a thorough review of existing records. We would add that intensive efforts should be made to gather more information through interviews with parents and through the use of social workers, teachers, and others from the school district who are members of the minority group to which the student belongs. Perhaps the most important thing to remember is that assessment of students from diverse cultural backgrounds requires extra attention. These five sociocultural factors just discussed provide a point of focus for such attention.

Qualifications of Assessment Personnel

Qualified examiners are essential to meaningful results in the administration of psychological/psychoeducational tests. In a similar manner, teachers who conduct informal assessment must know what to do and how to do it. If examiners are well qualified, the following problem areas will be less likely to result in inappropriate assessment practices.

Testing/Assessment Conditions

The conditions under which assessment takes place are important in any assessment procedure but are especially important in certain types of assessment. For example, the testing space should be large enough to be comfortable, but not too large. The space should be well lighted, without undue visual distraction, either by virtue of too many interesting pieces of equipment in the room or playground activities plainly visible through the windows. Assessment of auditory acuity in particular should not take place in an environment with a significant amount of background noise, and in fact all testing should be conducted in an area where extraneous sound is at a minimum. While testing is taking place, there should be no interruptions. Generally speaking, testing should not take place at the close of a long school day; this is especially important with younger children.

The use of test materials in which a separate answer sheet is required may lower test scores, particularly with younger children. And finally, the examiner's appearance and mannerisms may influence test results (a good examiner will be able to sense this).

These are only a few of the conditions or variables that may affect test results. When test conditions are such that they might influence the results of the assessment (and thus the interpretation and application of the results in the student's life), all unusual testing conditions and deviations from normal test procedures must be carefully recorded.

Validity and Reliability of Measurements

The concepts of validity and reliability were discussed in chapter 2. Validity is absolutely essential, but too often no absolutely valid measure may exist for some given need, and thus a measurement of marginal validity is used. If this is the case, for whatever reason(s), the examiner should note and consider this when all assessment data are assembled and reviewed. Reliability also must be taken into account when considering the implications of any one measuring instrument or procedure. In general, the more questions about either validity or reliability, the greater will be the depth of assessment required before making any critical decisions.

Test Anxiety

College students may overdo their claims about test anxiety (as a reason for low scores on tests), and some do so in jest. But test anxiety is a real phenomenon. If anxiety results in a grade of C rather than an A in freshman biology, that has serious implications. But if test anxiety results in an under-estimation of level of intellectual functioning, which in turn results in (for example) lack of eligibility for needed intervention in a learning disabilities resource room or improper classification as mentally handicapped, that is much more serious. With respect to either of these possible circumstances, additional assessment information should greatly reduce the possibility of inaccurate conclusions. Test administrators must be alert to test anxiety, and if it appears to exist, it should be prominently noted along with test scores or other test results.

Test Practice, Training, and Sophistication

Test practice, training to take a particular test or type of test, and general test sophistication have a potential impact on test results. These factors are more likely to influence the results of tests taken by older students than those of tests taken by elementary school students. A review of records, plus the examiner's observations, should indicate whether these factors are likely involved. If so, test results should be considered in the light of this possibility.

Lack of Motivation or Rapport

Unmotivated students and students with whom the examiner cannot establish rapport have been mentioned or inferred previously. These variables are interwoven with many others, but they do deserve this brief mention. The examiner should make notes regarding lack of motivation or rapport, which the assessment team should consider. For additional specific information regarding establishing rapport with infants and very young children, see chapter 7.

Multidisciplinary Team Deliberations

Public Law 94-142 established guidelines for the composition of the teams of professionals who are to consider assessment information and attempt to decide on classification (if that is appropriate) and intervention strategies. This multidisciplinary team deliberation is, in essence, the conclusion of *initial* assessment efforts with respect to any given student. Often these teams are composed of the proper combination of individuals, representing sufficient expertise to complete the task acceptably. At other times, however, they do not have the needed expertise or representation of sufficient professional disciplines.

In the case of students from culturally diverse backgrounds, no one may fully understand the culture under consideration. In other instances, parents may not attend, or if they do attend, their cultural background might lead them not to participate. Whatever the reason(s), if the multidisciplinary team has insufficient or inappropriate representation, the assessment process may break down, leading to inaccurate conclusions. This possibility must be guarded against lest all of the previous efforts in the assessment process be wasted.

Shortcomings in Continuing Assessment

If it is viewed as purely obligatory, continuing assessment may take the path that involves the least time, effort, and dollars. The IEP dictates certain assessment, which probably will relate to the most serious potential problems targeted in the staffing and program planning. Sometimes the modified programming (intervention) involves restructuring daily instructional activities, which shortchanges other areas of the student's broader educational needs. In making significant changes in a student's educational program, care must be exercised so as to not cause difficulties in areas that previously were judged to be satisfactory. These difficulties might be in either the cognitive or affective

59

domains, and the first step toward guarding against such a possibility is *observational alertness* on the part of the student's teachers. The second step is *additional assessment,* if the observations suggest it.

Litigation Relating to Assessment

If educators fail to consider the potential problems outlined in this chapter, as a practical matter they may find themselves involved in litigation relating to assessment practices. In fact, litigation relating to the use of inappropriate tests and resulting inappropriate decisions (often misclassification of students) were major factors in the development of the federal assessment guidelines outlined in chapter 1. Some of the historic assessment-related litigation might have incorporated an element of overreaction, but school officials unquestionably were making decisions based on flawed information or, at best, too little information, which altered the lives of students.

Assessment-related litigation involved concerns such as using tests that were normed on a population quite different from that to which the student being tested belonged, administering tests in a language other than the student's primary language, making highly important decisions based on only one measure (or on too few data), not involving parents, using tests for purposes other than those for which they had been developed, using only parts of tests, having as test administrators persons with questionable qualifications, and others. The *Lora* v. *Board* case cited earlier in this chapter is just one example of the litigation; there are many, many others.

As a potential problem area in assessment, litigation is quite different from most other assessment-related problems. It is not so much a problem in and of itself as it is a problem that results when educators do not respond intelligently to other assessment concerns. Some litigation in the field of education may be viewed as spurious and with little inherent merit. But most litigation relating to assessment has been founded on facts relating to inappropriate or inadequate assessment practices or outright abuses and has been won by the plaintiffs. Careful consideration and attention to the potential assessment problems discussed in this chapter can significantly reduce this problem.

Introduction to
Chapters 5 Through 15

Chapters 5 through 15 contain descriptions of a variety of tests and assessment instruments or techniques. These are presented to acquaint the reader with the varied content of assessment tools ranging from screening devices to comprehensive instruments that focus on individual skills or characteristics. Before initiating any assessment, the *purpose* of the assessment must be clearly defined. The next step is to select specific assessment instruments to achieve these defined purposes. Questions relating to validity and reliability of selected instruments should be answered through a review of information available in reference works such as the *Mental Measurements Yearbooks, Tests in Print,* and similar sources.*

---

* The *Mental Measurement Yearbooks, Supplements to Mental Measurement Yearbooks, Tests in Print,* and other volumes relating to specialized assessment areas are prepared by the Buros Institute of Mental Measurements, University of Nebraska–Lincoln, and published by the University of Nebraska Press. They are available in most college/university libraries.

Measures of Cognitive Ability and Adaptive Behavior

A first reaction to the mix of tests discussed in this chapter may be: Why are these two classes of assessment considered in the same chapter? They *are* very different types of measures—a fact that will be highlighted in the following presentation. But there are very logical reasons to consider them in a single chapter. For one thing, in the practical school setting, we *must* use a measure of adaptive behavior if the use of a test of intelligence leads to a tentative conclusion that a student is mentally retarded; adaptive behavior measures are required to corroborate a classification of mental retardation.

The American Association on Mental Deficiency (AAMD) took the lead in this movement with a definition of mental retardation, in 1961, noting that mental retardation was always associated with deficits in adaptive behavior. Then, litigation, primarily in the 1960s, led to judicial declarations that directed schools to no longer place children in classes for the mentally retarded based in IQ scores alone. Most of these decisions related to minority children.

Various states adopted regulations requiring the use of adaptive behavior measures, along with measures of intelligence, to verify the existence of mental retardation, but the final step was inclusion of the following statement in Public Law 94-142:

> "Mentally retarded" means significantly subaverage general intellectual func-
> tioning existing concurrently with deficits in adaptive behavior and manifested
> during the developmental period, which adversely affects a child's educational
> performance.

Since that time (1975) it has been generally accepted that to establish the existence of mental retardation there must be acceptable evidence from both a valid test of intelligence indicating below-average mental ability (the degree to which it must be below average varies by states, as established by state regulations) and a measure of adaptive behavior indicating similarly low adaptive behavior. Since that time, these classes of measures, though very different in what and how they measure, have been constant "partners."

Cognitive Ability/Intelligence/Academic Aptitude

In chapter 1 the discussion of origins of present day assessment practices for the most part focused on testing efforts that have led to present day tests of intelligence. That is, the first tests to receive extensive, continuing attention were those designed to measure "mental ability." Since that time, tests of this nature have been called, or characterized, as, "mental tests," "mental ability tests," "IQ tests," "intelligence tests," "academic aptitude tests," and "tests of cognitive ability." A case might be made for and against any of these terms. But whatever terms are used, they refer to measures that correlate highly with academic achievement (though there are notable exceptions) and measures in which educators and psychologists continue to have considerable interest.

Tests of intelligence have generated criticism for many years. The most significant criticism has been directed against group-administered tests of intelligence, and both group and individual tests of intelligence used with students from culturally diverse populations. Many school districts no longer administer group intelligence tests, and if they do, these instruments are more likely to be called tests of academic aptitude or of cognitive ability. In actuality, however, they are simply group intelligence tests with another name.

Such tests may have value in that they identify some students who score very high on the test but who do not reflect this potential ability in their school work. In these cases, follow-up assessment should be initiated to determine whether the inferred, potential ability is truly that high. Individually administered measures of intelligence may be of substantial value if they are used with full knowledge of potential bias and if they are interpreted only in conjunction with other appropriate measures.

Stanford-Binet Intelligence Scale (SBIS), 4th edition

The Stanford-Binet Intelligence Scale was the original standard of excellence in the field of individual tests of intelligence. From the 1920s through the 1940s, the Stanford-Binet was the major individual test used to attempt to obtain reliable information about the level of intelligence of children who were having learning problems or those thought to be intellectually gifted. From the 1950s until about 1970, the Stanford-Binet and the WISC-R (discussed in the following section) were the two tests most often used by psychologists and other assessment personnel in the schools to attempt to measure levels of intellectual ability. Since the early 1970s the WISC-R has been steadily replacing the Stanford-Binet as the test of choice, and other individual tests also have gained prominence. The origins of the Stanford-Binet, in 1904, were mentioned briefly in chapter 1. We will continue that consideration here.

Most educators are familiar with the version of the Stanford-Binet that evolved from revisions of Binet's original efforts in Paris. In 1916 Dr. Lewis Terman, at Stanford University, developed a set of questions adapted to and normed on American children. Thus, the Stanford-Binet was born. This test survived through the years, with its 1973 edition simply being an update/modification of previous editions.

In 1986 a substantially modified Stanford-Binet was published which is still so new that its potential impact is difficult to determine. With the changes in the 1986 revision, the new Stanford-Binet is more similar to measures such as the WISC-R and others that have gained more recent recognition. Time and use by experienced practitioners will determine whether the 1986 edition will regain the prominence of earlier editions. Some assessment personnel continue to use the 1973 edition, and test data on student records prior to 1986 will relate to the earlier edition. The description that follows relates to the 1986 edition.

The Stanford-Binet is designed to meet four major objectives: (a) to help differentiate possible mental retardation and specific learning disabilities, (b) to help identify gifted students, (c) to assist in better understanding of why a student is having difficulties in school, and (d) to promote study of the development of cognitive skills of individuals ages two through adulthood.

The 1986 Stanford-Binet includes 15 subtests, which assess abilities in four broad areas of cognitive functioning: Verbal Reasoning, Short-Term Memory, Quantitative Reasoning, and Abstract/Visual Reasoning. These 15 subtests are outlined as follows:

Verbal Reasoning

1. *Vocabulary*—46 items (ages 2-adult). The first 14 are picture vocabulary items; the remaining 32 are presented orally and on a printed form and require an oral response.
2. *Comprehension*—42 items (ages 2-adult). The first 6 items require identification of various body parts on a picture card; the remaining 36 items are questions requiring a verbal response.
3. *Absurdities*—32 items (ages 2-17 years, 11 months). These items require

the subject to determine what is "silly" or wrong in each picture.

4. *Verbal Relations*—18 items (ages 10-adult). These ask how the first three or four words (given) are related but differ from the fourth word.

Quantitative Reasoning

1. *Quantitative*—40 items (ages 2-adult). The items relate to a broad range of arithmetic skills; tasks range from block counting to orally presented word problems.
2. *Number Series*—26 items (ages 5-adult). The items require discovering the rule or pattern according to which number sequences are arranged and naming the next numbers in the sequence.
3. *Equation Building*—18 items (ages 10-adult). These require rearranging numbers and arithmetic signs into a true equation.

Abstract/Visual Reasoning

1. *Pattern Analysis*—42 items (ages 2-adult). The items require duplication of patterns presented through use of a form board, an examiner's model, or pictured cube patterns.
2. *Copying*—28 items (ages 2-17 years, 11 months). The subject must use blocks to copy block designs or pencil and paper to copy line drawings.
3. *Matrices*—26 items (ages 5-adult). These items require selection of the appropriate shape, design, letter, etc., to fill a blank spot in a matrix.
4. *Paper Folding and Cutting*—18 items (ages 10-adult). These entail visual study of pictures that depict a paper-folding and cutting sequence; the subject must determine how a piece of paper would look after being folded and cut.

Short-term Memory

1. *Bead Memory*—42 items (ages 2-adult). The items require identification of colored bead shapes shown by the examiner for 2 seconds, and duplication of bead designs shown on stimulus cards exposed by the examiner for 5 seconds.
2. *Memory for Sentences*—42 items (ages 2-adult). The test taker must replicate orally presented phrases or sentences, or both phrases and sentences.
3. *Memory for Digits*—14 items (ages 5-adult). A series of digits must be repeated in the order stated; and 12 items require the repetition of a series of digits in reverse order.
4. *Memory for Objects*—14 items (ages 5-adult). The subject is shown several

pictures of objects, one at a time. Next the subject is shown a picture containing many different pictures and is asked to identify pictures shown earlier, in the correct order.

Raw scores are obtained for each test. These are converted to Standard Age Scores, which have a mean of 50 and a standard deviation of 8. Standard Age Scores (SAS) for each area are summed, and an Area SAS is derived. Area SASs can be summed, giving a Composite SAS score. The Area SAS and the Composite SAS have a mean of 100 and a standard deviation of 16.

Wechsler Scales: WISC–R, WAIS–R, WPPSI

Assessment authorities appear to agree that "in recent years the most widely administered test of cognitive ability with school-age children has been the WISC-R" (Witt, Elliott, Gresham, & Kramer, 1988, p. 166). The Wechsler Intelligence Scale for Children–Revised (WISC-R) is one of what McLoughlin & Lewis (1986) call "a family of tests that spans all age levels" (p. 155). It receives much more use than the Wechsler Preschool and Primary Scales of Intelligence (WPPSI), which is for ages 4-0 to 6-6, or the Wechsler Adult Intelligence Scale–Revised (WAIS-R), for ages 16 to 74. The WISC-R is generally accepted as an appropriate measure of global intelligence, with much of its early acceptance resulting from the fact that in addition to a global IQ, it provides a Verbal IQ and a Performance (non-verbal) IQ.

Each of the three Wechsler tests is composed of subtests, grouped within verbal and performance sections, with many similarities between the tests. The nature of the tasks or activities involved in the WISC-R is described as follows.

Verbal Scale

1. *Information*—30 questions. The answers require general, factual knowledge. This subtest includes questions a subject might answer correctly through general experience, but it also includes questions that relate highly to formal educational experience.
2. *Similarities*—17 word pairs. The test taker must indicate how the two words in each word pair are similar. This may indicate logical thinking ability and, like the Information subtest, may be influenced by formal schooling.
3. *Arithmetic*—18 items. These practical arithmetic problems require response without paper-and-pencil computation. Although intended to avoid dependence on reading skill and general verbal ability, school experience may play a role in this subtest.

4. *Vocabulary*—32 items. These consist of words requiring synonyms or meaningful definitions. This subtest requires the subject to indicate the meaning of words taken from a master list arranged in order of increasing difficulty. It directly reflects school experience and, particularly with younger children, the range of vocabulary used in the home.

5. *Comprehension*—17 items. Problem situations are posed for solution. This subtest was designed as a measure of "common sense." To be successful, the subject must possess practical information and have the ability to evaluate past experiences.

6. *Digit Span*. This is an "alternate test" that may be used as a substitute for any other Verbal Scale subtest when indicated. The subject must repeat a series of digits forward and backward after hearing them only once.

Performance Scale

1. *Picture Completion*—26 items. These consist of drawings of common objects. The subject is asked to identify missing elements in incomplete pictures. It is designed to measure ability to differentiate the essential from the nonessential and in some respects might be considered a test of visual memory.

2. *Picture Arrangement*—12 sets of pictures. The test taker must place sets of cartoon-style panels into the proper, logical sequence so as to tell a story. This subtest requires interpretation of social situations and is intended to measure ability to comprehend and size up a total situation in relation to its parts.

3. *Block Design*—11 designs. This subtest requires arranging sets of blocks, colored red and white, so that they match pictures of designs shown by the examiner. The ability to perceive and analyze forms is believed to reflect ability to analyze and synthesize information.

4. *Object Assembly*—4 jigsaw puzzles. The subject must assemble jigsaw puzzle pieces so as to complete pictures of commonly known objects. This involves visual and motor functions and also permits the examiner to observe the subject's general task approach and reaction to mistakes.

5. *Coding*—symbols to be copied by matching them to numbers. This requires matching numbers and symbols by referring to a code that the subject keeps in view. The subtest is scored for both speed and accuracy; motor speed is probably more important then motor coordination.

6. *Mazes*—8 mazes. The subject is required to "find the way out" without being blocked. An alternate for the Coding subtest, this subtest involves tracing on a paper maze. Success depends on planning capability and the ability to follow a visual pattern.

The various Wechsler subtests are scored differently; some are scored pass-fail; others involve a weighted scoring system related to quality of responses. Raw scores on the WISC-R (and the other two Wechsler tests) are transformed to scaled scores, then scaled scores for subtests are combined and transformed to provide Verbal, Performance, and Full-Scale IQs. These are deviation IQs, with a mean of 100 and a standard deviation of 15.

The WISC-R is "the standard against which other measures of cognitive abilities have been judged for the last three decades" (Witt et al., 1988, p. 168). Availability of the separate Performance section may be particularly valuable in assessing students who are culturally or ethnically different from the majority, middle class, Anglo population. The following generalizations relating to differences between Verbal and Performance IQ scores provide some additional insight into the content of the WISC-R.

1. Mentally retarded subjects (in general) are likely to score higher on the Performance than on the Verbal section.
2. Bilingual subjects for whom English is a second language tend to score higher on the Performance section than on the Verbal section. This difference tends to be greater than that observed in relation to mental retardation.
3. Urban subjects are more likely to score higher on the Verbal section (as opposed to the Performance) than are rural subjects. This difference may be slowly disappearing.
4. Subjects classified as having reading problems are more likely to score higher on the Performance section than on the Verbal section.
5. Emotionally disturbed subjects (or in some instances those who are *temporarily* emotionally distraught) may score lower on the Performance section than on the Verbal section.

Differences in scores must be approached with caution in regard to predicting specific causation. The above statements are generalizations, and exceptions are quite likely. Also, differences between scores must be large enough to be significant or they mean very little; in the Wechsler Scales, differences should be at least 1 standard deviation (15 IQ points) to be considered significant.

Kaufman Assessment Battery for Children (K-ABC)

The Kaufman Assessment Battery for Children (Kaufman & Kaufman, 1983) is an individually administered measure designed to assess both cognitive and achievement abilities. The K-ABC age range (ages 2-6 through 12-5) is narrower than many other measures, and it does not attempt to assess the broad range of cognitive abilities that the Stanford-Binet and the Wechsler tests do. The total battery has three scales: Sequential Processing, Simultaneous Processing,

69

and Achievement. The two cognitive ability scales are described here; the achievement scale will be considered in chapter 8.

The Sequential Processing Scale has three subtests: Hand Movements, Number Recall, and Word Order. The Simultaneous Processing Scale has seven subtests: Magic Window, Face Recognition, Gestalt Closure, Triangles, Matrix Analogies, Spatial Memory, and Photo Series. The activities involved in these 10 subtests are:

Sequential Processing Scale

1. *Hand Movements*(ages 2-6–12-5). The subject must repeat a series of hand movements in the correct order.
2. *Number Recall* (ages 2-6–12-5). This subtest requires recall of numbers in sequence.
3. *Word Order* (ages 4-0-12-5). The subject must point to pictures of common objects in the same order as named by test administrator.

Simultaneous Processing Scale

1. *Magic Window* (ages 2-6–4-1). The test taker must name an object that is only partially visible. (A wheel is rotated—thus the magic window.)
2. *Face Recognition* (ages 2-6–4-1). The subject is required to identify one or two faces from a group picture.
3. *Gestalt Closure* (ages 2-6–12-5). This subtest requires identification of common objects from incomplete inkblot drawings.
4. *Triangles* (ages 4-0–12-5). The subject copies designs through use of a number of rubber triangles.
5. Matrix Analogies (ages 5-0–12-5). This subtest requires selecting a picture or design that completes an analogy.
6. *Spatial Memory* (ages 5-0–12-5). The subject must recall the location of pictures on a page.
7. *Photo Series* (ages 6-0–12-5). This subtest requires organizing photographs into a series representing their proper time sequence.

The K-ABC may not require the same level of training for administration as the Stanford-Binet or Wechsler tests do; however, it does require specific training for appropriate interpretation of results. Designed for use by school psychologists or specialized assessment personnel, it is based on a somewhat different theoretical perspective than many other measures of cognitive ability. It purports to determine how a student thinks, how he or she approaches problem solving and information processing, with less interest in what the student has learned previously. The K-ABC provides normalized standard scores for each subtest, which can be transformed into a Sequential Processing Scale score, a Simultaneous Processing Scale score, and a Mental Processing Composite score (Sequential plus Simultaneous scores). In addition, a Nonverbal Scale score can be calculated for subjects who have language or communication problems.

Woodcock–Johnson Psycho-Educational Battery, Revised (WJ-R)

WJ-R Tests of Cognitive Ability

The Woodcock-Johnson Psycho-Educational Battery (Woodcock & Johnson, 1989) consists of two parts—one group of subtests, which are collectively referred to as the Tests of Cognitive Ability, and a second part, the Tests of Achievement, which will be reviewed in chapter 8.

Twenty-one subtests are included in the Cognitive Ability Battery—seven in the Standard Battery and 14 in the Supplemental Battery. The Standard Battery permits the measurement of seven cognitive factors in less than 40 minutes. The Supplemental Battery provides one to three additional measures of each of these basic cognitive factors, allowing in-depth assessment of any factor that appears to require additional assessment. The seven tests included in the Standard Battery and the cognitive factors they measure are:

1. *Memory for Names*—assesses long-term memory.
2. *Memory for Sentences*—assesses short-term memory.
3. *Visual Matching*—assesses processing speed.
4. *Incomplete Words*—assesses auditory processing.
5. *Visual Closure*—assesses visual processing.
6. *Picture Vocabulary*—assesses comprehension-knowledge.
7. *Analysis-Synthesis*—assesses fluid reasoning.

The 14 tests included in the Supplemental Battery and the cognitive factors they measure are:

8. *Visual-Auditory Learning*—assesses long-term memory.
9. *Memory for Words*—assesses short-term memory.
10. *Cross Out*—assesses processing speed.
11. *Sound Blending*—assesses auditory processing.
12. *Picture Recognition*—assesses visual processing.
13. *Oral Vocabulary*—assesses comprehension-knowledge.
14. *Concept Formation*—assesses fluid reasoning.
15. *Delayed Recall-Memory for Names*—assesses long-term memory.
16. *Delayed Recall-Visual Auditory Learning*—assesses long-term memory.
17. *Numbers Reversed*—assesses short-term memory.

18. *Sound Patterns*—assesses auditory processing.
19. *Spatial Relations*—assesses both visual processing and fluid reasoning.
20. *Listening Comprehension*—assesses comprehension-knowledge.
21. *Verbal Analogies*—assesses both comprehension-knowledge and fluid reasoning.

English language skills are necessary for the WJ-R, but a Spanish language version is also available (Woodcock, 1982). Assessment is oral, and a test tape is used to present items on some subtests. If a student has difficulty with the taped presentation, however, the tester may present questions orally. The Woodcock-Johnson Tests of Cognitive Ability, which may be used with individuals ages 2 to 90+ years, provide a wide variety of scores and profiles. They also give discrepancy norms for making aptitude/achievement comparisons when used with the Woodcock-Johnson Tests of Achievement.

Other Measures of Cognitive Ability

Various of other measures of cognitive or intellectual ability may be used to provide a quick estimate of cognitive ability or in other special circumstances. Examples of these measures are briefly described in the following paragraphs.

Columbia Mental Maturity Scale (CMMS)

The Columbia Mental Maturity Scale (Burgemeister, Blum, & Lorge, 1972) is an individually administered test of general reasoning ability that requires no verbal response and minimal motor response from the subject. It is for use with children ages 3 years, 6 months through 9 years, 11 months, usually requires no more than 20 minutes to administer, and includes directions for administration in Spanish.

This is a "response to drawings" test, utilizing 92 items arranged in eight overlapping levels. The child actually is presented only 51 to 65 items, depending upon the level administered. Items are printed on 6" x 19" cards, and the child must select, from a series of drawings, the one that does not belong. The CMMS is particularly useful with children who have impaired verbal or physical abilities, and with children at the preschool or kindergarten levels. Test results provide an estimate of "general reasoning ability."

Detroit Tests of Learning Aptitude 2 (DTLA-2)

The Detroit Tests of Learning Aptitude 2 (Hammill, 1985) measure general aptitude (ability) plus certain discrete abilities. The subtests (ability areas) measured are: vocabulary, grammar, following commands, repeating words, storytelling, drawing from memory, order recall, reasoning, relationship knowledge, and Gestalt-closure function. A general intelligence quotient is also derived. The DTLA-2 is an individually administered test that may be useful in diagnosing learning disabilities and mental retardation. It is suitable for ages 6 through 17.

Differential Ability Scales (DAS)

The Differential Ability Scales (Elliott, 1989) is an assessment battery based on the *British Ability Scales*. Eight to 12 of the 18 subtests are appropriate for use at any age from 2½ through 17 years. The DAS measures specific cognitive abilities, including speed of information processing, verbal, nonverbal, and quantitative reasoning, spatial imagery, perceptual matching, short-term memory (both verbal and nonverbal), vocabulary, and verbal comprehension. Raw scores are converted to "ability scores" to provide potential for diagnostic assessment and planning of appropriate educational interventions.

The DAS has American-based age-norms (standard scores and percentiles) and out-of-level norms (for certain subtests) for use with gifted or developmentally delayed subjects. Three DAS subtests are optional achievement tests: Word Reading, Spelling, and Basic Number Skills. Excluding these three subtests, testing time is 60 to 90 minutes.

Hiskey-Nebraska Test of Learning Aptitude (HNTLA)

The Hiskey-Nebraska Test of Learning Aptitude (Hiskey, 1976) is a nonverbal, non-timed test for individuals with hearing handicaps, but norms are also available for children with normal hearing. This test is composed of 12 subtests: Bead Patterns, Memory for Color, Picture Identification, Picture Associations, Paper Folding (patterns), Visual Attention Span, Block Patterns, Completion of Drawings, Memory for Digits, Puzzle Blocks, Picture Analogies, and Spatial Reasoning. For use with students age 3 through 16, the HNTLA provides a generalized measure of learning potential.

Leiter International Performance Scale (LIPS)

A nonverbal measure of general intelligence, the Leiter International Performance Scale (Leiter & Arthur, 1955) does not require speech by either the examiner or the subject. The LIPS (more often called the "Leiter") is designed to measure intelligence through matching of colors, forms, and pictures; copying a block design; picture completion; number estimation; analogies; series completion; spatial relation; similarities; and other tasks of this nature. Test

73

materials and procedures are available for ages 2 through 18. The Leiter provides an estimate of mental ability.

McCarthy Scales of Children's Abilities (MSCA)

The McCarthy Scales of Children's Abilities (McCarthy, 1972a) measure general ability, auditory and visual short-term memory, and motor ability in children ages 2 years, 6 months to 8 years, 6 months. The MSCA includes 18 subtests, which may be grouped, for interpretation, into 6 scales (scores from certain subtests become part of more than one of these 6 scales): Verbal, Perceptual-Performance, Quantitative, General Cognitive Index, Memory, and Motor. The first three scales and the fourth (a composite of the first three) are pertinent to this chapter.

The Verbal scale includes pictorial memory, word knowledge, verbal memory, verbal fluency, and opposite analogies subtests. The Perceptual-Performance scale includes block building, puzzle solving, tapping sequence, right-left orientation, draw-a-design, draw-a-child, and conceptual grouping subtests. The Quantitative scale includes number questions, numerical memory, and counting and sorting subtests. The ability to attend, concentrate, and hold information in short-term memory are important factors in this scale, in addition to math skills, which are tapped more directly.

Raven Progressive Matrices (Raven)

The Raven Progressive Matrices (Raven, 1938, 1947, 1976—three different tests) are nonverbal tests that require the subject to find the missing segment of a design or matrix. Subjects are shown the incomplete design and are asked to select the piece that completes the design. This entire task can be completed by pointing. The three versions of the Progressive Matrices are: the Standard Progressive Matrices, for ages 8-65; the Colored Progressive Matrices, for ages 5-11 and for mentally retarded adults; and the Advanced Progressive Matrices, for adolescents and adults. Norms on these tests have been questioned for application in the United States because they were standardized in England. The Raven provides a general estimate of mental ability.

Slosson Intelligence Test (SIT)

The Slosson Intelligence Test (Slosson, 1983) is an individual test designed to provide a quick, screening type of estimate of general intelligence. Test questions are similar to those in the 1973 version of the Stanford-Binet, including vocabulary, verbal reasoning, memory, numerical reasoning, general information, and visual-motor items. Additional items related to the Gesell Developmental Schedules are included for use with very young children. Applicable from 1 month of age to age 27 years, the assessment of school children requires verbal responses. The SIT provides deviation IQ scores that can be converted to percentiles or stanines.

Test of Nonverbal Intelligence (TONI)

The Test of Nonverbal Intelligence (Brown, Sherbenou, & Dollar, 1982) is a measure of nonverbal problem-solving ability. The administrator gives instructions through pantomime, and the subject responds by pointing. Sets of figures are shown, and the subject first must determine whether it is a matter of matching, of analogies, or of progressions. He or she then selects the figure (from a number of options) that best completes the set. The TONI is for ages 5-85+, may be given individually or in small groups, and yields percentile ranks and a TONI quotient.

Adaptive Behavior

Adaptive behavior may be defined in a variety of ways, but all definitions relate to the level of development of personal living skills or social ability. That is, if an individual has well developed personal living skills and adapts to social demands so as to "fit" well within peer groups and with significant adults and authority figures, his or her adaptive behavior would likely be considered acceptable. Some teachers have observed that students with adequate adaptive behavior are "street smart."

Taylor (1985) has noted that adaptive behavior is age-specific, and, to some extent, culture-specific. Perhaps more important, he notes, "It is a difficult construct to operationalize and, subsequently, to measure" (1985, p. 1). Earlier, much less might have been said about adaptive behavior—either as a concept or with respect to specific assessment tools—but today, with the requirement that adaptive behavior must be measured before a classification of mental retardation is made, it is an important concept.

Adaptive behavior instruments are quite different from most other assessment tools in several ways. First, most adaptive behavior instruments depend on information from an informant (as contrasted to the subject being assessed). In most cases, the informant is parent(s) or teachers. Second, adaptive behavior instruments may be standardized on a population that is deliberately different from most of the subjects with which the instrument is likely to be used. Some have been standardized on individuals without handicaps even though the targeted population for adaptive behavior tests is primarily the population

75

having handicaps. Other adaptive behavior instruments have been standardized on a population with more severe handicaps.

Adaptive behavior scales are generally less reliable and less valid than most of the measures outlined in this text—not because test developers are not careful or competent, but because of the nature of the construct and the manner in which information must be gathered. The review of adaptive behavior instruments that follows will help explain both the construct of adaptive behavior and reasons why these measures may be less valid and reliable than most would desire.

AAMD Adaptive Behavior Scale—School Edition (ABS–SE)

The American Association on Mental Deficiency (AAMD), now renamed The American Association on Mental Retardation (AAMR), has historically related to "personal independence and social responsibility" in its consideration of adaptive behavior. The content of the AAMD Adaptive Behavior Scale—School Edition (Lambert, Windmiller, Tharinger, & Cole, 1981) provides an illustration of what typically is included in a definition/description of adaptive behavior. The domains and subdomains of the AAMD Scale are:

Domain 1. Independent Functioning
    eating
    toilet use
    cleanliness
    appearance
    care of clothing
    dressing and undressing
    travel
    other independent functioning
Domain 2. Physical Development
    sensory development
    motor development
Domain 3. Economic Activity
    money handling and budgeting
    shopping skills
Domain 4. Language Development
    expression
    comprehension
    social language development
Domain 5. Numbers and Time
Domain 6. Prevocational Activity

Domain 7. Self-Direction
  initiative
  perseverance
  leisure time
Domain 8. Responsibility
Domain 9. Socialization
Domain 10. Aggressiveness
Domain 11. Antisocial vs. Social Behavior
Domain 12. Rebelliousness
Domain 13. Trustworthiness
Domain 14. Withdrawal vs. Involvement
Domain 15. Mannerisms
Domain 16. Interpersonal Manners
Domain 17. Acceptability of Vocal Habits
Domain 18. Acceptability of Habits
Domain 19. Activity Level
Domain 20. Symptomatic Behavior
Domain 21. Use of Medications

The original AAMD Scales were standardized on institutional populations; the ABS-SE was standardized on a school-based population and is intended for use with subjects ages 3-16. Part One of the ABS-SE (Domains 1 through 9) for the most part involves evaluation of behavior on a dependence-independence continuum. The domains in Part Two (Domains 10 through 21) are designed for indications of whether various behaviors are exhibited occasionally, frequently, or not at all.

Scoring procedures permit comparison to a normal, an educable mentally retarded, or a trainable mentally retarded population. Percentile ranks are determined for each domain, and the domains are grouped into five factors: Personal Self-Sufficiency, Community Self-Sufficiency, Personal-Social Responsibility, Social Adjustment, and Personal Adjustment, for further evaluation. The ABS-SE may be used for screening purposes, for diagnosis and placement purposes, for IEP evaluation, or for progress evaluation. As with most other adaptive behavior measures, its value is dependent on the degree to which the respondent's information reflects the subject's behavior in an objective, informed manner.

Other Measures of Adaptive Behavior

The inventories and scales that have been developed have considerable similarity in assessing adaptive behavior, both with respect to behaviors assessed and in how they are assessed. There are, however, some differences. Several adaptive behavior measures are described next, illustrating these differences.

Adaptive Behavior Inventory (ABI)

Developed for completion by the classroom teacher and other school staff members, the Adaptive Behavior Inventory (Brown & Leigh, 1986) includes five scales: Self-Care Skills, Communication Skills, Social Skills, Academic Skills, and Occupational Skills. These may be used individually, or, if four or more scales are administered, a full-scale Adaptive Behavior Quotient can be calculated. (The ABI Short Form, a quick-scoring, 50-item version of the ABI, is also available.)

The ABI was standardized on a sample of normal students and another of students with mental retardation. It is intended to distinguish between persons without and with retardation and differentiate persons with mild, moderate, and severe/profound retardation. It also may be useful in diagnosing emotional disturbance.

Adaptive Behavior Inventory for Children (ABIC)

The Adaptive Behavior Inventory for Children (Mercer & Lewis, 1978) was developed as part of the System of Multicultural Pluralistic Assessment (SOMPA), reviewed in chapter 15. The ABIC is based on the belief that adaptive behavior can be best evaluated as it relates to role expectations of the family, the peer group, the school, and the community; thus, it is administered to the child's parent or caregiver.

The first section of the ABIC is administered to all respondents; administration of the remaining questions is determined by the student's age. The ABIC provides scores of six scales: Family, Community, Peer Relations, Nonacademic School Roles, Earner/Consumer, and Self-Maintenance. Either professionals or trained paraprofessionals can administer the measure, preferably in the home. Scaled scores for each of the six scales are obtained, as well as an Average Scaled Score. The ABIC classifies a student as "at risk" if scaled scores fall at 21 or below (approximately the 3rd percentile). The ABIC is available in both English and Spanish editions.

Children's Adaptive Behavior Scale (CABS)

The Children's Adaptive Behavior Scale (Richmond & Kicklighter, 1980) is different from many other adaptive behavior measures in that it directly assesses a child's ability to perform, rather than assessing through an informant. During the one-to-one testing five domains are assessed: Language Development,

Independent Functioning, Family Role Performance, Economic-Vocational Activity, and Socialization. The CABS is for use with children 5 to 10 years of age. Subjects' responses are in the form of answers to questions and the performance of various tasks. The CABS provides measures of both skill development and adaptive behavior in children who have mental retardation.

Comprehensive Test of Adaptive Behavior (CTAB)

Designed to be both a descriptive and a prescriptive test for individuals of all ages, the Comprehensive Test of Adaptive Behavior (Adams, 1984a) assesses in six areas: Self-Help Skills (separate male, female subtests), Home Living Skills, Independent Living Skills, Social Skills, Sensory and Motor Skills, and Language Concepts and Academic Skills. The parent/guardian provides information on the first three areas; school personnel provide information on the last three areas.

The CTAB was standardized on a handicapped sample, including children and adults, in schools, community-based programs, and institutions. The test is intended for use both in placement decisions and in follow-up, progress analysis.

Normative Adaptive Behavior Checklist (NABC)

Also by Adams, the Normative Adaptive Behavior Checklist (Adams, 1984b) evaluates the same six areas as the Comprehensive Test of Adaptive Behavior, above. The parent is the informant for this checklist, designed to identify those who need further evaluation. In contrast to the CTAB, the NABC was normed on normally achieving individuals. It is intended for use from birth to age 21.

Scales of Independent Behavior (SIB)

The Scales of Independent Behavior (Bruininks, Woodcock, Weatherman, & Hill, 1984) test is considered to be part of the Woodcock-Johnson Psycho-Educational Battery (reviewed earlier in this chapter); it is organized to relate to those cognitive measures. These scales are appropriate for persons 3 months through 40 + years of age. The SIB is similar to other scales of adaptive behavior and includes a section on maladaptive behavior. The SIB may be administered as a total battery or as an abbreviated scale; as examples, the Early Development Scale or the Problem Behavior Scale may be administered separately. Various scores are available; percentile ranks, standard scores, Maladaptive Behavior Indexes, and others. All can be related directly to the other elements of the Woodcock-Johnson system.

79

Pyramid Scales (PS)

The Pyramid Scales (Cone, 1984) provide a measure of adaptive functioning in 20 skill areas. The PS is both criterion- and curriculum-referenced. Items are curriculum-referenced to sources such as the Brigance Inventory, the Uniform Performance System, and others. Administration is by interview, by an informant, by direct observation, or some combination of these three modes. The Pyramid Scales can be used from birth to age 78.

Vineland Adaptive Behavior Scales (VABS)

The Vineland Adaptive Behavior Scales (Sparrow, Balla, & Cicchetti, 1984) include two interview editions and one classroom edition. The interview editions, administered by trained interviewers, are for children from birth to 18 years, 11 months; they also may be used with low-functioning adults. The classroom scale, to be completed by the teacher, is for ages 3 to 12 years, 11 months. All three editions include four adaptive behavior domains: Communication (subdomains Receptive, Expressive, and Written), Daily Living Skills (subdomains Personal, Domestic, and Community), Socialization (subdomains Interpersonal Relationships, Play and Leisure Time, and Coping Skills), and Motor Skills (subdomains Gross and Fine). The interview edition includes an optional domain—Maladaptive Behavior. Standard Scores are obtained for each of the domains and for the Composite Score.

Weller-Strawser Scales of Adaptive Behavior: For the Learning Disabled (Elementary Scale & Secondary Scale) (WSSAB)

Developed for use with students already identified as learning disabled, both of the Weller-Strawser Scales of Adaptive Behavior (Weller & Strawser, 1981) include assessment of social coping, relationships, pragmatic language, and production. Scores obtained, which define problems as mild to moderate or moderate to severe, are intended to provide guidance for instruction, not as a placement device. The authors emphasize that the WSSAB is to be used only with students who are already identified as learning disabled. The WSSAB Elementary Scale is for students in grades 1 to 6; the Secondary Scale is for students in grades 7 to 12.

Informal Assessment

We noted earlier that informal assessment includes procedures or techniques such as sytematic observation, work sample analysis, task analysis, error analysis, inventories, diagnostic teaching, checklists, interviews, questionnaires, analysis of records, and other similar approaches to data gathering. Curriculum-based evaluation (CBE) also is usually considered to be informal assessment. McLoughlin and Lewis (1986) have pointed out several important differences between formal and informal measures:

1. Informal measures are designed to gather information about current status; formal measures are usually thought to be predictive of future performance.
2. The standard of reference of informal measures is usually specific instructional concerns or performance in a given classroom; the standard of reference of formal measures (of norm-referenced tests) is a much larger, theoretical norm group.
3. Most informal measures are not standardized, and there is no information about validity or reliability; most formal measures are standardized, with information about both validity and reliability.
4. Informal measures often require more time and effort by educational personnel to design the instrument; formal, norm-referenced measures are "ready to use" and are thus more time-efficient.
5. Informal measures vary with respect to specificity but often are more specific and focused than are formal measures; formal measures are broader in nature and tend to assess in a selective manner intended to represent a broad area of the curriculum or a broad personal characteristic.

One additional characterization of the differences between formal and informal assessment has been outlined by Guerin and Maier (1983). They indicate that such differences "center on six basic testing dimensions: setting, activities, dialogue, statistics, data, and format" (p. 7). As for setting, formal assessment is structured while informal is naturalistic; activities are ordered in formal assessment and flexible in informal assessment; dialogue is prescribed in formal assessment and open in informal assessment; statistics are standardized in formal asssessment and idiosyncratic in informal assessment; data are codified in formal assessment and enumerated in informal assessment; and format is numerical in formal assessment, descriptive in informal assessment. They also noted that "informal assessment encompasses information that is ongoing and cumulative rather than information that is drawn from a fixed point in time and is static" (p. 7).

Exceptions to these generalized differences between formal and informal measures exist, of course. Some checklists, for example, have been developed by recognized experts, used with many thousands of subjects, and thus can be put to use immediately by the teacher or other assessment personnel. They are "informal," but they seem to have some of the characteristics of formal measures. Many authorities suggest that teachers should make greater use of informal measures that they develop and that are specific to their unique needs. Salvia and Ysseldyke (1988) believe that "Increasingly, educators are advocating informal over formal assessment, especially in instructional decision making and in evaluating pupil progress" (p. 22). They also suggest that some informal assessment may be called "diagnostic teaching," because with such procedures "teachers or diagnostic specialists have an opportunity to modify several aspects of instruction and to study the impact of such adaptations on pupil performance" (p. 23).

In this chapter we discuss a sample of informal measures that represent the wide variety of informal assessment techniques and procedures teachers may elect to use in their classrooms. With respect to these and other informal assessment procedures, it should be noted that although a technique may be illustrated with respect to its use in spelling or writing, it also might be used with respect to other academic areas. In comparison to the finite number of formal measures of language development, for example, a thousand or more informal language development assessment techniques might be developed.

Curriculum-Based Assessment*

Curriculum-based assessment (CBA) and curriculum-based evaluation are terms applied to a variety of informal assessment procedures that are directly related to the classroom curriculum. This is informal assessment that will assist the teacher to more effectively plan to meet the unique needs of individual students. In an introduction to a special issue of *Exceptional Children,* totally dedicated to curriculum-based assessment, Tucker (1985) noted, "There is nothing new about curriculum-based assessment. In many respects it is like coming home to traditional classroom instruction" (p. 199). He further noted that "*in curriculum-based assessment the essential measure of success in education is the student's progress in the curriculum of the local school*" (p. 199).

In the Preface to their text, *Curriculum-based Evaluation for Special and Remedial Education,* Howell and Morehead (1987) stated, "Curriculum-based evaluation draws much of its strength from the *principle of alignment.* This principle states that greater learning will occur in programs that ensure that evaluation and instruction are both aligned with the curriculum" (p. vi). Gickling and Thompson (1985) also speak of "alignment," indicating that CBA permits the alignment of assessment practices with what is being taught in the classroom. As they noted, this makes it possible to "determine the need for curriculum adaptations quickly and to initiate instruction that will provide low-achieving and mainstreamed handicapped students with a better chance for success" (p. 207).

CBA does not eliminate the potential need for other assessment. Tucker (1985) stated that when discussing CBA, "a mistaken conclusion is often drawn that the CBA proponents believe that all students who show problems in school can be helped by better teaching and that there is no need to perform the more traditional clinical assessments . . ." (p. 201). He then stated that this conclusion is unwarranted and that some students require "the cooperative skills of a number of different professions working together to determine what factors are involved and how best to help a particular student" (p. 202).

In a discussion of how to use CBA to make curriculum decisions, Blankenship (1985) stated that "the aim is to produce a device to measure pupil performance and to develop a plan for administering and interpreting the results of the assessment" (p. 234). She provided a series of steps for implementation of curriculum-based assessment:

1. List skills involved in the targeted material.
2. Analyze the list to see if all important skills are included.
3. Make certain the edited skill list has the skills in logical order.
4. Develop a written objective for each skill in the list.
5. Develop items to test each objective.
6. Prepare testing materials.

---

* This discussion of curriculum-based assessment is adapted from B. Gearheart and C. Gearheart (1989), *Learning Disabilities: Educational Strategies* (5th ed., pp. 71-73). Columbus, OH, Charles Merrill.

7. Decide how the tests will be administered.
8. Give the test just prior to starting instruction on the curriculum topic under consideration.
9. Evaluate the results to determine:
   a. which students have already mastered which skills.
   b. which students have the necessary prerequisite skills.
   c. which students must be helped with prerequisite skills.
10. Plan instruction based on the above information; after completing instruction, readminister the test to determine which students have mastered the skills.
11. Modify instructional planning based on the new assessment results, and repeat the procedure.

Although "curriculum-based assessment" is somewhat established as the terminology of choice with this type of assessment system, some writers refer to the approach as "curriculum-based measurement" (CBM) (Deno & Fuchs, 1987). In their text on assessing special students, McLoughlin and Lewis (1990) include curriculum-based measures as one of three major types of informal assessment. (The other two types or categories are (a) observation, work sample analysis, and task analysis, and (b) procedures using informants.) In their categorization, CBM includes inventories, criterion-referenced tests, diagnostic probes, and diagnostic teaching.

According to Deno and Fuchs (1987), "What makes CBM distinct from traditional psychoeducational measurement . . . is that the stimulus material that provides the occasion for student responses is the actual curriculum of the local school rather than a set of independent items or problems created by commercial test developers" (p. 2). Whether referred to as CBA or CBM, the essential feature is that the local school curriculum is the starting point. Many teachers recognize that these concepts are not entirely new.

Systematic (Direct) Observation

Direct observation has been used for a variety of purposes, but questions about both the reliability and the accuracy of the results have always been raised. Unplanned or indirect observations can have value, but our focus will be on planned, systematic observation.

Direct observation ordinarily should include the following characteristics:
1. Developing a specific plan for observing.
2. Developing a specific method and format for recording observations.
3. Reducing potential ambiguities as much as possible.
4. Training observers.

5. Observing and recording behaviors. (If behaviors cannot be recorded concurrently, they must be recorded as quickly as possible following the event.)

Guerin and Maier (1983) have outlined four methods of observation that may be of value in the classroom. These are briefly described.

Chronolog

The chronolog is especially useful when it is difficult to determine what events in a student's life are influencing his or her behavior. The chronolog states objective observations in short phrases or sentences, in nonjudgmental language. The observer avoids words that evaluate, draw conclusions, or suggest intent. (Example: Avoid "he was mad at John"; instead, state, "He spoke in a loud voice and swung the bat at John.") Relevant details (such as time, location, activity) are recorded, along with the name of other major "players" in the setting. The chronolog provides a basis for later evaluation by the observer or by others on an evaluation team. Several chronologs on the same student, but in different settings or in the company of different "players," may provide significant insights. If it is properly completed, the chronolog is an objective, meaningful informal assessment tool.

Frequency Recording

Frequency recording provides a means to establish patterns of behavior. Recording may represent the total number of times a behavior occurs or the number of times it occurs during various time intervals. If the behavior is well defined, this recording can provide useful quantitative data about changes in behavior. This may be particularly useful in evaluating the effectiveness of various intervention programs.

Sequence Sample

In the sequence sample, behavior is recorded at the moment the targeted problem occurs. What happens immediately after the problem is recorded and, to the extent possible, what happened immediately before the problem. This type of observation, intended to separate behavior into its stimuli, event, and response components, may be valuable in planning interventions. If the teacher carefully records his or her own behavior, this also will be of value in determining the teacher's role in the sequence.

Trait Sample

The trait sample requires an established system with predetermined "trait" categories. In most cases a third person (not the teacher) must give full attention to observing, categorizing, and recording observed behavior. For example, one such system might include three aggressive trait categories: direct physical aggression (e.g., hitting, kicking, pushing), verbal aggression, and aggressive acts against property/inanimate objects. Other behavior, such as various types of attention-getting behavior and manipulating/controlling behavior, would complete the system. Systems of this nature have been developed by various authorities, and the observer must be trained to do this type of observation.

A type of direct observation that does not fit neatly into Guerin and Maier's four categories of observation is illustrated in the following vignette.

Assume that the problem is Mike's difficulty in producing acceptable, legible writing products. If other interventions have not worked, the teacher should observe Mike while he is writing—considering his degree of tenseness, speed of writing, pressure applied to writing tools, interest level, ease with which he is distracted by noise or movement, onset of fatigue, and any other factors the teacher's experience indicates are important. Such observation, on several occasions, may provide useful clues (assessment) of what help Mike may need to improve his writing.

Direct, systematic observations are an important form of assessment. Preplanning is *essential* to success in the use of this tool.

Checklists

Various types of checklists may be used effectively in informal assessment. Some require the teacher to analyze the student's academic efforts; others require observation of student behavior and response to a list that calls to the teacher's attention behaviors that might influence the targeted performance. Unlike standardized tests, some checklists can be modified to fit the present need, age of student, and so on. Various published checklists are useful in a given situation, but some cannot be modified. Many master teachers have developed checklists of their own to accomplish specific types of assessment. The samples that follow illustrate how checklists may be used.

Temple and Gillet (1984) developed a detailed checklist to analyze a student's writing. It includes 20 major questions, with three to five subquestions under most of these questions. Major subparts of this checklist include: The Writing Process, The Functions of Writing, Qualities of Writing Style (Fluency of Writing), Mechanics of Writing, and Enjoying Writing. One example, under the subpart "Mechanics of Writing,," illustrates how such a checklist works. In regard to spelling:

— Does the writer misspell words in the first draft?
— Does the writer correct the spelling of many words between the first and second drafts?
— What does the writer do when he or she is uncertain of how to spell a word? (p. 292).

A number of checklists have been developed in the area of mathematics—perhaps because of the relatively predictable/logical sequential nature of basic arithmetic skills. Reisman (1978) developed a list of 46 common arithmetic errors; examples of each are provided along with the written description of the errors. Teachers may find this type of assessment tool quite helpful in attempts to better understand (assess) the nature of and reasons for a particular student's difficulties in arithmetic. For example, one item on Reisman's checklist relates to errors in division resulting from incomplete subtraction. Another item relates to errors in division as a result of stopping at the first partial quotient. Such analysis statements, along with examples of each type of error, provide a useful informal assessment tool that assists the classroom teacher in determining the student's specific difficulty.

Checklists are of the greatest value in assessment that is directly related to planning intervention or remediation or in determining whether to refer a particular student for formal assessment by the assessment team.

Error Analysis

Error analysis is one informal technique that is described quite precisely through its title. The use of a checklist in relation to errors in mathematics, described in the previous section, is also an example of error analysis. In fact it provides an excellent example of how one assessment approach may involve at least two of the informal assessment techniques listed at the start of this chapter. Other types of error analysis may be applied in spelling, handwriting, and other areas of the curriculum.

The basic idea is simple: The concern must be with what the student did incorrectly, what aspects of his or her answers are wrong or confused, what incorrect processes or misunderstandings are involved, and similar questions. To say that a student writes poorly or illegibly, or misses 12 of 50 basic

87

arithmetic problems, or scores at the 3.5 level in arithmetic when the student is in grade 6, or cannot read a "third-grade" reading book although the student is in the sixth grade, is of very little help for instructional purposes.

Error analysis is an attempt to systematically analyze what the student is doing right and wrong and where confusion, lack of skill development, lack of understanding, and other, similar factors are preventing successful performance. In most instances, error analysis involves establishing categories of reasons why the student was not successful, and through analysis of the student's work, determining which of these categories are most significant. Error analysis may be quite precise or relatively judgmental, but the intent and the thrust are always the same.

As an example, spelling errors generally can be categorized as omissions, additions, substitutions, sequencing errors, or some combination of these four categories. A frequency count of errors can be tabulated and types of errors categorized. An attempt to find the cause of errors can be made, providing a basis for remediation. But there may be disagreement as to how the causes should be categorized for analysis. In error analysis as applied to spelling, the assessors must decide how they will categorize cause(s), and then relate the types of errors to causes. (For example, there may be a question as to whether a particular group of errors consists of phonetic/nonphonetic errors or revisualization errors.)

Whatever the causal assumptions, the process of error analysis which applies to many academic areas is:
1. Classify as to type of errors.
2. Classify as to cause of errors.
3. Establish a matrix or chart with types of errors on one axis and causes on the other.
4. Record errors.
5. Based on where the major problems are concentrated, initiate a program designed to help the student overcome the errors.

One additional factor should be considered in error analysis. For some academic areas certain skills may be prerequisites for other learning in that area. When this is the case, indication (through error analysis) that these skills are underdeveloped requires an immediate focus on these prerequisites. Ignoring the unusual level of influence of such prerequisites may greatly reduce the student's learning. The process of task analysis, described next, can provide the teacher with information regarding prerequisite skills.

Clearly, error analysis and, for that matter, several other informal assessment techniques place more responsibility on the teacher and assume more teacher knowledge about how learning takes place than do other, formal techniques that "prescribe" certain interventions. This is a characteristic of informal assessment.

Task Analysis

Task analysis may be referred to as a process, a point of view, or a model. The task analysis process is based on the assumption that most tasks are made up of many components and subcomponents, and that a student who cannot complete a task successfully has likely not mastered all of its essential subcomponents or has not learned to integrate them. When we engage in task analysis, we attempt to identify all of the activities (subcomponents) required to complete whatever task is under investigation.

Investigation of a given task can be approached in various ways. One way is to perform the task yourself. Some teachers may not be sufficiently objective or perceptive to see all that is involved. With practice, however, most can learn to observe all aspects of a task. One way to increase one's own objectivity and perception is to enlist the help of a coworker; one of you performs the task, and the other observes. This process will lead to much more accurate observations.

Other approaches to task analysis also involve careful observation. In one, the teacher observes the student completing the task (e.g., an arithmetic problem or a written assignment in social studies). Another approach involves observing someone who is highly skilled at a given task (an expert). This latter approach may be particularly useful with respect to physical tasks (e.g., tossing up a tennis ball and swinging a tennis racquet so as to hit the ball with accuracy). Whatever the initial approach, one will likely proceed somewhat as follows in completing task analysis:
1. Define the task with a high degree of specificity, and establish the acceptable level of performance.
2. Identify the subtasks (smaller tasks or components involved in the larger task) and the sequence in which they must occur to achieve success. (In some instances more than one sequence will be acceptable.)
3. Determine the minimum skill level necessary in each of the smaller tasks, to permit integration of such components.
4. Identify strategies (rules, procedures, etc.) that must be understood and mastered in order to combine/integrate the smaller tasks or components into larger tasks.
5. Determine the components in which the student is not proficient.
6. Initiate instruction, remediation, intervention, or adaptive measures as required.

Many good teachers have successfully used task analysis for years without identifying this logical approach as task analysis. Nevertheless, a teacher's almost unconscious application of this method may not provide the useful insights that are obtained when teachers understand what they are doing and why they are doing it.

89

Work Sample Analysis

Work sample analysis involves studying samples of a student's work and determining correct and incorrect responses or components so as to permit the development of a meaningful plan for remediation. It involves error analysis (see the discussion earlier in this chapter) and usually involves task analysis (described in the preceding section). Work samples provide a highly practical instrument for determining the areas in which the student is most in need of help, although just one or two work samples do not provide a sufficient base for decisions about interventions.

If, after analysis of a few work samples, a particular problem appears to be present, it is helpful to make another work assignment structured so as to provide more information about the apparent source of the difficulty. *The purpose of work sample analysis is to discover patterns of errors that may be further sorted into categories.* In some instances, discovering patterns may be difficult; the errors may be apparently random. When this is the case, further investigation is required, because random errors provide very little guidance for remediation.

When thinking of work samples, one naturally thinks of written work, and this is the product most often "analyzed" using this procedure. But oral products also may be analyzed. For example, if a student has difficulties in oral reading, a tape recording of his or her work becomes the product that is subject to analysis. As with any teaching or assessment procedure, ingenuity is required to make work sample analysis a successful assessment technique.

Interviews

Interviews constitute one of two major ways in which we may gain information from informants. (The other, questionnaires, will be discussed next.) Interviews with parents, teachers, or students may be of great value, but their value depends upon the accuracy of the informant's answers. Inaccurate information may be deliberate, but, more often, inaccurate or partially accurate information is the result of factors such as poor memory, the informant's inability to understand and report what they saw, know, or experienced, built-in observer bias resulting from self-interest, or poor judgment. Interviewer bias may also be a problem.

Conducting a successful interview is a skill that must be learned, and until an interviewer develops considerable competence, information obtained through an interview may be of questionable value. Teachers who want to utilize this technique must practice, just as they would need special training to administer some of the more complex psychological tests.

Interviews provide the teacher with insights from another person's point of view. An interview with the parent may indicate that a particular problem, demonstrated in school, does or does not exist at home (e.g., the student may avoid reading anything in the home, or the student may be an avid reader of sports or beauty magazines). This information, in the first case, would lead the teacher to further examine why the student avoids reading, or, in the second case, whether the reading material used in school can be made more relevant to the student's interests.

Interviewing other teachers provides similar information, whereas interviews of the student may provide insights that cannot be gained from other sources. The student's interests, motivations, and perceptions are critical in providing meaningful intervention. Significantly different interventions are indicated if the teacher finds that Tom dislikes reading because he believes he is "too dumb" to learn to read well, as opposed to discovering that he wants to learn to read but "can't remember the words."

Questionnaires

The questionnaire may be considered a written interview. But unlike the interview, which can be expanded and take almost any path or direction, the questionnaire is obviously limited to the topics included in written form. A questionnaire is a simple, effective way to obtain information, but good questionnaires are *not* simple to construct.

Questionnaires do have several possible shortcomings; for example: questions can be misinterpreted, and the fixed format limits the options for respondents. Questionnaires do, however, provide a permanent product for analysis/comparisons on a within-student basis (compared to other information on a given student) or for comparisons among students. As compared to interviews, questionnaires may permit more freedom in responses in that the student may be very aware that "someone is waiting for an answer" in the interview but can take more time in completing a questionnaire.

Inventories

Inventories usually are thought of as comprehensive listings of some sort (e.g., the year-end inventory of items in a hardware store). Teachers may construct and use informal inventories that will relate to a particular class, curriculum, or student. Self-concept inventories may be constructed to permit the student to inventory his or her own strengths and weaknesses, or beliefs or feelings.

A number of published interest and "preference" inventories are used in relation to career or vocational counseling (see chapter 14), as well as those relating to preferred learning style, preferred teacher style, and others. Informal, teacher-constructed inventories on any topic provide a systematic way to list—so as to provide more objective evaluation—whatever characteristics, abilities, or interests are under consideration. Reading ability may affect the potential value and effectiveness of inventories.

Modified Assessment Techniques

Modified assessment techniques (Hargrove & Poteet, 1984) are adjustments that the tester may make to further determine the student's capabilities. After completing a test, following standardized administration procedures, the test administrator "selects those items or tasks on which the student gave incorrect, inefficient, or inappropriate responses" (p. 54), for further investigation. Based on the student's response, the tester modifies aspects of test items to determine whether the modification will enable the student to successfully respond. The usual components that are modified are modality, language, complexity, space, and time.

Modality relates to how the student receives information and provides a response. For example, a test item that is provided verbally may be modified so as to be visual (2 apples and 3 apples equals how many apples? presented verbally, may be presented visually as $2 + 3 =$ ____). Similarly, test items presented visually may be modified so that presentation is verbal. Other modifications include the manner in which the student responds—for example, writing a response rather than responding verbally.

Language complexity may be reduced by using concrete objects. And overall *complexity* may be reduced by simplifying the task. Additional modifications relate to *space*—for example, transferring knowledge of the concept of "under" into a concrete form. If the child has difficulty marking an x "under" a given word in the assessment setting, it can be determined whether the child understands the concept with respect to getting "under" a table. *Time* can be modified by allowing as much time as required to complete test tasks, or the rate of presentation can be changed.

The need for modified assessment techniques is determined during administration of standardized tests. The key factor is for the tester to determine whether a modification might provide educationally relevant information.

Diagnostic Probes and Diagnostic Teaching

"Diagnostic Probes are typically brief, one-time measures of a single instructional option. Diagnostic teaching . . . takes place over an extended time period to investigate fully the differential effects of various instructional interventions" (McLoughlin & Lewis, 1990, p. 117). A diagnostic probe ordinarily involves modifying some one aspect of instruction to see if the student will perform more satisfactorily under the modified approach. It requires very little time and involves trying an idea that the teacher's experience indicates might be helpful or more effective.

Teachers are admonished regularly to adapt instruction to meet students' needs. The diagnostic probe is a type of informal assessment that permits the teacher to assess the relative effectiveness of standard instructional practice as compared to an adapted instructional procedure. Modifications might include changing how a student is taught (oral versus written presentation), how the student is asked to respond (formal written—e.g., essay type paragraphs versus phrases in outline form versus recorded oral responses), how much information is presented at one time, how much response is asked for at one time, how feedback is provided, how success is rewarded, and many others. If two or three alternatives are to be assessed, a number of successive probes will be required.

Diagnostic teaching is a longer term version of the diagnostic probe, and it allows for more trial modifications and an opportunity to determine longer term effectiveness. It requires more involved planning, is a more comprehensive process, and entails more detailed record keeping. Both diagnostic probes and diagnostic teaching require accurate information about the baseline (current) instructional condition, and results obtained under this condition, in order to give meaning to results obtained under the modified condition.

In conclusion, one reason informal assessment has received much added attention since the early 1970s is that during the period of time when standardized (norm-referenced) tests were receiving considerable criticism for their contribution to inappropriate classification and placement practices, informal measures received little criticism and were recommended as part of the solution to the problem of test bias. But they are not without negative aspects. Teachers may not be skilled, and they are not always unbiased in constructing informal assessment tools. The value of informal assessment is that it provides information about the student that formal, standardized instruments cannot provide.

Assessment in Early Childhood

Early childhood education has a long and varied history. The emphasis of educational efforts with young children has ranged from that of *Plato* (427-347 B.C.), who believed that children should be removed from the home as soon as possible and placed in state-run schools, to the beliefs of John *Dewey* (1859-1952), which involved social interaction to develop cooperation and encourage intellectual growth and emphasized the vital role of parental involvement and nurture. After Dewey's theories became generally recognized, interest in the processes of learning in young children increased, and from the study of these processes came the maturationist views of individuals such as Arnold *Gesell* (1880-1961).

At about the same time as maturationist theories were becoming popular, the behavioral theories, as advocated by B. F. *Skinner* (1904-), were influencing many educators, including those whose primary interest was education in early childhood. These opposing points of view, plus increasing interest in the concept of intelligence and its measurement in young children, converged into an intensified interest in early childhood education. The work of Jean *Piaget* (1896-1980), which emphasized cognitive development and a blending of maturationist and interactionist views, led to accelerated interest and emphasis in the 1960s. Throughout this evolution of thought, and the development of various early childhood programs, most efforts were directed toward children in general rather than children from disadvantaged backgrounds or handicapped children.

In the 1960s the Head Start programs were developed in response to a national belief that early childhood compensatory programs could make a difference in children's success in later school years. A major component of

Head Start programs was assessment of the progress of these young children. The national commitment to early childhood intervention was reemphasized with passage of Public Law 94-142 and its incentives for preschool-age children, and again with passage of Public Law 99-457 in 1986, which required the states to provide services for handicapped preschool children aged 3 to 5 by 1991. Another section of this law provided for monetary incentives to states that provided services to infants and toddlers (birth through age 2).

The components of PL 94-142 relating to assessment by a multidisciplinary team and development of an individualized education program (IEP) apply to preschool children (see chapter 3). PL 99-457 uses the more inclusive term "developmental disabilities" in place of individual categories such as learning disabilities, behavior disorders, and mental retardation—recognizing the dangers and difficulties inherent in specifically labeling young children.

Under current legislation, a preschooler who experiences developmental delays or is at risk in physical development, cognitive development, language or speech development, or some combination of these, may be considered developmentally delayed.

The Child Find provision of PL 94-142 requires school districts to develop a plan to actively search for handicapped children at both the preschool and school age levels. PL 99-457 has extended this to infants and toddlers through monetary incentive grants to individual states.

PL 99-457 includes specific regulations that relate to assessment and provision of services for infants and toddlers. Relevant sections of PL 99-457 are included here.

In a departure from PL 94-142 and the requirement of an IEP, PL 99-457 requires a more inclusive individualized family service plan (IFSP). Recognizing that infants and toddlers are influenced by the family environment, this plan provides for assessment of the child *and* the family, as well as the provision of services for the child *and* family. A description of the components of an individualized family service plan are reprinted here from the Regulations for PL 99-457.

In addition to assessing the infant or toddler in the areas of physical development, cognitive development, psychosocial development, and self-help skills to determine his or her needs, family strengths and needs also must be assessed. This is significantly different from PL 94-142. The provision of support services to the family to enhance the infant's or toddler's development is an additional departure from PL 94-142. Figure 7.1 provides a comprehensive overview of the system of identification processes or services that should be provided for the families of young handicapped and at-risk children. It also permits a comparison to similar provisions for school-age children as required by PL 94-142 and previously outlined in chapter 3.

An essential component of the individualized family service plan (IFSP) is the identification of a case manager at the initial meeting. This individual is to coordinate the services of the various individuals who may be involved: special educators, physical or occupational therapists, psychologists, speech therapists, audiologists, medical personnel, family trainers or counselors, and others. The intent of this mandate is to ensure unified, coordinated multidisciplinary services that meet the needs of the family and the child.

Assessment of the Family

Recognizing the vital role the family plays in child development, the authors of PL 99-457 have included assessment of the family in order to provide services for them as well as the at-risk or handicapped child. Although family assessment is not an entirely new concept, it has received less attention than assessment of children (Jordan, Gallagher, Hutinger, & Karnes, 1988).

Bailey and Simeonsson (1988a) have identified several major areas of potential difficulty in assessment of the family. The first relates to a "lack of functional models for conceptualizing families and their needs" (p. 6). Models that conceptualize the *child's* needs have been developed and are in use, but models that identify the essential components of *family functioning* and the means to assess those components to develop appropriate goals have yet to be developed.

A second area of concern relates to the instruments available. Assessment instruments that are available tend to identify deficits and areas of stress but not how to deal with conflicting values and problems with spousal interaction, feelings, and lifestyle practices. Such assessment provides few data for building on the strengths of the family and may even create problems of dissension or trust.

The third barrier to appropriate family assessment may be the individuals delegated to carry out the assessment. Many persons trained to provide services for the child have not received comprehensive training in family assessment. Effectively teaching children requires a different set of skills than interviewing families, identifying priorities, or accommodating to the values of the family.

Last, the family may resist assessment, viewing it as intrusive, irrelevant to the child's needs, or of much lower priority. Parents who have only recently found that their child is handicapped may be unable to deal with any more than that or may deny that the handicap exists (Pollner & McDonald-Wiler, 1985).

The intent of family assessment is to establish the goals required for the IFSP that will enhance the child's development, building on family strengths, not merely identifying weaknesses. If the team is not aware of differing cultural influences, values, or priorities, the goals set for the family may be incongruent with family priorities and values, which will lead to a lack of ownership or

97

Sec 672. As used in this part—

(1) The term "handicapped infants and toddlers" means individuals from birth to age 2, inclusive, who need early intervention services because they—

(A) are experiencing developmental delays, as measured by appropriate diagnostic instruments and procedures in one or more of the following areas: Cognitive development, physical development, language and speech development, psychological development, or self-help skills, or

(B) have a diagnosed physical or mental condition which has a high probability of resulting in developmental delay.

Such term may also include, at a State's discretion, individuals from birth to age 2, inclusive, who are at risk of having substantial developmental delays if early intervention services are not provided.

(2) "Early intervention services" are developmental services which—

(A) are provided under public supervision,

(B) are provided at no cost except where Federal or State law provides for a system of payments by families, including a schedule of sliding fees,

(C) are designed to meet a handicapped infant's or toddler's developmental needs in any one or more of the following areas:

(i) physical development,

(ii) cognitive development,

(iii) language and speech development,

(iv) psycho-social development, or

(v) self-help skills,

(D) meet the standards of the State, including the requirements of this part,

(E) include—

(i) family training, counseling, and home visits,

(continued)

"compliance." As a result, professionals involved may think of the family as disinterested or uncaring (Turnbull & Turnbull, 1985).

Assessment of family needs must be conducted frequently because of the growth and development of the child and the modification of family dynamics (McGonigal & Garland, 1988). The type of instrument selected will be determined by the information required; for example, certain information is necessary upon identification of the presence of a handicap, different information is required during transitions, still different information is mandatory when attempting to determine progress, and still different information is necessary when comparing one program with another (Peterson, 1987). Interventionists must carefully analyze the specific information necessary, use of the informa-

(continued)

      (ii) special instruction,

      (iii) speech pathology and audiology,

      (iv) occupational therapy,

      (v) physical therapy,

      (vi) psychological services,

      (vii) case management services,

      (viii) medical services only for diagnostic or evaluation purposes,

      (ix) early identification, screening, and assessment services, and

      (x) health services necessary to enable the infant or toddler to benefit from the other early intervention services,

    (F) are provided by qualified personnel, including—

      (i) special educators,

      (ii) speech and language pathologists and audiologists,

      (iii) occupational therapists,

      (iv) physical therapists,

      (v) psychologists,

      (vi) social workers,

      (vii) nurses, and

      (viii) nutritionists, and

    (G) are provided in conformity with an individualized family service plan adopted in accordance with section 677.

    (3) The term 'developmental delay' has the meaning given such term by a State under section 676(b)(1).

    (4) The term 'Council' means the State Interagency Coordinating Council established under section 682.

(Federal Register, 1987, pp. 1146-1147)

tion, and which instruments are least instrusive while still providing the needed data.

Instruments for Family Assessment

Critical Events Checklist (CEC)

The Critical Events Checklist (Bailey et al., 1986) is an eight-question screening checklist designed to be used at regular intervals to determine recent or future potentially stressful events in the families of handicapped children. The

Individualized Family Service Plan

Sec. 677. (a) ASSESSMENT AND PROGRAM DEVELOPMENT. — Each handicapped infant or toddler and the infant or toddler's family shall receive —

(1) a multidisciplinary assessment of unique needs and the identification of services appropriate to meet such needs, and

(2) a written individualized family service plan developed by a multidisciplinary team, including the parent or guardian, as required by subsection (d).

(b) PERIODIC REVIEW. — The individualized family service plan shall be evaluated once a year and the family shall be provided a review of the plan at 6-month intervals (or more often where appropriate based on infant and toddler and family needs).

(c) PROMPTNESS AFTER ASSESSMENT. — The individualized family service plan shall be developed within a reasonable time after the assessment required by subsection (a)(1) is completed. With the parent's consent, early intervention services may commence prior to the completion of such assessment.

(d) CONTENT OF PLAN. — The individualized family service plan shall be in writing and contain —

(1) a statement of the infant's or toddler's present levels of physical development, cognitive development, language and speech development, psycho-social development, and self-help skills, based on acceptable objective criteria,

(2) a statement of the family's strengths and needs relating to enhancing the development of the family's handicapped infant or toddler.

(3) a statement of the major outcomes expected to be achieved for the infant and toddler and the family, and the criteria, procedures, and timelines used to determine the degree to which progress toward achieving the outcomes are being made and whether modifications or revisions of the outcomes or services are necessary.

(4) a statement of specific early intervention services necessary to meet the unique needs of the infant or toddler and the family, including the frequency, intensity, and the method of delivering services.

(5) the projected dates for initiation of services and the anticipated duration of such services.

(6) the name of the case manager from the profession most immediately relevant to the infant's and toddler's or family's needs who will be responsible for the implementation of the plan and coordination with other agencies and persons, and

(7) the steps to be taken supporting the transition of the handicapped toddler to services provided under part B to the extent such services are considered appropriate.

(*Federal Register*, 1987, pp. 1149-1150.)

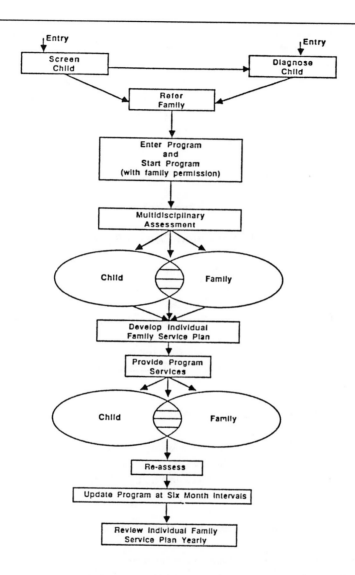

From P. Hutinger (1988), "Linking Screening, Identification, and Assessment with Curriculum," in *Early Childhood Special Education: Birth to Three,* edited by J.B. Jordan, J.J. Gallagher, P.L. Hutinger, & M.B. Karnes, Reston, VA: Council for Exceptional Children and DEC. (An ERIC Clearinghouse on Handicapped and Gifted Children Publication)

Figure 7.1

A System of Identification Processes and Services for Families of Handicapped and At-Risk Children

parents indicate events relating to factors such as anticipated transitions from home-based programs to preschool or to kindergarten, anticipated surgery, when the family learned of the existence of the handicap, and various developmental milestones including self-feeding, toileting, walking, and talking. Items marked "yes" are indicators for further assessment and discussion by the interventionist to set goals or provide additional services.

Dyadic Adjustment Scale (DAS)

The Dyadic Adjustment Scale (Spanier, 1976) is designed to measure family strength. It consists of 32 questions, is self-reporting, and relates to various marital interactions such as agreement, cohesion, satisfaction, and affection.

Dyadic Parent-Child Interaction Coding System (DP-CICS)

The Dyadic Parent-Child Interaction Coding System (Robinson & Eyberg, 1981) is a system for counting behaviors during 5-minute, 1-week-apart play sessions to evaluate the interaction between parents and child. Examples of behavior assessed include the child's degree of compliance, parents' commands, praise provided for the child, and types of physical contact. The DP-CICS is to be administered in a setting other than the home and is designed for parents of children 2 to 7 years of age. The DP-CICS has been used primarily with children who have behavior problems.

Family Adjustment Survey (FAS)

The Family Adjustment Survey (Abbott & Meredith, 1986) is a survey designed to evaluate areas of family strength relating to unique family problems and strengths, coping skills, sources and nature of support. The FAS is self-reporting on open-ended questions.

Family Information Preferences Inventory (FIPI)

The Family Information Preferences Inventory (Turnbull & Turnbull, 1986) is an inventory of 37 items designed to assess the needs of families and their preferences regarding how those needs might best be met. Topics considered in the FIPI include planning for the future, locating and using support, working with professionals, teaching the child at home, and helping the family enjoy the child. The 37 items are statements of specific informational needs, and parents first rate their needs on a point scale of 0-4 (0 indicates no interest in the information and 4 indicates a high priority). The parents then indicate how they would best like to receive the information—through parental group meetings, individual meetings, or written materials. Usefulness of the FIPI is related to identifying and prioritizing parental needs.

Family Needs Survey (FNS)

The Family Needs Survey (Bailey & Simeonsson, 1988b) consists of 35 items relating to family needs such as assistance in explaining their handicapped child to others, reading material, how to teach or play with their child, financial needs, and community resources. Parents respond separately to each item using the scale: 1—no help needed, 2—not sure, or 3—definitely need help. Differences in parental perceptions and agreed-upon needs are discussed at family conferences and used to develop interventions.

Family Resource Scale (FRS)

The Family Resource Scale (Dunst & Leet, 1987) is designed to assess the areas of support available to families. Parents indicate the adequacy of resources relating to nutritional resources, resources of personal growth, and intrafamily support. The FRS, consisting of 30 items, identifies specific needs of the family.

Family Roles Scale (FRS)

The Family Roles Scale (Gallagher, Scharfman, & Bristol, 1984) addresses 20 roles that parents may assume related to food preparer, social planner, child disciplinarian, clothing selector, provider, home care of equipment, moral leader, and others. The respondent indicates who does perform the role, who should, and the degree of satisfaction with the role divisions. Information from the profile is used to determine the family's satisfaction with the division of responsibilities.

Home Observation for the Measurement of Environment (HOME)

A set of procedures called the Home Observation for the Measurement of Environment (Caldwell & Bradley, 1979) consists of observations and interviews designed to evaluate the stimulation a child receives and the environment of the home. This includes concepts such as maternal involvement, physical environment, variety of stimulation, and disciplinary practices. The HOME has two forms—one consisting of 6 subscales for 0-3 year-olds and another for 3-6 year-olds consisting of eight subscales.

Home Quality Rating Scale (HQRS)

The Home Quality Rating Scale (Meyers, Mink, & Nihira, 1977) is designed to assess factors relating to child-rearing attitudes and practices such as quality of the residential environment and area, harmony in the home and quality of parenting, openness of the respondent, and concordance in marriage and parenting. An interview is conducted, with the assessor indicating responses on a 5-point rating scale and fixed-choice responses.

Maternal Behavior Rating Scale (MBRS)

The Materal Behavior Rating Scale (Mahoney, Finger, & Powell, 1985) is designed for use with a 10-minute videotape that was done in the home. The MBRS is to be used with children 1 to 3 years of age. The rating scale is completed to determine the quality of interaction between parents and child, including behaviors such as sensitivity to the child, effectiveness in providing stimulation, parents' warmth toward the child, child's activity level and attention span, and parent and child enjoyment. The MBRS has been used primarily with children who are mentally retarded.

Parent As A Teacher Inventory (PAAT)

The Parent As A Teacher Inventory (Strom, 1984), for parents of children 3 to 9 years of age, assesses parents' attitudes about parent-child interactions, standards for child behavior, value preferences regarding child behavior, and frustrations related to child behavior. The parent is able to complete the PAAT in approximately 30 to 40 minutes. The PAAT is available in English and Spanish.

Parent Behavior Progression (PBP)

The Parent Behavior Progression (Bromwich, 1981) is a checklist of behaviors designed to be used by the assessor after informal interactions with the parents. The PBP has two forms—one for children 0-9 months and another for those 9 months to 3 years of age. After observing the family interactions, the assessor marks on the checklist behaviors such as providing stimulation, parental pleasure in the child, appropriate activities, physical proximity, and awareness of child stress or comfort.

Parent/Caregiver Involvement Scale (PCIS)

The Parent/Caregiver Involvement Scale (Farran et al., 1987) is a rating scale

104

used primarily with children who are multiply handicapped, mentally retarded, or at-risk. Rating is designed to assess parent or caregivers' behaviors including physical interactions, providing stimulating environment, verbal interactions, level of effective climate, and responsiveness to the child. The PCIS is to be used with children aged 2 to 57 months during actual interactions or with videotaped interactions of 20 minutes in length.

Parenting Stress Index (PSI)

The Parenting Stress Index (Abidin, 1986) is a self-reporting rating scale of 101 items relating to child characteristics (6 subscales) and parent characteristics (7 subscales). The child characteristics subscales include areas such as mood, adaptability, distractibility, hyperactivity, and demandingness. The parent characteristics subscales include topics such as social isolation, depression, relationship with spouse, attachment, and parental health. Percentile scores are derived from the parental responses. The PSI may be used with children 0-10 years of age. An additional Life Stress Scale may be used to determine stress factors other than the parent-child factors—such as recent deaths or financial problems.

Questionnaire on Resources and Stress (QRS)

The Questionnaire on Resources and Stress (Holroyd, 1974, 1986) is a self-reporting, true-false questionnaire used to determine the perceived degree of stress experienced by the family of the handicapped child. The long form of the QRS consists of 285 items, which address issues such as difficult personality traits, lack of family integration, lack of social support, excessive time demands, financial problems, poor health, and others. The short version consists of 66 items and, according to its author, is to be used only as a screening instrument. A profile is developed from the parental responses and compared to a profile of scores developed from a normative population of families who did not have a handicapped child.

Social Interaction Assessment/Intervention (SIAI)

A procedure for counting certain types of behavior to document change in parent-child interaction, the Social Interaction Assessment/Intervention system (McCollum & Stayton, 1985) is designed to be used before and after interventions with the parents. These interventions assess behaviors such as imitation, social interaction, and vocalization. The SIAI has been used with parents of children who have severe motor and cognitive delays. The procedure consists

105

of counting behaviors demonstrated in 4-minute videotaped play sessions in the home before and after interventions.

Teaching Skills Inventory (TSI)

The Teaching Skills Inventory (Rosenberg, Robinson, & Beckman, 1984) is a rating scale designed to assess the parents' skill in teaching their child. The TSI is to be used before and after training of the parent in skills relating to the parents' ability to maintain the child's interest, modify tasks when necessary, provide clear instructions to the child, and others. Four-minute videotapes that record the parent-child interaction before intervention and after intervention are provided for the parents.

Screening and Assessment Processes for Children

If services are to be provided, the children who need such services must be identified. Children of school age are routinely assessed in relation to achievement, vision, hearing, and other areas. Infants and some preschool-age children are not a part of such an organized system of evaluation; consequently, states and local areas have developed processes for screening infants and toddlers. They usually include:

1. A developmental history provided by the parents; usually obtained through a structured interview, a checklist, or a questionnaire.
2. Problems or concerns regarding the child, as described by the parent.
3. Evaluation of the child's developmental status through the use of one or more screening instruments. Areas assessed include cognitive development, motor development, self-help and adaptive skills, emotional development, auditory and visual perception, visual acuity, hearing acuity, and speech and language development.

Screening instruments used in the programs are, in general, rather easy to administer and typically are not lengthy. The intent is to identify infants, toddlers, and preschoolers who may require additional assessment. Not all children who are identified in the initial screening actually turn out to have significant problems.

The screening process, in most cases, will identify a number of children for whom additional assessment will be required to confirm or deny the presence of a problem. The assessment process then is put into action. A wide variety of information is collected to determine the child's strengths and weaknesses, abilities and disabilities. This further assessment also may identify at-risk children—those who may potentially develop delays unless services are provided. The general areas to be assessed are similar to those in screening, but they may take very different forms depending on the child's age.

To achieve the best results, the assessment of infants and very young children requires unique abilities on the part of assessment personnel. Very young children cannot be expected to simply comply with a request. They have not learned test behavior and rarely are concerned with the correctness of a response or feedback from the examiner. Ulrey & Rogers (1982) have identified four characteristics of effective examiners of young children. First, experience with and enjoyment of infants is an essential characteristic. Ease in handling infants, talking to them, and communicating with them by facial expressions are all aspects for developing a rapport that will lead to effective assessment.

A second characteristic is the examiner's ability to accommodate the infant's readiness for interaction, which may involve several stages. The examiner is first a stranger who stays on the sidelines while the child adjusts to the new environment by exploring the room. The examiner must be able to determine the appropriate time to move into the stage of offering interesting items, making tentative requests, and praising performance. After the child demonstrates readiness, the examiner moves to the third stage, which entails active involvement with the child, requesting performance, inhibiting or controlling certain behaviors, always eliciting the best performance. Some children who are shy or have difficulties with control or autonomy may never allow the examiner to progress to the stage of active involvement.

Closely related to the issues of rapport are those of respect for physical touch and physical distance. The third characteristic of the effective examiner includes an understanding and respect for these issues and allows the child to set distance limits and to decide when to approach the examiner. Many young children do not like to be touched by strangers and only gradually arm up enough to allow patting or light physical contact.

Last, effective examiners are able to put parents at ease. Allowing parents to express concerns, answering their questions, explaining the assessment procedures, where they should sit, whether they should talk to the child during the assessment—all contribute to putting them at ease. Small children interpret the facial expressions, vocal tone, and gestures to determine the safety or pleasure of a situation. Therefore, putting parents at ease often leads to more accurate assessment of the child.

In summary, because effective evaluations of infants and young children require somewhat different skills than do assessments of older children, these usually are not taught to early childhood specialists. With practice, individuals are able to upgrade their skills in this area. Screening and assessment tools that may be used with children at the infant and toddler stages, the ages for which they are useful, and a brief description of each follow.

107

Instruments for Assessment of Infants and Toddlers

Adaptive Behavior Scale for Infants and Early Childhood (ABSI)

The Adaptive Behavior Scale for Infants and Early Childhood (Leland, Shoace, McElwain, & Christie, 1980) was designed for children from birth to 6 years of age and measures the ability of a child to cope with environmental demands. The ABSI is a behavior rating scale that is untimed.

APGAR Rating Scale

The APGAR Rating Scale (Apgar, 1953) is a screening instrument administered at birth and again at 5 and 10 minutes after birth. Nurses or obstetricians usually administer the APGAR to determine heart rate, muscle tone, color, reflex irritability, and respiratory effort. The newborn is rated on a scale of 0, 1, or 2 for a total of 10 points; a low total is an indicator of some potential problem.

Assessing Linguistic Behaviors (ALB)

The test Assessing Linguistic Behaviors (Olswang, Stoel-Gammon, Coggins, & Carpenter, 1987) is for assessing early language disorders. The ALB is for children from 9 through 24 months of age and includes five separate scales for measuring cognitive-social and linguistic development. These scales are: Cognitive Antecedents to Word Meaning, Play, Communication Intention, Language Comprehension, and Language Production. The time required for administration varies.

Battelle Developmental Inventory (BDI)

The Battelle Developmental Inventory (Newborg, Stock, Wnek, Guidubaldi, & Suinicki, 1984) is an assessment tool designed to be administered individually to children from birth through 8 years of age. The BDI assesses information through structured settings, direct observation, and interviews with parents and teachers (when appropriate for the age). The manual provides for modifications required by children with various handicaps. Areas assessed are Cognitive, Motor, Adaptive, Personal-Social, and Communication, generating 30 profile scores that indicate the child's strengths and weaknesses. Administration requires 1 to 2 hours and yields standard scores, percentile ranks, and age equivalents.

Battelle Developmental Inventory Screening Test (BDIST)

The Battelle Developmental Inventory Screening Test (Newborg, Stock, Wnek, Guidubaldi, & Suinicki, 1988) is a short form of the BDI consisting of 956 items addressing the same domains. Administration time is 10 to 30 minutes. Scores attained are cutoff scores and age equivalents.

Bayley Scales of Infant Development (BSID)

An individually administered assessment tool, the Bayley Scales of Infant Development (Bayley, 1984) is used with children 2 to 30 months. It has two scales, Mental and Motor. The 30 behavior ratings assess areas such as degree of body control, coordination of large muscles, manipulatory skills of the hands and fingers, sensory-perceptual acuities, sensory discrimination, memory, learning and problem-solving ability, beginnings of verbal communication, and evidence of the ability to form generalizations and classifications.

Brazelton Behavioral Assessment Scale
(See Neonatal Behavior Assessment Scale, p. XXX.)

Brigance Diagnostic Inventory of Early Development (BDIED)

The Brigance Diagnostic Inventory of Early Development (Brigance, 1978) is an individual test designed for children of developmental ages 0 to 7 years. It assesses the major skill areas of preambulatory motor, gross and fine motor, self-help, pre-speech, speech and language, general knowledge and comprehension, readiness, basic reading, writing, and math. The BDIED provides criterion-based assessment that correlates with instructional objectives.

Cattell Infant Intelligence Scale (CIIS)

The Cattell Infant Intelligence Scale (Cattell, 1969) is an individually administered extension of the Stanford-Binet Intelligence Scale for younger children (3 months to 30 months). CIIS tasks are selected for administration, based on the child's age, and yield mental age scores and IQ. The CIIS requires 20 to 30 minutes for administration.

Child Behavior Checklist for Ages 2-3 (CBC/2-3)

The Child Behavior Checklist for ages 2-3 (Achenbach, 1986) is a downward extension of the Child Behavior Checklist for ages 4-16. The CBC/2-3 consists of 99 items, which yield measures of competencies and problem areas. Parents rate the child. Administration time varies.

Cognitive Abilities Scale (CAS)

Designed for children 2 and 3 years of age, the Cognitive Abilities Scale (Bradley-Johnson, 1987) measures cognitive development in skills related to language, imitation, memory, reading, mathematics, and handwriting. The CAS has 88 items and provides an overall measure of performance for children who will not talk or whose speech is unintelligible.

Denver Developmental Screening Test—Revised (DDST-R)

The Denver Developmental Screening Test—Revised (Frankenburg, Dodds, & Fandal, 1981) may be used with infants from 2 weeks old to children 6 years of age, yielding gross motor, fine motor, personal-social, and language scores. DDST-R scores are classified in normal, questionable, or abnormal ranges; responses may be either verbal or nonverbal. Administration requires approximately 20 minutes.

Developmental Activities Screening Inventory—Revised (DASI-II)

Designed for children 1 month to 60 months of age, the Developmental Activities Screening Inventory (DuBose & Langley, 1984) may be administered verbally or visually and includes adaptations for use with children who have visual impairments. Skills measured include sensory intactness, means-end relationships, causality to memory, reasoning, and seriation. The DASI-II may be administered in two settings and in different sequences.

Developmental Profile II (DPII)

Designed for screening children from birth to 9 years, the Developmental Profile II (Alpern, Boll, & Shearer, 1980) has an administration time of 20 to 40 minutes. The DPII assesses five major areas: physical, self-help, social, academic, and communication. Scoring is accomplished by direct observation or report of parents in an interview. Norms are provided at 6-month intervals for children ages birth to 4 years, and at yearly intervals for ages 4-9 years.

Early Intervention Developmental Profile (EIDP)

The Early Intervention Developmental Profile (Schafer & Moersch, 1981) assesses perceptual and fine-motor skills, cognition, language, social-emotional, self-care, and gross motor areas in children birth through 3 years of

110

age. Curriculum activities are included, with adaptations suggested for children who have hearing, motor, or visual impairments.

Early Language Milestone Scale (ELMS)

The Early Language Milestone Scale (Coplan, 1987) is a screening instrument designed for children from birth through 36 months of age. The ELMS consists of 42 items and assesses three domains: Auditory Expressive, Auditory Receptive, and Visual. It requires 4 minutes for administration.

Early Learning Accomplishment Profile (E-LAP)

The Early Learning Accomplishment Profile (Sanford, 1981) is designed to assess the areas of emotional, social, self-help, language cognition, and gross and fine motor skills. For children birth through age 3, the E-LAP provides guidance in programming for severely handicapped young children.

Hawaii Early Learning Profile (HELP)

The Hawaii Early Learning Profile (Furuno et al., 1979) examines 650 skills in the following major areas: cognitive (with receptive language), language (expressive), fine and gross motor, social-emotional, and self-help. The HELP is for children birth through 3 years of age and includes an assessment-related curriculum.

Milani-Comparetti Developmental Scale (MCDS)

The Milani-Comparetti Developmental Scale (Milani-Comparetti & Gidoni, 1977) is designed to measure motor development, including areas such as ability to move about, stand from a supine position, control head and body, and move from one position to another. The MCDS is for children birth through age 2.

Minnesota Child Development Inventory (MCDI)

The Minnesota Child Development Inventory (Ireton & Thwing, 1979) was developed as an assessment tool to identify children (birth through age 6) whose development is below that expected for their gender and age. It consists of an interview with the parent, requiring yes-no responses, and encompasses the areas of general development, gross and fine motor, expressive language, comprehension-conceptual, situation comprehension, self-help, and personal-social.

111

Neonatal Behavior Assessment Scale (NBAS)

The Neonatal Behavior Assessment Scale (Brazelton, 1973)—also referred to as the Brazelton Behavioral Assessment Scale—is designed to evaluate infants from 4 days to 4 weeks of age. The NBAS yields 47 scores related to the infant's responsiveness to the environment and specific stimuli, as well as stages from deep sleep to crying.

Ordinal Scale of Psychological Development
(See Uzgiris-Hunt Scales of Psychological Development, p. XXX.)

Peabody Developmental Motor Scales (PDMS)

The Peabody Developmental Motor Scales (Folio & Fewell, 1983), individually administered, measure gross and fine motor skills of children through 6 years, 11 months of age. The PDMS measures reflexes, balance, nonlocomotor, locomotor, receipt and propulsion of objects, grasping, hand use, eye-hand coordination, and manual dexterity. It requires approximately 60 minutes to administer.

Portage Guide to Early Education (PGEE)

The Portage Guide to Early Education (Shearer et al., 1976) provides a checklist for current levels of performance in the areas of infant stimulation, socialization, language, self-help, cognitive, and motor. The PGEE is designed for children from birth through age 6. In addition to the checklist, a manual and 850 activity cards for skill development are available.

Preschool Attainment Record (PAR)

A screening device using parent interview techniques, the Preschool Attainment Record (Doll, 1966) provides attainment age scores and quotients. The PAR is designed for use from birth through 7 years of age and samples behavior at 6-month intervals in the physical, social, and intellectual areas.

Preschool Language Scale (PLS)

Designed to be administered by a diagnostician, the Preschool Language Scale (Zimmerman, Steiner, & Pond, 1979) measures language development in children 1 to 7 years of age. It measures verbal ability and auditory comprehension, providing a "language age" and also identifying strengths and weaknesses. A Spanish version of the PLS is available.

Receptive-Expressive Emergent Language Scale (REEL)

The Receptive-Expressive Emergent Language Scale (Bzock & League, 1971) is designed for children birth through 3 years of age. Through parental interview, the REEL assesses receptive and expressive language, including communicative, vocal, and symbolic behaviors. Scores obtained include receptive language age, expressive language age, and combined language age.

Revised Gesell Developmental Schedules (RGDS)

The Revised Gesell Developmental Schedules (Knoblach, Stevens, & Malone, 1980) provide a norm-referenced assessment of overall development in children 1 through 36 months of age. The RGDS measures adaptive behavior, gross and fine motor, language, and personal-social areas. It yields developmental quotients and maturity age scores for each of the five domains.

Rockford Infant Developmental Evaluation Scales (RIDES)

The Rockford Infant Developmental Evaluation Scales (Project RHISE, 1979) include 308 developmental behaviors arranged by age range into five areas: personal-social, self-help, fine motor/adaptive, receptive language, expressive language, and gross motor. RIDES provides a skill-by-skill picture of the child's developmental pattern across these five areas. Administration time varies.

Scale of Social Development (SSD)

The Scale of Social Development (Venn, Serwatka, & Anthony, 1987) is for children birth through age 6. It is designed to assess three skill clusters: participates/socializes, investigates/identifies, and prefers/complies. The SSD may be used with students who are deaf or have multihandicaps, and to measure progress.

Scales of Independent Behavior
(See chapter 5.)

Scales of Socio-Emotional Development (SSED)

The Scales of Socio-Emotional Development (Lewis & Michalson, 1983) provide an observational procedure for assessing a child who is in a program with other children. The SSED measures emotional functioning in areas such as competence, happiness, affiliation, and fear. Administration consists of observation by a rater over one day. The SSED is for children from birth to 3 years of age.

113

Sequenced Inventory of
Communication Development—Revised (SICD)

The Sequenced Inventory of Communication Development (Hedrick, Prather, & Tobin, 1984) is a diagnostic test designed to evaluate communication abilities in children 4 months to 4 years of age. The 92-item receptive language section assesses sound and speech discrimination, awareness, and understanding. The 118-item expressive language section assesses imitating, initiating, and responding and measures verbal output for length, articulation, and grammatic and syntactic structure. The SICD is available in English and Spanish.

Uniform Performance Assessment System (UPAS)

The Uniform Performance Assessment System (White et al., 1981) is a criterion-referenced test designed specifically to assess the skills of handicapped children from birth to 6 years of age. The UPAS measures adaptive behaviors in four areas: preacademic/fine motor development, communication, social/self-help skills, and gross motor development. A fifth section addresses the issue of maladaptive behaviors.

Uzgiris-Hunt Ordinal Scales of Psychological Development (OSPD)

The Uzgiris-Hunt Ordinal Scales of Psychological Development (Uzgiris & Hunt, 1975) is a test designed to measure cognitive functions in the areas of visual pursuit, permanence of objects, means for obtaining desired environmental events, imitation, operational causality, construction of object relations in space, and schemes for relating to objects—all of which are based on Piagetian theory. The OSPD is to be used with children from birth to age 2 to determine sensorimotor development.

Instruments for the Assessment of Preschool Children

The procedure for screening preschool-age children is described in chapter 3, as are procedures for further assessment. Tests that may be useful for screening and diagnostic purposes follow.

Adaptive Behavior Scale for Infants and Early Childhood
    (See previous Infant and Toddler section.)

114

Arizona Basic Assessment and Curriculum Utilization System for Young Handicapped Children (ABACUS)

The Arizona Basic Assessment Utilization System for Young Children (McCarthy, Bos, Lund, Glattke, & Vaughn, 1985) is designed to screen and assess in the areas of body management, self-care, communication, pre-academics, and socialization for children of functional ages of 2 to 5½ years. The ABACUS is a criterion-referenced instrument that may be used in home or school environments and is keyed to curricular programs in the same five developmental areas.

Assessment of Children's Language Comprehension (ACLC)
(See chapter 11.)

Autism Screening Instrument for Educational Planning
(See chapter 12.)

Barber Scales of Self-Regard for Preschool Children (BSSRPS)

The Barber Scales of Self-Regard for Preschool Children (Barber, 1975) consist of a set of seven rating scales that are completed by the parents, teachers, or others who are familiar with the child. The dimensions measured include: purposeful learning skills, completing tasks, coping with fears, cooperating with parental requests, dealing with frustration, social adjustment, and developing imagination in play. The BSSRPS is for children ages 3 through 5. Administration time varies.

Bankson Language Screening Test
(See chapter 11.)

Basic School Skills Inventory—Diagnostic (BSSI-D)

The Basic School Skills Inventory—Diagnostic (Hammill & Leigh, 1983a) is designed as both a norm-referenced and criterion-referenced measure of readiness skills. It is composed of 110 items, assessing six areas: daily living skills, spoken language, reading readiness, writing readiness, math readiness, and classroom behavior. For children ages 4 through 7½ years, the BSSI-D is individually administered, with varied time for administration.

115

Basic School Skills Inventory—Screen (BSSI-S)

A companion to the Basic School Skills Inventory—Diagnostic, the Basic School Skills Inventory—Screen (Hammill & Leigh, 1983b) is a 20-item observational screening instrument for children ages 4 through 7 years. It examines daily living skills, spoken language, reading readiness, math readiness, and classroom behavior. The BSSI-S requires 5 to 8 minutes for completion by the examiner.

Battelle Developmental Inventory
(See previous Infant and Toddler section.)

Boehm Test of Basic Concepts—Preschool (BTBC-P)

The Boehm Test of Basic Concepts—Preschool (Boehm, 1986) is a downward extension of the Boehm Test of Basic Concepts—Revised, to be used with children ages 3 to 5 years. Administration time, on an individual basis, is 10 to 15 minutes. The BTBC-P measures 26 relational concepts, requires only a pointing response, and yields percentile age bands for 3, 3½, 4, 4½, and 5 years.

Boehm Test of Basic Concepts—Revised (BTBC-R)
(See chapter 11.)

Bracken Basic Concept Scale (BBCS)

The Bracken Basic Concept Scale (Bracken, 1984) consists of two forms to be used in screening, and a diagnostic scale. The screening forms are primarily for children 5 to 7 years of age whose concept development is below age-level expectations; the diagnostic scale is to be used with children ages 2½ to 7 years. The BBCS measures 258 concepts in 11 categories: color, letter identification, numbers/counting, comparisons, shapes, direction/position, social/emotional, size, texture/material, quantity, and time/sequence. An instructional program for teaching the concepts is available.

Brigance Diagnostic Inventory of Early Development
(See previous Infant and Toddler section.)

Burks' Behavior Rating Scales
(See chapter 12.)

Carolina Developmental Profile (CDP)

The Carolina Developmental Profile (Lillie & Harbin, 1975) provides a combination of assessment and learning activities. The CDP assesses 83 skill areas arranged into seven major categories: fine motor, gross motor, visual perception, receptive language, expressive language, reasoning, and social-emotional. The profile is designed to be used with children 2 to 5 years of age and requires 15 minutes for administration. A criterion-referenced checklist includes instructional objectives.

Carolina Picture Vocabulary Test
(See chapter 15.)

Carrow Elicited Language Inventory
(See chapter 11.)

Child Behavior Checklist for Ages 4-16
(See chapter 12.)

Child Behavior Rating Scale
(See chapter 12.)

CID Preschool Performance Scale (CIDPPS)

The CID Preschool Performance Scale (Geers & Lane, 1984) is for use with children ages 2 to 5½ years of age who may have hearing or language impairments. The CIDPPS is nonverbal in both administration and response. Areas measured are part/whole relations, manual planning, preschool skills, manual dexterity, perceptual-motor skills, and form perception.

Clark-Madison Test of Oral Language
(See chapter 11.)

Columbia Mental Maturity Scale
(See chapter 5.)

Comprehensive Identification Process (CIP)

The Comprehensive Identification Process (Zehrback, 1987) is a screening instrument for children 2 to 6 years of age. It assesses seven areas: cognitive-verbal, fine motor, gross motor, speech and expressive language, hearing, vision, and social/affective behavior, and it requires a medical history. The CIP yields 24 scores plus final recommendations, which are categorized into "pass," "rescreen," or "refer to agency or program," and requires approximately 30 minutes to administer.

Del Rio Language Screening Test (DRLST)

The Del Rio Language Screening Test (Toronto, Leverman, Hanna, Rosengweis, & Maldonado, 1975) is a receptive language screening instrument for children ages 3 to 7 who speak either English or Spanish. The DRLST measures receptive language in five areas: receptive vocabulary, sentence repetition length, sentence repetition complexity, oral commands, and story comprehension.

Denver Developmental Screening Test
(See Infant and Toddler section.)

Detroit Tests of Learning Aptitude—Primary (DTLA-P)

Designed for children ages 3 through 9, the Detroit Tests of Learning Aptitude—Primary (Hammill & Bryant, 1986) indicate intra-individual strengths and weaknesses. Administered individually, the DTLA-P includes 130 items that provide eight subtest scores and one total score in the areas of motor, attention, verbal, and conceptual.

Developmental Activities Screening Inventory—Revised
(See Infant and Toddler section.)

Developmental Indicators for
the Assessment of Learning—Revised (DIAL-R)

The Developmental Indicators for the Assessment of Learning—Revised (Mardell-Czudnowski & Goldenberg, 1983) is a screening instrument for children ages 2 through 6. It yields four scores: motor, concepts, language, and a total. The DIAL-R requires 25-30 minutes per child and may be used with children who are experiencing difficulty or indicate signs of giftedness.

Developmental Profile II
(See Infant and Toddler section.)

Developmental Test of Visual Motor Integration
(See Chapter 13.)

Early Language Milestone Scale
(See Infant and Toddler section.)

Early Screening Inventory (ESI)

The Early Screening Inventory (Meisels & Wiske, 1983), a screening instrument for children ages 4-6, examines perceptual, cognitive, language, and motor development. The ESI requires 15 to 20 minutes for administration and includes information from a medical examination, vision and hearing screening, and an interview with the parents.

Evaluating Acquired Skills in Communication
(See chapter 11.)

Evaluation and Programming System for Infants and Young Children (EPS)

A criterion-referenced instrument, the Evaluation and Programming System for Infants and Young Children (Bricker, Bailey, & Gentry, 1985) measures gross and fine motor, communication, cognition, self-help, and social areas. The EPS allows for adaptations for sensory and motor impairments and is for children birth through 3 years. The EPS uses observation, direct testing, and parent report and includes functional goals and objectives.

Expressive One-Word Picture Vocabulary Test
(See chapter 11.)

Frostig Developmental Test of Visual Perception
(See chapter 13.)

Goldman-Fristoe Test of Articulation
(See chapter 11.)

Goldman-Fristoe-Woodcock Test of Auditory Discrimination
(See chapter 13.)

Goodman Lock Box (GLB)

The Goodman Lock Box (Goodman, 1981) is a system of observations of play activities that yields scores on competence, organization, and aimless actions. The GLB is for children 2½ to 5½ years of age. It is nonverbal and requires 6.5 minutes of observation.

Illinois Test of Psycholinguistic Abilities (ITPA)

The Illinois Test of Psycholinguistic Abilities (Kirk, McCarthy, & Kirk, 1978) is a diagnostic test designed to assess children from 2 to 10 years of age in auditory reception, visual reception, visual sequential memory, auditory association, auditory sequential memory, visual association, visual closure, verbal expression, grammatic closure, and manual expression. Two subtests—auditory closure and blending—are optional. The ITPA is administered individually.

Kaufman Assessment Battery for Children
(See chapters 5 and 8.)

Kohn Problem Checklist
(See chapter 12.)

Kohn Social Competence Scale
(See chapter 12.)

Learning Accomplishment Profile—Revised (LAP-R)

The Learning Accomplishment Profile—Revised (LeMay, Griffin, & Sanford, 1981) has both a screening and a diagnostic edition. The diagnostic edition, for birth through 6 years, measures gross motor, fine motor, pre-writing, cognitive, language, self-help, and personal/social areas. The kindergarten screening edition requires 15 minutes for administration and addresses similar concepts.

Leiter International Performance Scale
(See chapter 5.)

Let's Talk Inventory for Children
(See chapter 11.)

McCarthy Scales of Children's Abilities
(See chapter 5.)

McCarthy Screening Test (MST)

The McCarthy Screening Test (McCarthy, 1972b), drawn directly from the McCarthy Scales of Children's Abilities, requires approximately 20 minutes to administer. Cognitive and sensorimotor functions measured include verbal memory, right-left orientation, leg coordination, draw-a-design, numerical memory, and conceptual grouping. The MST is for children ages 4 to 6½ years and yields either "satisfactory development" or "need for further assessment" status.

Miller Assessment for Preschoolers (MAP)

The Miller Assessment for Preschoolers (Miller, 1982) is a screening instrument designed to identify mild to moderate developmental delays in five areas: neural foundations, coordination, verbal, nonverbal, and complex tasks. The MAP yields a score in each area measured, and a total score. It is for children 2 years, 9 months to 5 years, 8 months of age. Individually administered, the MAP requires approximately 20 to 30 minutes.

Miller-Yoder Language Comprehension Test
(See chapter 11.)

Minnesota Child Development Inventory
(See previous Infant and Toddler section.)

Northwestern Syntax Screening Test
(See chapter 11.)

Patterned Elicitation Syntax Test
(See chapter 11.)

Peabody Mathematics Readiness Test
(See chapter 10.)

Peabody Picture Vocabulary Test—Revised (PPVT-R)

The Peabody Picture Vocabulary Test—Revised (Dunn, 1981) is an individually administered test consisting of two forms, for children from 2½ years of age to adult. The PPVT-R, assessing receptive language, is untimed (typical time is 15-20 minutes) and allows for verbal or nonverbal responses.

Porch Index of Communicative Ability in Children
(See chapter 11.)

Portage Guide to Early Education
(See previous Infant and Toddler section.)

Pragmatics Screening Test
(See chapter 11.)

Preschool Attainment Record
(See previous Infant and Toddler section.)

Preschool Language Scale
(See previous Infant and Toddler section.)

Preverbal Assessment Intervention Profile
(See chapter 11.)

Rhode Island Test of Language Structure
(See chapter 11.)

Scale of Social Development
(See previous Infant and Toddler section.)

Scales of Independent Behavior
(See chapter 5.)

School Readiness Test (SRT)

The School Readiness Test (Anderhalter, 1989) is for students who are completing kindergarten or just entering first grade. The SRT assesses the student's readiness for formal instruction in seven skill areas: word recognition, identifying letters, visual discrimination, auditory discrimination, comprehension and interpretation, handwriting readiness, and number readiness. Results of the SRT indicate at which of six readiness levels the student is functioning. The SRT requires 60 minutes for administration and the *Manual of Directions* is available in English and Spanish.

Screen Kit of Language Development (SKOLD)

The Screening Kit of Language Development (Bliss & Allen, 1983) is designed to measure language development in children who speak either Black English or Standard English. It assesses vocabulary, comprehension, story completion, individual and paired sentence repetition with pictures, individual sentence repetition without pictures, and comprehension of commands. The SKOLD consists of six subtests—three for Black English and three for Standard English—in each of the following age ranges: 30-36 months, 37-42 months, and 43-48 months. It requires 15 minutes for administration.

Screening Children for Related Early Educational Needs (SCREEN)

Screening Children for Related Early Educational Needs (Hresko, Reid, Hammill, Ginsburg, & Baroody, 1988) is a screening test for children 3 through 7 years of age. SCREEN provides scores in areas related to language, reading, writing, and mathematics, plus a global quotient.

Screening Test for Auditory Processing Disorders
(See chapter 11.)

Sequenced Inventory of Communication Development—Revised
(See previous Infant and Toddler section.)

Slosson Intelligence Test
(See chapter 5.)

Stanford-Binet Intelligence Scale
(See chapter 5.)

Test of Articulation Performance—Diagnostic
(See chapter 11.)

Test for Auditory Comprehension of Language—Revised
(See chapter 11.)

Test of Early Language Development (TELD)

The Test of Early Language Development (Hresko, Reid, & Hammill, 1981) evaluates the form (syntax, phonology, and morphology), content (word and concept knowledge), and interpretation of meaning of both expressive and receptive language. The 38 items of the TELD are administered individually and require about 15 minutes. This test is for children ages 3 through 8 years.

Test of Early Mathematics Ability (TEMA)

The Test of Early Mathematics Ability (Ginsburg & Baroody, 1983) is an individually administered measure of formal mathematics concepts (mathematic conventions, number facts, calculation, and base-ten concepts) and informal concepts (counting, informal calculations, and relative magnitude). It is designed for children 4 to 12 years of age and requires about 20 minutes for administration.

Test of Early Reading Ability (TERA)

The Test of Early Reading Ability (Reid, Hresko, & Hammill, 1981) is designed to measure the reading ability of children in three areas: knowledge of the alphabet, comprehension, and the conventions of reading. An individually administered, 50-item test, the TERA is suited for children ages 3 to 8 years.

Test of Early Socioemotional Development (TESED)

A downward extension of the Behavior Rating Profile, the Test of Early Socioemotional Development (Hresko & Brown, 1984) has four major components: a 30-item student rating scale, a 34-item parent rating scale, a 36-item teacher rating, and a sociogram. It is used with children 3 through 7 years of age and is administered individually or in an ecological battery.

Test of Early Written Language (TEWL)

The Test of Early Written Language (Hresko, 1988) is designed to measure emerging written skills as conventions of print, communication, creative expression, and transcription. The TEWL, for children ages 3 to 7 years, yields both standard scores and percentiles.

Test of Language Development-2 Primary (TOLD-2, Primary)

The Test of Language Development (Newcomer & Hammill, 1988) assesses spoken language in children ages 4 to 12 years. Areas measured include picture vocabulary, oral vocabulary, grammatic understanding, grammatic completion, word articulation, and word discrimination. The TOLD-2 primary is untimed, but it requires 30 to 60 minutes to complete.

Test of Pragmatic Skills
(See chapter 11.)

Test of Relational Concepts (TRC)

The Test of Relational Concepts (Edmonston & Thane, 1988) is an individually administered test requiring 15 minutes for administration. The TRC tests 56 concepts including spatial, temporal, and quantitative words and dimensional adjectives. It is for children of 3 to 8 years of age.

Tree/Bee Test of Auditory Discrimination
(See chapter 11.)

Uniform Performance Assessment System
(See previous Infant and Toddler section.)

Utah Test of Language Development
(See chapter 11.)

Vineland Adaptive Behavior Scales
(See chapter 5.)

Walker Problem Behavior Identification Checklist
(See chapter 12.)

Wechsler Intelligence Scale for Children—Revised
(See chapter 5.)

Wechsler Preschool and Primary Scale of Intelligence (WPPSI)

The Wechsler Preschool and Primary Scale of Intelligence (Wechsler, 1974) is the downward extension of the Wechsler Intelligence Scale for Children—Revised (see chapter 5). The WPPSI yields a performance IQ, a verbal IQ, and a total measure of general intelligence. It requires 60 to 90 minutes for administration.

Woodcock-Johnson Psychoeducational Battery—Revised
(See chapters 5 and 8.)

Woodcock Language Proficiency Battery
(See chapter 11.)

Tests of Academic Achievement

In the minds of most parents and teachers, academic achievement is the major yardstick of success in the schools. Peer acceptance, social skills, and, for some, athletic accomplishment, are important factors in school performance, but reading, mathematics, and the sciences (including social science) have been accepted as the major, legitimate targets of the schools. If we were to add to the above list spelling, correctness of expression, and development of an adequate vocabulary, we would have summarized what educators say they are doing, what critics say they are not doing, and what most of our special educational efforts (special programs for the handicapped, for culturally different, and the like) are all about.

Almost since the beginning of formal educational programs, academic achievement tests have been part of the school program. In the last 40 to 50 years, group achievement batteries have been big business, with keen competition among major test publishers. In this chapter we will review a number of achievement batteries—which are actually just a collection of tests representing various subject or skill areas, integrated into one "super-test". Theoretically, *an achievement test measures the results of earlier instruction.* That instruction may have taken place at home, in the school, or elsewhere, but the achievement test battery purports to measure what has been learned. For the sake of convenience, the school curriculum is divided into areas such as reading, mathematics, spelling, written language, and science. The achievement test then is designed to assess, by sampling, what has been learned within these areas.

Group Achievement Tests

The vast majority of our discussion in this chapter relates to individually administered tests of achievement, but group achievement tests do have their proper place in assessment. They can be given to large groups of students at one time, by one test administrator. They can be scored with relative ease, by computers. Thus, they are highly cost-effective. If they are valid for the purposes under consideration, they provide one important indication of the effectiveness of instruction. In some instances they pinpoint potential strengths and weaknesses, in an individual student, that for some reason the teacher had not noted. In general, however, they are not of any great value in efforts with students who are known to have learning handicaps, or those suspected of having such handicaps.

Achievement tests are *not* acceptable for identification or classification purposes because:

1. Usually they require reading ability, even though they are not supposedly measuring reading skills.
2. Group administration assumes that students can, and will, work independently.
3. They are often timed.
4. Ordinarily students must write or otherwise record their answers; sometimes they must "translate" from a test booklet to an answer sheet.

As a result, scores on group tests may not be particularly meaningful for handicapped students (except to indicate that they are not good test takers). Group tests, however, may have some value in relation to special education programs. They may, for example, be of value as a screening device. A low score may or may not be meaningful. At least, it may indicate the need for individual assessment. Also, when a student is referred for individual assessment, the record of past group test scores may be useful as a clue to when school difficulties first began to emerge, and it may provide other, similar information.

In general, very low scores on a group test of achievement tend to be less meaningful than scores near the mean. But very high scores may be useful in screening for potentially gifted students. Very significant differences between scores on different sections of a group achievement test battery may lead to further investigation of potential causes of this variation, which in turn may lead to information that will be helpful in program planning for that student.

Before proceeding to our primary concern in this chapter—individually administered achievement tests—we will list some of the major group achievement tests, indicate the grade levels for which they are available, and their scope, in terms of subject areas assessed. Table 8.1 summarizes this information

Table 8.1

Comprehensive, Group-Administered, Academic Achievement Tests

Name	Grades	Subject / Skill Areas Assessed								Publisher
Title (Year)		Reading	Math	Spelling	Language	Social Studies	Science	Reference Skills	Study Skills	
American School Achievement Test (1988)	K-9	●	●	●	●	●	●			Pro-Ed
California Achievement Tests (1985)	K-12	●	●	●	●	●	●	●		CTB/McGraw Hill
Comprehensive Tests of Basic Skills (1981-82-83)	K-12	●	●	●	●	●	●	●		CTB/McGraw Hill
Educational Development Series (1984)	K-12	●	●	●	●	●	●	●		Scholastic Testing Service
Iowa Tests of Basic Skills (1986)	K-9	●	●	●	●	●	●	●	●	Riverside
Iowa Tests of Educational Development (1981)	9-12	●	●	●	●	●	●			Science Research Associates
Metropolitan Achievement Tests (1984)	K-12	●	●	●	●	●	●			Psychological Corp.
Sequential Tests of Educational Progress (STEP III) (1979)	3-12	●	●	●	●	●	●	●	●	CTB/McGraw Hill
SRA Achievement Series (1978)	K-12	●	●	●	●	●	●	●		Science Research Associates
Stanford Achievement Test Series (1982)	K-13	●	●	●	●	●	●			Psychological Corp.

for 10 comprehensive, group-administered tests of academic achievement. Most group tests provide test results in terms of grade equivalents, percentile ranks, and stanines. They offer the school administration a way to report student achievement to parents, the school board, and the general public, and are undoubtedly here to stay.

Major Individually Administered Achievement Tests

Many individually administered achievement tests are available, ranging from those that assess achievement in only three or four areas, to much broader instruments. Some are "free-standing"; others are part of some more comprehensive assessment battery. The four tests reviewed in the following section are among the most commonly used individual achievement instruments.

Kaufman Assessment Battery for Children (K-ABC)

The Kaufman Assessment Battery for Children (Kaufman & Kaufman, 1983) incorporates tests of general cognitive ability and of achievement. The cognitive ability sections were reviewed in chapter 5; we will briefly outline the achievement sections here.

The six achievement subtests of the K-ABC are: expressive vocabulary, faces and places, arithmetic, riddles, reading/decoding, and reading/understanding. Subtest scores and a global achievement scale score provide measures of academic/educational achievement. This section of the K-ABC is often used when the cognitive sections are used, because it provides a series of convenient measures, subject to similar interpretation. Just two years after publication of the K-ABC, however, a more comprehensive achievement test was published by the same authors. Its description follows.

Kaufman Test of Educational Achievement (K-TEA)

The Kaufman Test of Educational Achievement (Kaufman & Kaufman, 1985) was developed to correct what some users perceived to be weaknesses in the achievement section of the K-ABC. The Kaufman Test of Educational Achievement (K-TEA) is published in two forms: The Brief Form and The Comprehensive Form. The Brief Form provides a global assessment of reading, mathematics, and spelling, as well as a Composite Score. The Comprehensive Form provides information in five areas, through the following subtests:
1. Mathematics Applications—60 orally presented items.
2. Reading Decoding—60 items in letter identification and word pronunciation.

3. Spelling—50 items to be written by the student; the administrator reads aloud and uses in a sentence.
4. Reading Comprehension—50 items relating to paragraphs read by subjects; oral answers and some gestural responses required.
5. Mathematics Computation—60 written items ranging from simple arithmetic to algebra.

The K-TEA is appropriate for grades 1 through 12 and has the advantage of providing for error analysis of the subject's mistakes within any subtest.

Peabody Individual Achievement Test—Revised (PIAT-R)

The Peabody Individual Achievement Test—Revised (Dunn & Markwardt, 1989) is a current revision of a test that has been in use for many years. McLoughlin and Lewis (1986) indicate that it "is most commonly used in special education for identifying academic deficiencies" (p. 127). The PIAT-R has six subtests: mathematics, reading recognition, reading comprehension, spelling, written expression, and general information. The PIAT is intended for use with children ages 5 through adult and requires 60 minutes to complete. Subtest content may be described as follows:
1. Mathematics—tasks range from matching numerals through word problems requiring basic arithmetic operations, to algebra, geometry, and trigonometry.
2. Reading Recognition—tasks range from matching objects, letters, and words, to reading words in isolation.
3. Reading Comprehension—tasks include a variety of reading comprehension items.
4. Spelling—tasks begin with letter recognition and conclude with selection of the properly spelled words.
5. Written Expression—tasks incorporate a variety of means to screen written expression.
6. General Information—items test information in social studies, science, sports, and fine arts; student must respond orally to questions posed by examiner.

In a majority of the PIAT-R (excluding the General Information subtest), the student chooses answers from a multiple-choice format. In most, the student can respond by pointing, saying a number, or saying the answer. Reading is not required for the Mathematics and General Information subtests, because the examiner reads the questions aloud.

PIAT-R scores include age- and grade-based standard scores, age and grade equivalents, and percentile ranks and stanines for all subtests except written expression. Grade-based stanines are provided for both levels of Written Expression, and developmental scaled scores are available for Written Expression, Level 2 (grades 2-12). The total test score is considered an overall index of academic achievement.

Woodcock-Johnson Psycho-Educational Battery—Revised (WJ-R) WJ-R Tests of Achievement

The Woodcock-Johnson Revised Tests of Cognitive Ability were discussed in chapter 5. The WJ-R Tests of Achievement (Woodcock & Johnson, 1977) complement the cognitive ability tests, providing discrepancy norms for making aptitude comparisons. The WJ-R Tests of Achievement include five achievement clusters: reading, mathematics, written language, knowledge, and skills. These tests are numbered consecutively with tests included in the Cognitive Ability part of the total WJ-R Battery; thus, they start with number 22. Tests in the Standard Battery and the curricular area they measure are:

22. Letter-Word Identification—assesses reading.
23. Passage Comprehension—assesses reading.
24. Calculation—assesses mathematics.
25. Applied Problems—assesses mathematics.
26. Dictation—assesses written language.
27. Writing Samples—assesses written language.
28. Science—assesses knowledge.
29. Social Studies—assesses knowledge.
30. Humanities—assesses knowledge.

Nine additional tests included in the Supplemental Battery, and the curricular area in which they measure, are:

31. Word Attack—assesses reading.
32. Reading Vocabulary—assesses reading.
33. Quantitative Concepts—assesses mathematics.
34. Proofing—assesses written language.
35. Writing Fluency—assesses written language.
36. Punctuation and Capitalization—assesses written language.
37. Spelling—assesses written language.
38. Usage—assesses written language.
39. Handwriting—assesses written language.

The WJ-R Tests of Achievement may be used with individuals ages 2 to 90+ years. They provide a variety of measures, including intra-achievement discrepancies, and are available in alternate forms, A and B.

Wide Range Achievement Test—Revised (WRAT-R)

The WRAT-R (Jastak & Wilkinson, 1984) is the fifth revision of the individual achievement test sometimes known as the "Granddaddy of them all." The original WRAT (often called the "Jastak" [referring to the author] by assessment personnel) first came into use in the 1930s and quickly became the favorite of psychologists who wanted a fast individual achievement measure. It remains an accepted "quick" measure of achievement, but it does not assess some essential areas of academic achievement and involves limited sampling of the areas included in the test. The WRAT-R, intended for use with subjects ages 5-0 to 74-11, takes from 15 to 30 minutes to administer. Academic areas assessed are:

1. Reading—Prereading section includes matching and naming letters; reading involves reading aloud, words presented in isolation (i.e. word recognition).
2. Spelling—Prespelling includes copying geometric shapes and writing (or printing) their name; spelling involves writing words that are dictated and used in sentences.
3. Arithmetic—Prearithmetic includes counting, reading numbers, and oral addition and subtraction; arithmetic includes computation ranging from simple arithmetic to problems involving algebra and geometry.

WRAT-R-derived scores include grade equivalents, standard scores, and percentile ranks. Other scores (for example, stanines) also may be derived. The WRAT-R is used primarily for screening rather than for diagnostic purposes.

Other Individually Administered Tests of Academic Achievement

Individually administered tests of academic achievement are available for a variety of purposes. Some are for general screening purposes; some have diagnostic potential. Some are K-12 instruments; others were designed for a more limited age and grade range. The tests described in the following section provide a sample of these instruments.

Basic Achievement Skills Individual Screener (BASIS)

The Basic Achievement Skills Individual Screener (Sonnenschein, 1983) was designed to provide initial diagnostic assessment of academic strengths and needs in reading, mathematics, and spelling. BASIS yields both criterion-referenced and norm-referenced information. In addition, an optional writing exer-

133

cise is available. Reading, mathematics, and spelling questions are grouped in grade-referenced clusters. BASIS is intended for use with individuals from grade 1 through post high school, whose academic performance is at grade levels 1 through 8. BASIS is intended for program planning, IEP development, and related purposes, and scores may be converted to standard scores, age- or grade-based percentile ranks, stanines, grade or age equivalents.

Diagnostic Achievement Battery (DAB)

The Diagnostic Achievement Battery (Newcomer & Curtis, 1984) provides achievement measures in reading, writing, and math and also includes subtests in listening and speaking, and an index of spoken language. To give a measure of listening skills, the student listens to the examiner read short stories, after which the student answers questions and responds to true-false statements the examiner poses. These statements are intended to be within the listener's realm of knowledge, and thus can be answered correctly if the listener carefully attends to them. To determine the student's speaking skills, he or she supplies synonyms for words the examiner reads, and completes unfinished sentences, which the examiner also reads.

Assessment results are provided through percentile ranks and standard scores for each subtest, a total achievement quotient, and various other composite scores reflecting combinations of subtest scores. The DAB is for students aged 6-0 through 14-11.

Diagnostic Achievement Test for Adolescents (DATA)

The Diagnostic Achievement Test for Adolescents (Newcomer & Bryant, 1986) is designed to measure the achievement level of students in grades 7 through 12. DATA includes tests in reading, mathematics, writing, science, social studies, and reference skills. Individual subtests are provided in word identification, reading comprehension, math calculations, math problem solving, spelling, writing composition, science, social studies, and reference skills. Two subtests—spelling and writing composition—may be administered to small groups; the remainder of DATA must be administered individually. Test results are provided in percentiles, and standard scores with the normal interpretation possibilities.

Test of Academic Progress (TAP)

The Test of Academic Progress (Adams, Erb, & Sheslow, 1988) is a norm-referenced, individually administered test of achievement for use in grades K through 12. TAP includes subtests in mathematics, reading, and spelling.

Though intended for individual use, the math and spelling subtests may be administered to small groups. TAP was developed as a quick test of academic progress, to check annual progress or to determine if more intensive diagnostic assessment is required. TAP provides within-grade standard scores, percentile ranks, and grade equivalents.

Criterion-Referenced Achievement Tests

Criterion-referenced tests are intended to assess student performance (achievement) with respect to specific instructional objectives. Sections of some of these tests will be referenced in later chapters, but we will mention one, to illustrate the difference between the traditional achievement tests—such as those outlined in this chapter—and criterion-referenced tests, which also assess achievement in academic areas.

The Brigance tests are among the more often used criterion-referenced tests that can illustrate our point. For example, the *Brigance Diagnostic Comprehensive Inventory of Basic Skills (Brigance, 1983)* assesses skills in spoken language, reading, spelling, writing, and mathematics. That certainly sounds like an achievement test, but, instead of measuring broad levels of achievement, the Brigance targets student performance on tasks that relate to specific instructional objectives. These tests are designed to analyze strengths and weaknesses in specific skill areas, as a basis for instructional planning, and take much more time to administer. Achievement tests, as they are generally defined, might more likely be used in initial assessment. Criterion-referenced tests are more likely to be used as part of the later assessment that is done to establish a basis for specific instructional planning.

Reading Assessment Instruments

The definition of reading in its simplest form indicates that the reader understands or is gaining the meaning the author intends. Therefore, reading, is another facet of the total communication process. An author provides information or writes about an idea or concept, uses conventional form (correct spelling, appropriate grammatical constructs, and so forth), and thus conveys a message. The reader decodes the message (using various methods) and achieves meaning.

The efficient reader must possess knowledge regarding words and letters, syntax, and semantics. To read efficiently, one need not be able to state rules regarding phonics, syntax, or semantics but must have an awareness of these rules. Students who are learning to read or have developed a degree of reading proficiency are aware of the rules governing the English language through their use of oral language. Reading then relates to applying this knowledge to print.

The Focus of Reading Assessment

Assessment of reading centers on vocabulary (word recognition) and meaning. Once the reader has developed a degree of proficiency, factors related to speed of reading may be the focus of assessment. Determining a student's ability to recognize or decode words is not particularly difficult. But comprehension—not simple recognition or decoding words—is the essence of reading. Witt, Elliott, Gresham, & Kramer (1988) have stated that as yet we "do not have sophisticated methods of measuring reading comprehension because it seems to involve so many cognitive skills" (p. 239). Assessment efforts must center on the use of tests, "both formal and informal, that require subjects to behave as they do in typical learning situations" (p. 239).

Finally, we must systematically isolate the skills and situations in which students do or do not succeed. Each individual approaches the reading task differently, and only through a thorough assessment of that individual approach can the teacher develop appropriate interventions to assist the less efficient reader.

Assessment in reading ranges from measuring a student's ability in a single skill area—for example, a list of words that the student reads—to more comprehensive assessment, which also might include word attack skills, different levels of comprehension, comprehension in various academic areas, and attitudes toward reading. Selection of the appropriate test is guided by the information the teacher requires.

Standardized, Criterion-Referenced, and Informal Reading Inventories

Advanced Reading Inventory (ARI)

The Advanced Reading Inventory (Johns, 1982) is an informal reading instrument consisting of graded word lists, graded reading passages, and comprehension questions. The ARI is intended for students grades 1 through 6. Administration time varies.

Analytic Reading Inventory (ARI)

The Analytic Reading Inventory (Woods & Moe, 1989) is a 170-item, graded assessment utilizing word lists and reading passages. The ARI measures strengths and weaknesses in word attack and comprehension skills. Designed for students grades 1 through 9, the ARI is untimed.

Bader Language and Reading Inventory (BLRI)

The Bader Language and Reading Inventory (Bader, 1983) is an informal reading inventory designed to assess reading ability in word recognition, reading graded passages, and comprehension. The BLRI is for students in grades 1 through 6.

Basic Achievement Skills Individual Screener

(See chapter 8.)

Basic School Skills Inventory—Diagnostic
(See chapter 7.)

Basic School Skills Inventory—Screen
(See chapter 7.)

Boder Test of Reading-Spelling Patterns (BTRSP)

The Boder Test of Reading-Spelling Patterns (Boder & Jarrico, 1982) is designed for students from preschool age through adulthood. The Reading Test assesses sight vocabulary and phonetic word analysis skills. The Spelling Test uses known and unknown words from the student's reading test. The two tests assess the central visual and auditory processes required for reading and spelling. Results of the BTRSP may be used to diagnose developmental dyslexia.

Botel Reading Inventory (BRI)

The Botel Reading Inventory (Botel, 1978) is designed to assess skills in word recognition, word opposites, and phonic application. The BRI provides information regarding the student's instructional and frustration levels. It requires 30 minutes to administer and is for students from first grade through junior high levels.

Brigance Diagnostic Comprehensive Inventory of Basic Skills (CIBS)

Designed to assess students from prekindergarten through ninth grade, the Brigance Diagnostic Comprehensive Inventory of Basic Skills (Brigance, 1983) is a 203-multiple-item test organized into 22 skill areas that address reading, spelling, writing, and mathematics. Assessment using the CIBS begins at the level at which the student is known to be successful and continues until the student attains the level of achievement for that skill. Several methods of assessment (appraisal of student performance in daily work, teacher observation, parent interview) may be used to collect appropriate information. Two forms of the CIBS are available for 51 of the skill sequences, allowing for pre- and post-testing. The CIBS is a criterion-referenced instrument. The following skills are assessed:
1. Speech and listening
2. Readiness
   Word recognition grade placement
   Oral reading
   Reading comprehension

Functional word recognition
Word analysis
3. Reference skills
4. Graphs and maps
5. Spelling
6. Writing
7. Math grade placement
Numbers
Number facts
Whole number computation
Fractions and mixed numbers
Decimals
Percents
Word problems
Metrics
Math vocabulary

Brigance Diagnostic Inventory of Basic Skills (IBS)

The Brigance Diagnostic Inventory of Basic Skills (Brigance, 1977) is an earlier, shorter version of the Brigance Diagnostic Comprehensive Inventory of Basic Skills. The IBS is a 143-item test that assesses student mastery in 14 major skill areas. It is designed for students in kindergarten through 6th grade. Skill areas assessed include:
1. Reading Readiness
Word recognition
Reading (fluency and level)
Word analysis
Vocabulary
Reference skills
2. Handwriting
Grammar and mechanics
Spelling
3. Math Placement
Numbers
Operations
Measurement
Geometry

Brigance Diagnostic Inventory of Early Development
(See chapter 7.)

Brigance Diagnostic Inventory of Essential Skills
(See chapter 14.)

California Achievement Test
(See chapter 8.)

Classroom Reading Inventory (CRI)

The Classroom Reading Inventory (Silvaroli, 1986) is designed to assess word recognition and comprehension skills in students from first grade through adulthood. The CRI provides information regarding student' independent, instructional, and frustration reading levels, as well as information regarding skills related to consonants, vowels, and syllabication. In the area of comprehension, the CRI provides information regarding the student's abilities in understanding vocabulary, and literal and inferential comprehension. The CRI is available in four forms. Forms A and B are for students in grades 1 through 6, Form C is for junior high age students, and Form D is for high school age and adult persons. The CRI requires 12 minutes for administration.

Cloze Procedure (CP)

The Cloze Procedure (Clary, 1976; Karlin, 1973) is an informal method of determining the difficulty a student will have in reading specific materials. In administering the CP the teacher selects a passage of 250-350 words and omits every tenth word. The student reads the passage, filling in the missing words, which the teacher records. Scoring is completed by converting errors to percentages. A score of 61% or more indicates an independent level of reading; 40%-60% indicates the instructional level; 40% or less indicates the frustration reading level.

Criterion Test of Basic Skills
(See chapter 10.)

Diagnosis: An Instructional Aid (DAIA)

Diagnosis: An Instructional Aid (Shub et al., 1973) consists of two levels and is to be used for assessing a variety of reading skills. The DAIA is a criterion-referenced system addressing reading skills such as phonetic analysis, structural analysis, comprehension, vocabulary, and dictionary skills. Level A is for use with students whose reading skills are at the kindergarten through third grade level, and Level B is for those whose reading level is at the 4th through 6th grade level.

Diagnostic Achievement Battery
(See chapter 8.)

Diagnostic Achievement Battery for Adolescents
(See chapter 8.)

Diagnostic Reading Scales—Revised (DRS-R)

The Diagnostic Reading Scales—Revised (Spache, 1981) are designed to assess oral and silent reading skills and auditory comprehension. They consist of a series of graded word lists, graded reading selections, and phonetic and word analysis tests. The DRS-R provides information regarding the student's instructional level, a measurement of oral reading and comprehension, independent level, a measurement of silent reading and comprehension, and a potential level of measurement of auditory comprehension. The scales are to be used with students in grades 1 through 7 or with older students whose reading skills are below normal levels.

Doren Diagnostic Test of Word Recognition (DDTWR)

The Doren Diagnostic Test of Word Recognition (Doren, 1973) assesses word recognition skills of students in grades 1 through 6. The DDTWR measures the following skill areas: letter recognition, beginning sounds, whole-word recognition, words within words, speech consonants, blending, rhyming, vowels, spelling, and sight words.

Durrell Analysis of Reading Difficulty—Third Edition (DARD)

The Durrell Analysis of Reading Difficulty (Durrell & Catterson, 1980) is designed for use with students who are at nonreader or prereading level to the sixth grade level. The DARD assesses the following reading skills: oral and silent reading, listening vocabulary and comprehension, word recognition and analysis, spelling, auditory analysis of words and word elements, visual memory of words, pronunciation of word elements, and prereading phonic abilities. An individually administered test, the DARD requires 30 to 45 minutes for administration.

Ekwall Reading Inventory (ERI)

The Ekwall Reading Inventory (Ekwall, 1979) is an individually administered assessment of decoding skills and comprehension. The ERI is for students whose functional reading ability is from the preprimer to ninth grade level. Four forms are available.

Formal Reading Inventory (FRI)

A method of assessing silent reading comprehension and diagnosing oral reading miscues, the Formal Reading Inventory (Wiederholt, 1985) has four forms, each with 13 sequenced passages containing lateral, inferential, critical, and affective comprehension questions. Forms A and C require the student to read silently and then respond to comprehension questions. The student orally reads Forms B and D, and the examiner notes miscues. The miscues noted are: meaning similarity, function similarity, graphic/phonemic similarity, multiple sources (when the miscue fits more than one of the above miscue types), and self-correction. Forms C and D may be used for post-tests.

Fountain Valley Teachers Support System in Reading (FVTSSR)

The Fountain Valley Teachers Support System in Reading (Zweig, 1971) is a criterion-referenced measure of 367 reading skills. The reading skills measured are: phonetic analysis, structural analysis, vocabulary development, comprehension, and study skills. All of the tests are arranged in order of difficulty and color-coded.

Gates-MacGinitie Reading Tests (GMRT)

The Gates-MacGinitie Reading Tests (MacGinitie, 1978) are a series of norm-referenced tests to assess the reading skills of students in kindergarten through twelfth grade. The GMRT has seven levels, and each level has two forms, except levels D and F, which have three apiece. Each level measures vocabulary and reading comprehension; the forms for first grade also assess letter recognition and sound-letter association. Each of the levels requires an hour for administration. The GMRT may be scored by hand or by computer.

Gates-McKillop-Horowitz Reading Diagnostic Tests (GMHRDT)

The Gates-McKillop-Horowitz Reading Diagnostic Tests (Gates, McKillop, & Horowitz, 1981) are contained within an 11-part battery of tests measuring oral reading, spelling, and writing abilities. The target population is grades 1 through 6. Reading skill areas examined include: isolated word recognition, knowledge of word parts, recognizing and blending common word parts, giving letter sounds, letter recognition, auditory blending, identifying vowel sounds, discrimination of sounds, and writing. The GMHRDT is individually administered and requires 1 hour.

Gilmore Oral Reading Test (GORT)

The Gilmore Oral Reading Test (Gilmore & Gilmore, 1968) is designed to assess three aspects of oral reading: accuracy, comprehension, and rate of reading. The GORT is available in two forms, is individually administered, and requires 20 minutes for administration. The test is used with students in grades 1 through 8.

Gray Oral Reading Test—Revised (GORT-R)

Designed to measure reading ability from early 1st grade through college, the Gray Oral Reading Test—Revised (Wiederholt & Bryant, 1986) has four forms, each with developmentally sequenced passages that are read orally. Scores are derived from the reading rate and reading errors. Comprehension questions are included, as are directions for analyzing student errors. The GORT-R requires 30 minutes for administration.

Hudson Educational Skills Inventory
(See chapter 10.)

Informal Reading Assessment (IRA)

The Informal Reading Assessment (Burns & Roe, 1980) is an instrument designed to assess word recognition and comprehension. Included in the IRA are graded passages to determine the student's independent, instructional, and frustration reading levels.

McCullough Word Analysis Tests (MWAT)

The McCullough Word Analysis Tests (McCullough, 1963) are for students in grades 4 through 6. The MWAT is individually administered and measures skills in the following areas: identifying initial blends and diagraphs, phonetic discrimination, matching letters to vowel sounds, sounding whole words, dividing words into syllables, and identifying root words in affixed form.

Metropolitan Achievement Tests
(See chapter 8.)

Multilevel Academic Skills Inventory: Reading Program (MASI)

The Multilevel Academic Skills Inventory: Reading Program (Howell, Zucker, & Morehead, 1982b) is intended to measure skills in reading, handwriting, and spelling. The Survey Test measures a wide range of skills; the Placement Test measures specific skills in greater detail; and a Specific Level Test measures subskill abilities. The MASI includes assessment of decoding skills, reading vocabulary, and comprehension. Designed for students in grades 1 through 8, the time for administration varies.

Multilevel Academic Survey Test (MAST)

The Multilevel Academic Survey Test (Howell, Zucker, & Morehead, 1982c) provides two methods of assessing performance in reading and mathematics. The Grade-Level Tests contain a primary form for kindergarten through grade 2 and an extended form for grades 3 through 12. The Grade-Level Tests are nationally normed, and deficits indicate inadequate grade level skills. Skills assessed in the Reading domains include decoding and comprehension. (The Mathematics Domains are described in chapter 10.) The Curriculum Level Tests, designed to measure specific strengths and weaknesses in Reading and Mathematics, are to be used in conjunction with the Grade-Level Tests. The Curriculum-Level Tests assess oral reading, decoding, vocabulary, and comprehension in the Reading portion. The Grade-Level Tests require 30 to 60 minutes for administration, depending on the form used, and the Curriculum-Level Tests require 30 minutes per subject for administration. The MAST is used with students in kindergarten through 12th grade.

New Sucher-Allred Reading Placement Inventory (NSARPI)

The New Sucher-Allred Reading Placement Inventory (Sucher & Allred, 1981) is for students in grades 1 through 6. The NSARPI has two parts; the Word Recognition Test is administered first and is used to select a beginning point for the Oral Reading Test. The Inventory measures word recognition, oral reading, and oral and silent reading comprehension. It also provides information regarding the student's independent, instructional, and frustration reading levels. The NSARPI requires 20 minutes for administration.

Peabody Individual Achievement Test—Revised
(See chapter 8.)

Prescriptive Reading Inventory (PRI)

A criterion-referenced test, the Prescriptive Reading Inventory (CTB/McGraw-Hill, 1972) is for students in grades 1 through 8 and consists of 568 items, which measure 90 objectives. The PRI measures skills in decoding, comprehension, and oral and silent reading.

Reading Comprehension Inventory (RCI)

The Reading Comprehension Inventory (Giordano, 1988) consists of six progressively more complex passages that the student reads either orally or silently for each grade level. Results of the students' responses to questions related to each passage are analyzed, and a reading comprehension profile is developed. The RCI is for students in kindergarten through 6th grade. Time required for administration varies.

Reading Miscue Analysis (RMA)

The Reading Miscue Analysis (Goodman, 1973; Goodman & Burke, 1972) is a method of analyzing students' oral reading strategies. The miscues are analyzed according to three major categories: semantic—words miscalled that are similar in meaning; syntactic—words miscalled that are the same part of speech; and graphic—word or letter(s) that is similar to the miscalled word or a substitution of letter sounds. The purpose of analyzing the miscues is to determine whether they interfere with the student's comprehension. The RMA may be used with students from grade 1 through high school.

Regional Resource Center
Diagnostic Reading Inventory (RRCDRI)

The Diagnostic Reading Inventory (Regional Resource Center, 1971) is a measure of a student's phonetic analysis skills and oral reading. The test uses 1-minute behavior samplings from each of the subtests: consonant sounds, vowel sounds, blending, and reading from a classroom reader. It is recommended that each subtest be administered five times over a period of several days to promote more reliable data.

Slosson Oral Reading Test (SORT)

The Slosson Oral Reading Test (Slosson, 1963) is a screening test of reading ability. The SORT contains lists of words of increasing difficulty, which the student must read. Form A of the SORT is in large print for persons with visual impairments. The SORT requires 5 minutes for administration and may be used with school-age students and in adult literacy programs.

Spadafore Diagnostic Reading Test (SDRT)

The Spadafore Diagnostic Reading Test (Spadafore, 1983) is a screening and diagnostic test for students in grades 1 through 12 and can be used with adults. Criterion-referenced, the SDRT measures word recognition, oral reading and comprehension, silent reading comprehension, and listening comprehension. At each grade level the independent, instructional, and frustration levels are designated. The Screening portion, requiring 30 minutes for administration, provides information regarding reading difficulties that may exist. The Diagnostic portion of the test requires 60 minutes for administration.

SRA Achievement Series
(See chapter 8.)

Stanford Diagnostic Reading Test—Third Edition (SDRT)

The Stanford Diagnostic Reading Test (Karlsen & Gardner, 1984) is designed to measure the reading skills of students in grades 1 through 12. The SDRT assesses auditory discrimination, phonetic analysis, and structural analysis at all levels. The Comprehension section of the SDRT provides separate scores for comprehension of textual, functional, and recreational reading passages. The SDRT is normed for fall and spring so that yearly progress may be assessed.

Test of Early Reading Ability
(See chapter 7.)

Test of Reading Comprehension (TORC)

The Test of Reading Comprehension (Brown, Hammill, & Wiederholt, 1986) contains four subtests: General Vocabulary, Syntactic Similarities, Paragraph Reading, and Sentence Sequencing. The TORC also includes supplementary subtests for measuring the student's abilities in reading the vocabularies of math, science, and social studies material. The TORC requires 1 hour and 45 minutes for administration. It is for students in grades 2 through 12.

Wide Range Achievement Test—Revised
(See chapter 8.)

Wisconsin Tests of Reading Skill Development (WTRSD)

The Wisconsin Tests of Reading Skill Development (Kamm, Miles, Van Blaricon, Harris, & Stewart, 1972) have 38 short tests at four levels of difficulty. Word-attack skills are assessed for students in kindergarten through 3rd grade. The WTRSD assesses the comprehension skills of students in kindergarten through sixth grade. Comprehension skills assessed include cause and effect, relationships, drawing conclusions, and judging relevance. These are criterion-referenced tests.

Woodcock Language Proficiency Battery
(See chapter 11.)

Woodcock Reading Mastery Tests—Revised (WRMT-R)

The Woodcock Reading Mastery Tests (Woodcock, 1987) are a battery of five individually administered tests for persons in kindergarten through adulthood. Reading readiness, vocabulary, and comprehension skills are assessed. Reading vocabulary in General Reading, Science-Mathematics, Social Studies, and Humanities is also measured. Forms G and H of the WRMT-R may be used for test and retest. Screening for overall reading ability may be accomplished in 15 minutes by using scores from the Word Identification and Passage Comprehension tests.

Woodcock-Johnson Psychoeducational Battery—Revised
(See chapter 8.)

Mathematics
Assessment Instruments

Although the terms arithmetic and mathematics are frequently used interchangeably, they are actually different concepts. Mathematics is the broader term; it refers to classifying, comparing, ordering, quantified relationships, prediction, estimation, and the application of these concepts. Arithmetic is concerned primarily with computation (addition, subtraction, multiplication, division). Problem solving relates to both, although it is frequently narrowed to mean only "story problems." It must be recognized, however, that students are involved in problem solving when they use systems of classification—for example, when a student classifies a group of blocks based first on color (red and yellow blocks) and later on size (big and little blocks).

The content of mathematics has a logical, sequential structure, beginning with simpler tasks and proceeding to more complex tasks. Many teachers consider an understanding of concepts, for example as described by Piaget (1965), as a prerequisite to formal math instruction. According to Piaget, classification must precede meaningful work with numbers. Classification involves the recognition and understanding of relationships, whether of size, color, shape, texture, function, or others. Ordering and seriation relate to understanding relative differences—for example, arranging pencils from shortest to longest or blocks from smallest to largest. Understanding one-to-one correspondence is essential to computation. For example, there is the understanding that one object in a set is the same number as one object in a different set, no matter what characteristics the objects possess. Conservation refers to the understanding that the number of objects in a set remains constant regardless of their arrangement.

Concepts in Mathematics

Other conceptual understanding is also essential for students to effectively manipulate numbers. For example, regardless of the order in which the same set of numbers is combined, the sum remains constant. Also, the same numbers being multiplied may be in any order, and the product remains the same. These are generally taught in the same manner as the basic operations of addition, subtraction, multiplication, and division, but students often focus their attention on mastering facts and do not learn the mathematical axioms.

Some authors (Underhill, Uprichard, & Heddens, 1980) believe that students must progress through several levels of learning in order to master mathematics. These levels are: concrete, semiconcrete, and abstract. The *concrete* level consists of manipulation of actual objects that aid in developing the mental images and understanding the symbolic processes. The *semiconcrete* level is a transition; illustrations of objects or dots, lines, and tallies relate to the mathematical task. The *abstract* level involves the exclusive use of numerals. Underhill et al. (1980) suggest that when students count on their fingers or make tallies, they are indicating the level at which they are performing. A thorough understanding of mathematical concepts is necessary; otherwise computation is merely a task performed by rote memory (Reid, 1988).

Assessment of computational skills is easier and may be accomplished more quickly than assessment of mathematics concepts, but understanding the *processes* a student uses is more important than a particular test score (Witt, Elliott, Gresham, & Kramer, 1988). For example, some students have difficulty remembering that addition or subtraction processes begin on the right and move left—just the opposite of what they have learned in the reading process. Other students may have difficulty *reading* mathematics. For example, they may be unable to read graphs, charts, or the individual words related to the problems or directions.

Still other students may experience difficulty in understanding *quantitative language*—words related to position or direction, geometric words (triangle, octagon), relative words (smaller, nearest), and others. Other mathematical factors relating to a concept of time (not merely telling time) or money (which includes equivalency and part-whole relationships) may pose problems for students. Clearly mathematics includes more than computation.

Assessment in mathematics is traditionally product-oriented; that is, it is concerned with whether the student finds the correct answer. To gain insights into a student's specific mathematical abilities and understandings, however, it also must be process-oriented—concerned with how the student arrived at the answer. This attention to process may be necessary even when students derive correct answers, especially at early stages of mathematical learning. They may be using processes or methods that enable them to get correct answers as long as the computation is simple, but that will fail as problems become increasingly complex. In addition to the formal instruments discussed next, informal strategies of assessment, discussed in chapter 6, also may be required to determine the full range of a student's abilities and difficulties.

Instruments Used in Mathematics and Computational Assessment

Adston Mathematics Skill Series: Common Fractions (AMSSCF)

The Adston Mathematics Skill Series: Common Fractions (Adams, 1979) is a criterion-referenced test designed to assess the skills of students (in any grade) who have received instruction in common fractions. The AMSSCF includes a survey test, a fact test, and an operations test.

Adston Mathematics Skill Series: Decimal Numbers (AMSSDM)

The Adston Mathematics Skill Series: Decimal Numbers (Beeson & Pellegrin, 1979) is a criterion-referenced test designed to measure skills in decimal numbers. The AMSSDN has a survey test, fact test, and operations test and is for students (in any grade) who have received instruction in decimal numbers.

Adston Mathematics Skill Series: Readiness for Operations (AMSSRO)

The Adston Mathematics Skills Series: Readiness for Operations (Adams & Sauls, 1979) is a criterion-referenced test to determine a student's readiness for operations. The test is pictorial and includes items at the semiconcrete level. The AMSSRO is for students in preschool through 2nd grade.

Adston Mathematics Skill Series: Working with Whole Numbers (AMSSWWN)

The Adston Mathematics Skill Series: Working with Whole Numbers (Adams & Ellis, 1979) is a criterion-referenced test to assess skills in each of the operations: addition, subtraction, multiplication, and division. This series is designed for students who have received instruction in any of the operations. It includes a survey test, fact test, and operations test.

Assessment of Early Mathematical Language
(See Early Mathematical Language, p. 154.)

Basic Achievement Skills Individual Screener
(See chapter 8.)

Basic School Skills Inventory—Diagnostic
(See chapter 7.)

Basic School Skills Inventory—Screen
(See chapter 7.)

Brigance Diagnostic Comprehensive Inventory of Basic Skills
(See chapter 9.)

Brigance Diagnostic Inventory of Early Developlment
(See chapter 7.)

Brigance Diagnostic Inventory of Essential Skills
(See chapter 14.)

California Achievement Tests
(See chapter 8.)

Classroom Learning Screening Manual (CLSM)

The Classroom Learning Screening Manual (Koenig & Kunzelmann, 1980) is designed to assess the skills of students in kindergarten through 6th grade. The CLSM is a criterion-referenced test that assesses skills in numbers, addition facts, subtraction facts, multiplication facts, and division facts through divisors of 9. The CLSM uses probes to assess each fact, and the number of correct and incorrect responses per minute is recorded.

Criterion Test of Basic Skills (CTBS)

The Criterion Test of Basic Skills (Lundell, Brown, & Evans, 1976) is designed to assess reading and arithmetic skills of students in grades 1 through 6. The Arithmetic subtest measures skills in numbers and numerical recognition, addition, subtraction, multiplication, and division. The CTBS is criterion-referenced and requires 15 minutes for administration.

Diagnostic Achievement Battery
(See chapter 8.)

Diagnostic Achievement Battery for Adolescents
(See chapter 8.)

Diagnostic Mathematics Inventory (DMI)

The Diagnostic Mathematics Inventory (Gessell, 1977) is a multiple-choice test assessing 325 objectives. The DMI, for students from grades 1.5 through 8.5, has seven levels. The objectives assessed in the DMI are cross-referenced to mathematics textbooks and supplemental materials. The materials available include practice exercises and learning activities for the objectives.

Diagnostic Screening Test: Math (DSTM)

The Diagnostic Screening Test: Math (Gnagey, 1980) has two sections—Basic Processes and Specialized—and an optional 9-item pretest for an estimate of computational skills. The Basic Processes section measures skills in addition, subtraction, multiplication, and division. Supplemental categories assessed are: process, sequencing, simple computation, special manipulations, use of zero decimals, simple fractions, and manipulation in fractions. The Specialized section evaluates conceptual and computational skills in money, time, percent, U.S. measurement, and metric measure. The DSTM is for students in grades 1 through 12 and requires 5 to 20 minutes for administration.

Diagnostic Test of Arithmetic Strategies (DTAS)

The Diagnostic Test of Arithmetic Strategies (Ginsburg & Mathews, 1984) is designed to evaluate the strategies students in grades 1 through 8 use in solving basic arithmetic calculations: addition, subtraction, multiplication, and division. The DTAS results in an individual profile of each student's faulty calculational strategies and potential strengths. The DTAS may be used individually or with groups.

Diagnostic Tests and Self-Helps in Arithmetic (DTSA)

The Diagnostic Tests and Self-Helps in Arithmetic (Brueckner, 1955) is a criterion-referenced set of tests designed to measure both general and specific areas of strength and weakness. The DTSA measures abilities in computation of whole numbers, fractions, decimals, percent, and operations in measurement. The DTSA is for students in grades 1 through 8.

DMI Mathematics System (DMIMS)

A set of criterion-referenced tests designed for use with students in kindergarten through 8th grade, the DMI Mathematics System (CTB/McGraw-Hill, 1983) measures four strands of mathematic content: whole numbers, fractions and decimals, measurement and geometry, and problem solving and special topics. The DMIMS is available in two formats: System 1 is a graded approach and assesses skills by level; System 2 is a multigraded approach and assesses skills across grade levels.

Early Mathematical Language (EML)

The Early Mathematical Language Test (Williams & Somerwill, 1982) is designed to assess students in first grade or older students who have difficulty in mathematics. The EML assesses students' knowledge and use of mathematical language in the following areas: position in space, weight and shape, number, volume and capacity, length, and time. The EML is nonverbal. Administration time varies.

Enright Diagnostic Inventory of Basic Arithmetic Skills (EDIBAS)

The Enright Diagnostic Inventory of Basic Arithmetic Skills (Enright, 1983) consists of four sets of multiple-item tests assessing 13 computational skill sections. Skills assessed are: addition, subtraction, multiplication, division of whole numbers, fractions, decimals, and conversion of fractions. A wide range placement test of 26 items is available in two forms. The skill placement tests, one for each of the 13 skills sections, are available in two alternative forms. Error patterns associated with each of the 144 skill areas are presented for diagnosing specific computational errors. The EDIBAS is criterion-referenced and may be administered individually or in groups.

Fountain Valley Teacher Support System in Mathematics (FVTSSM)

A criterion-referenced test, the Fountain Valley Teacher Support System in Mathematics (1976) is for students in grades 1 through 8. It assesses skills in numbers, operations, geometry measurement, application, probability, sets, functions, logical thinking, and problem solving.

Fundamental Processes in Arithmetic (FPA)

The Fundamental Processes in Arithmetic Test (Buswell & Johns, 1925) is designed to measure the student's arithmetic abilities as well as the student's mental processes while performing the calculations. Skills assessed include addition, subtraction, multiplication, and division.

154

Hudson Education Skills Inventory (HESI)

The Hudson Education Skills Inventory (Hudson, Colson, Welch, Banikowski, & Mehring, 1988) is a curriculum-based set of three tests for use with students in grades 1 through 12. The separate tests and subskills assessed in each are: (1) Mathematics—addition, subtraction, multiplication, division, fractions, decimals, percentages, time, money, measurement, statistics, graphs, tables, and word problems; (2) Reading—readiness, sight word vocabulary, phonic analysis, structural analysis, and comprehension; and (3) Writing—composition, spelling, and handwriting. The HESI is criterion-referenced and may be administered in its entirety or each test may be administered separately.

Individualized Criterion Referenced Testing—Mathematics (ICRTM)

The Individualized Criterion Referenced Testing—Mathematics (Strotman & Steen, 1977) is intended to measure student knowledge in operations, fractions, measurement, geometry, decimals, percentages, and special topics. The ICRTM presents a developmental continuum of 384 learning objectives for grades 1 through 9. The tests may be administered to students beyond the ninth grade because the ICRTM is designed to be taken at an individual's instructional level rather than grade level. Results of the ICRTM provide information regarding which skills have been mastered, which require review, and which must be learned.

Iowa Test of Basic Skills
(See chapter 8.)

Key Math—Revised (KM-R)

The Key Math—Revised (Connally, 1988), a revision of the Key Math Diagnostic Arithmetic Test, is designed to measure students' understanding and application of mathematic concepts and skills. For students in kindergarten through 9th grade, the KMR includes 13 subtests in three areas. The subtests and the skills addressed in each are: (1) Basic Concepts—numeration, rational numbers, and geometry; (2) Operations—addition, subtraction, multiplication, division, and mental computation; and (3) Applications—measurement, time and money, estimation, interpreting data, and problem solving. The KMR is individually administered, requires 50 minutes, and is available in two parallel forms.

Metropolitan Achievement Tests
(See chapter 8.)

Multilevel Academic Survey Test
(See chapter 9.)

Multilevel Academic Skills Inventory: Math Program (MASI-MP)

The Multilevel Academic Skills Inventory: Math Program (Howell, Zucker, & Morehead, 1982a) is designed for students in grades 1 through 8. The MASI-MP measures computation, application of skills with time and temperature, problem solving, metric measurement, addition, subtraction, multiplication, division, fractions, decimals, ratios, percent, and geometry. A Survey test samples a wide range of objectives. The Placement test assesses abilities in more detail, and a Specific Level test examines subskills in detail.

Peabody Individual Achievement Test—Revised
(See chapter 8.)

Peabody Mathematics Readiness Test (PMRT)

The Peabody Mathematics Readiness Test (Bassler, Beers, Richardson, & Thurman, 1979) is designed to measure the mathematic abilities of students in kindergarten and first grade or students with a mental age of 4 through 6 years. The readiness factors of number, containment, size, shape, configuration, and drawing are assessed. These factors are used to identify students who may later display poor mathematic achievement.

Progress Tests in Maths (PMT)

The Progress Tests in Maths (Hollands, 1983) are used to assess the mathematics achievement of students ages 7 through 12 and may be used with older students who are having difficulty with math. The PTM consists of six separate tests to measure yearly progress in the following areas: number concepts and knowledge; problems; computation skills in addition, subtraction, multiplication and division; shapes and pictorial representations; fractions; and decimals. The teacher may read the tests for the first three years to minimize problems caused by the students' limited reading abilities.

Regional Resource Center Diagnostic Math Inventories (RRCDMI)

A criterion-referenced set of tests designed to measure basic computational skills, the Regional Resource Center Diagnostic Math Inventories (1971) uses probe sheets for each individual arithmetic skill being assessed. Rates of correct and incorrect responses from 1-minute samples of behavior are used to determine strengths and weaknesses. Several samples taken over several days provide more reliable data than one sample.

Sequential Assessment of Mathematics Inventory (SAMI)

The Sequential Assessment of Mathematics Inventory (Reisman, 1985) is a 243-item test using varied response modes designed to assess the mathematic abilities of students in kindergarten through 8th grade. The SAMI measures performance in the following areas: math language, ordinality, number/notation, measurement, geometry, computation, word problems, and math applications. Most items are free-response rather than multiple-choice, allowing examiners to observe the students' problem-solving approach. The SAMI requires 30 to 60 minutes for individual administration.

SRA Achievement Series
(See chapter 8.)

Stanford Achievement Tests
(See chapter 8.)

Stanford Diagnostic Mathematics Test (SDMT)

The Stanford Diagnostic Mathematics Test (Beatty, Madden, Gardner, & Karlsen, 1984) is a multiple-item test measuring mathematic skills in three broad areas: number system and numeration, computation, and applications. The SDMT is both norm-referenced and criterion-referenced. Norms are fall and spring, so yearly growth may be measured. The SDMT may be administered in a group or individually.

Steenburgen Diagnostic-Prescriptive Math Program and Quick Math Screening Test (QMST)

The Steenburgen Diagnostic-Prescriptive Math Program and Quick Math Screening Test (Gelb, 1978) is both a screening test and a diagnostic-prescriptive program. The QMST measures the abilities of students in grades 1 through 6 in simple addition and subtraction, one-digit carrying, addition of mixed numbers, and long division. It requires 10 minutes for administration and may be used with older students who are at the elementary level. The diagnostic-prescriptive program consists of 55 reproducible worksheets for the student to use until the skill is mastered.

Test of Academic Progress
(See chapter 8.)

Test of Computational Processes (TCP)

The Test of Computational Processes (Kingston, 1985) measures computational skills in the following areas: addition, subtraction, multiplication and division of whole numbers, fractions, decimals, and knowledge of essential measurement unit. The TCP is designed for students in grades 3 through 8 and requires 30 minutes for administration. It may be administered individually or to a group.

Test of Early Mathematics Ability
(See chapter 7.)

Test of Mathematical Abilities (TOMA)

The Test of Mathematical Abilities (Brown & McEntire, 1984) is designed for students in grades 3 through 12. The TOMA measures knowledge, mastery, and attitudes in two major skill areas—story problems and computation—and four broad diagnostic areas—expressed attitudes toward mathematics, understanding of vocabulary as applied to mathematics, the functional use of mathematics as applied to our general culture, and the relationship between a student's attitudes and abilities and those of peers. The TOMA is individually administered.

Wide Range Achievement Test—Revised
(See chapter 8.)

Wisconsin Design for Math Skill Development (WDMSD)

The Wisconsin Design for Math Skill Development (Armenia, Kamp, McDonald, & Van Kuster, 1975) is a criterion-referenced test for students in grades 1 through 8. Skills assessed by the WDMSD include: numeration, place value, addition, subtraction, multiplication, division, fractions, geometry, measurement, time, money, and graphs.

Woodcock-Johnson Psychoeducational Battery—Revised
(See chapter 8.)

Oral and Written Language Assessment Instruments

Language, written and oral, is the essence of communication. An idea or concept that an individual develops is encoded into either oral language or written language, which is "sent" to a receiver. The receiver decodes the message either by listening and interpreting verbal messages or by reading what was written. The process may continue with the original receiver becoming the sender by responding, and so the cycle of communication continues. Continuation of the communication process is dependent upon the common understanding of language by both receiver and sender.

Speech is "verbal communication which includes the precise coordination of oral neuromuscular actions to form linguistic units. In addition to speech sounds, rate of speech and rhythm and intensity of sound also contribute to the speech process" (Bernstein & Tiegerman, 1985, p. 6). Language is a "socially shared code or conventional system for representing concepts through the use of arbitrary symbols and rule-governed combinations of those symbols" (Shames & Wiig, 1986, p. 31). The assessment process may address either or both of these aspects of communication. In some situations the focus will be on the production of speech sounds, rate, rhythm, and intensity of the sounds produced.

Components of Language and Communication

Rate, rhythm, and intensity, in conjunction with application of the rules of a particular language, form the basis of sophisticated language, which in turn leads to effective verbal communication. Language and its components may be the focus of the assessment process and, as such, the emphasis may be more on the ability to apply the rules of the language than on pronunciation.

The *structure* of any language has five components: phonology, morphology, syntax, semantics, and pragmatics. Assessment in language centers on these five areas, with some receiving more emphasis at one particular time.

Phonology is the set number of pronounceable sounds that a given language requires. The smallest units of speech sound are *phonemes,* which do not in and of themselves have meaning. The English language has 44 phonemes, which must be correctly pronounced or the communication process may be inhibited.

Morphemes are the smallest units of language that are meaningful; they allow for tense, plurality, and possession, and they extend word meanings. Morphemes may be categorized as *free* or *bound.* As examples, "girl" is a free morpheme and can stand alone; the suffix /s/, while denoting specific meaning, must be attached to a free-standing morpheme to have meaning.

Syntax relates to the rules that specify how words are arranged in phrases or sentences. Every language has rules that indicate the correct order of words, and if the rules are not followed, incorrect grammatic usage results. The order of words reflects a change in meaning, as in "Susan, will you sit down?" versus "Susan, you will sit down."

Semantics encompasses the meaning assigned to words or phrases. Whereas phonology, morphology, and syntax form the structures of a language system, semantics refers to the *meaning* of those structures. Semantics relates to the meaning attached to words (for example, *judge* the noun versus *judge* the verb) and provides for subtle nuances of language, as in glowing, gleaming, and shining.

Pragmatics refers to how language is used in varying situations. It implies the ability to recognize a specific situation, judge the listener's characteristics, determine the intent of the communication, and select the appropriate language based on these considerations.

Effective communicators have a command of all these components of language even though they may not be able to articulate definitions or rules relating to them. In assessing *oral language,* the focus may be on one or more of these components.

Written language is another aspect of the total communication process. It encompasses handwriting, spelling, and written expression or—as it is sometimes referred to—composition.

The assessment of *handwriting* relates primarily to legibility or conformity to some standard of correct formation of letters. With students who are learning to write, the emphasis may be on formation; later the assessment may examine whether the student can write legibly or is somewhat careless.

Spelling assessment relates to correct spelling, as well as noting patterns of errors. Misspellings inhibit the communication process in written language.

Composition, a term that encompasses all writing activities, relates to three major categories: (a) expressive, (b) transactional, and (c) poetic (Britton, 1970). *Expressive* writing is generally conversational and stems from personal feelings and experiences. *Transactional* writing includes all activities related to conducting business. It may be further subdivided into exposition, description, and persuasion (Reid, 1988).

Expository writing refers to writing activities such as science experiments, giving directions, book reports, and so on. *Descriptive writing* is used in writing letters, essays, stories, and other activities in which the author's intent is to help the reader visualize a subject. *Persuasive writing* is the type that provides a thesis and supporting evidence such as budget requests, business letters, public relations materials, and advertising. Finally, *poetic writing* is primarily meant to be enjoyed; it includes plays, stories, poetry, and the like.

Assessment of composition relates to the author's purposes, legibility, and appropriate use of conventions such as punctuation, spelling, grammatical construction, and style.

Language Assessment Instruments

Assessment of oral and written language may cover several aspects of communicative abilities, or it may focus on one specific aspect. Brief descriptions of assessment instruments related to oral and written language follow.

Adolescent Language Screening Test (ALST)

The Adolescent Language Screening Test (Morgan & Guilford, 1984) is designed for a quick (15-minute) screening of students' language. The ALST consists of seven subtests: phonology, morphology, sentence formulation, receptive and expressive vocabulary, concepts, and pragmatics. The ALST, for students ages 11 through 17 years, provides information regarding the need for further assessment and the dimensions on which such assessment should focus.

Assessment of Children's Language Comprehension (ACLC)

The Assessment of Children's Language Comprehension (Foster, Giddan, & Stark, 1973) identifies young children's receptive language difficulties. The ACLC is a 41-item list of language comprehension which measures understanding of core vocabulary and combinations of language elements. No oral responses are required for the ACLC as the child responds by pointing. The

161

ACLC is designed for children ages 3 to 6½ years. A 17-item Group Form has been developed for classroom screening. The ACLC is available in English and Spanish.

Auditory Discrimination Test—Revised (ADT)

The Auditory Discrimination Test (Wepman, 1973) is designed for children 5 to 8 years of age. The ADT is an oral response test requiring 10 to 15 minutes and assesses the ability of the child to discriminate between pairs of words. The test predicts articulatory speech defects and certain remedial reading problems.

Auditory Pointing Test (APT)

The Auditory Pointing Test (Fudala, Kunze, & Ross, 1974) measures short-term memory through visual-motor responses. It is normed for children in kindergarten through 5th grade. This test is appropriate for persons with oral communication problems and consists of two forms, for test and retest situations. The APT requires 20 minutes for administration.

Bankson Language Screening Test (BLST)

The Bankson Language Screening Test (Bankson, 1977) is designed to measure psycholinguistic and perceptual skills in the following areas: semantic knowledge, morphological rules, syntactic rules, visual perception, and auditory perception. The BLST, an oral-response test for children 4 through 8 years of age is untimed. The BLST consists of 17 subtests with nine items apiece that provide information for diagnostic assessment. It is untimed.

Basic Achievement Skills Individual Screener
(See chapter 8.)

Basic School Skills Inventory—Diagnostic
(See chapter 7.)

Basic School Skills Inventory—Screen
(See chapter7.)

Boder Test of Reading-Spelling Patterns
(See chapter 9.)

Boehm Test of Basic Concepts—Revised (BTBC)

The Boehm Test of Basic Concepts—Revised (Boehm, 1986) is designed to measure the concepts usually considered important in the student's understanding the teacher's directions during the first years of school. The BTBC, used with children in kindergarten through 2nd grade, has two equivalent forms. The revised version includes an Applications level for grades 1 and 2, in which children must respond to combinations of the basic concepts. The BTBC is available in both English and Spanish.

Brigance Diagnostic Comprehensive Inventory of Basic Skills
(See chapter 9.)

Brigance Diagnostic Inventory of Basic Skills
(See chapter 9.)

Brigance Diagnostic Inventory of Early Development
(See chapter 7.)

Brigance Diagnostic Inventory of Essential Skills
(See chapter 14.)

California Achievement Test
(See chapter 8.)

Carolina Picture Vocabulary Test
(See chapter 15.)

Carrow Elicited Language Inventory (CELI)

The Carrow Elicited Language Inventory (Carrow, 1974), a diagnostic tool, was designed to assess the expressive grammatical competence of children 3 to 8 years of age. The CELI consists of 52 orally presented items, which the student is to imitate. Responses are analyzed to determine the student's ability to use pronouns, prepositions, conjunctions, adverbs, questions, negatives, nouns, adjectives, verbs, infinitives, and gerunds. Administration time is about 5 minutes.

Clark-Madison Test of Oral Language (CMTOL)

The Clark-Madison Test of Oral Language (Clark & Madison, 1986) is an assessment of the expressive abilities of students ages 4 to 8 years. It elicits

163

97 targets in the context of 66 sentences. The categories assessed are: syntax, modifiers, verbs, pronouns, and inflections. The CMTOL is untimed and requires about 20 minutes for administration.

Clinical Evaluation of Language Functions: Diagnostic Battery (CELF)

The Clinical Evaluation of Language Functions Battery (Semel & Wiig, 1987) is an 11-category verbal test that measures language processing and production. The areas assessed are: phonology, syntax, semantics, memory and word finding, and retrieval. The CELF, for students in grades 1 through 12, requires 1 to 2 hours for administration.

Comprehensive Screening Tool for Determining Optimal Communication Mode (CST)

The Comprehensive Screening Tool for Determining Optimal Communication Mode (House & Rogerson, 1984) is a multiple-item battery of response tests used to systematically and objectively determine the individual's potential for using an augmentative system, its mode and code. The CST assesses oral skills, manual skills, and pictographic skills. It is untimed and is to be used with persons of any age over the developmental level of 6 months.

Detroit Test of Learning Aptitude—II
(See chapter 5.)

Diagnostic Achievement Battery
(See chapter 8.)

Diagnostic Achievement Battery for Adolescents
(See chapter 8.)

Diagnostic Screening Test: Spelling (DSTS)

The Diagnostic Screening Test: Spelling (Gnagey, 1979) is a 78-item paper-and-pencil test designed to measure the student's sight or phonics orientation for spelling instruction. The DSTS is for students in grades 1 through 12. A pretest for the DSTS is available to determine appropriate level of entry, as are two forms. The DSTS requires 5 to 10 minutes for administration.

Diagnostic Spelling Potential Test (DSPT)

The Diagnostic Spelling Potential Test (Arena, 1982) has four subtests: spelling, word recognition, visual recognition, and auditory—visual recognition. The DSPT, a multiple-item, paper-and-pencil assessment tool designed for persons 7 years of age through adulthood, requires 25 to 40 minutes for administration.

Dos Amigos Verbal Language Scales (DAVLS)

The Dos Amigos Verbal Language Scales (Critchlow, 1974) assesses the cognitive level of language functioning, for students ages 5-13, in both Spanish and English, and is used to determine the dominant language. The examiner must be proficient in both Spanish and English.

Early Language Milestone Scale
(See chapter 7.)

Evaluating Acquired Skills in Communication (EASIC)

Designed to evaluate the language abilities of severely handicapped children, Evaluating Acquired Skills in Communication (Riley, 1984b) consists of a five-level set of inventories. The EASIC assesses abilities in semantics, syntax, morphology, and pragmatics. The scoring system is qualitative and allows for responses that are spontaneous, cued, imitated, manipulated, noncompliant, or incorrect. This instrument, for persons from age 4 through adulthood, is untimed.

Evaluating Communicative Competence (ECC)—Revised

Evaluating Communicative Competence (Simon, 1987) provides an appraisal of communicative skills through use of a series of 21 informal evaluation tasks. In a process involving comprehension of directions, giving directions, storytelling, expression and justification of an opinion, and other such tasks, the student exhibits competencies both as a listener and a speaker. Information from these probes should allow a clinician to determine whether a student requires additional intervention and provide guidance as to the nature of the intervention. The ECC is appropriate for students ages 9 through 17 years. Time required for administration varies.

Examining for Aphasia (EFA)

Examining for Aphasia (Eisenson, 1954) is a multiple-item screener of expressive and receptive language functions that may be an indicator of aphasia in adolescents and adults. Fourteen plates of black-and-white stimulus materials are included, and the examiner assembles other common objects required for the examination. Administration requires 30 minutes to 2 hours.

Expressive One-Word Picture Vocabulary Test (EOWPVT)

The Expressive One-Word Picture Vocabulary Test (Gardner, 1979), available in English and Spanish, assesses the speaking vocabulary of students from 2 to 12 years of age. The EOWPVT is used for screening for speech defects, school readiness, and fluency in English. The subject is shown 110 picture cards, one at a time, and is asked to name each picture. The EOWPVT is untimed but usually requires about 20 minutes.

Goldman-Fristoe Test of Articulation (GFTA)

The Goldman-Fristoe Test of Articulation (Goldman & Fristoe, 1972) is a test that requires no reading and is for children ages 2 through 16 years. It is designed to assess the articulation of consonant sounds in the initial, medial, and final positions. The GFTA has three subtests: sounds-in-words, sounds-in-sentences, and stimulability. The GFTA is untimed.

Goldman-Fristoe-Woodcock Test of Auditory Discrimination
(See chapter 13.)

Hudson Educational Skills Inventory
(See chapter 10.)

Illinois Test of Psycholinguistic Abilities
(See chapter 7.)

Informal Writing Inventory (IWI)

The Informal Writing Inventory (Giordano, 1986) is intended to measure the ability of students in grades 3 through 12 to communicate through writing. Pictures are used to assist the student in developing writing samples, which are subsequently analyzed for handwriting, spelling, grammar, and communicative ability. The time required for administration varies.

Iowa Test of Basic Skills
(See chapter 8.)

Joliet 3-Minute Speech and Language Screen (JMSLS)

The Joliet 3-Minute Speech and Language Screen (Kinzler & Johnson, 1983) is designed for the quick screening of speech and language problems of individuals or groups in the range of kindergarten through 5th grade. The JMSLS is a multiple-item, individually administered, oral response assessment tool. The areas examined include: expressive syntax, voice, fluency, and phonological competence.

Kindergarten Language Screening Test (KLST)

The Kindergarten Language Screening Test (Gauthier & Madison, 1983) assesses the abilities of kindergartners in receptive and expressive language areas. This is a multiple-item, oral response screening device used for identifying children who may require further assessment. Verbal language abilities regarding knowledge of name, age, body parts, number concepts, ability to follow commands and repeat sentences, and spontaneous speech are assessed. The KLST requires 4 to 5 minutes for administration.

Language Inventory for Teachers (LIT)

The Language Inventory for Teachers (Cooper & School, 1982), designed to assist teachers in developing IEPs, assesses the spoken and written language development of students from preschool through junior high age. The LIT provides a paper-and-pencil sequence of more than 500 language tasks that correspond to five goals in spoken language and eight in written language. Administration time is 30 minutes.

Language Proficiency Test (LPT)

The Language Proficiency Test (Gerald & Weinstock, 1981) is designed to assess the ability of individuals from 9th grade through adulthood to use the English language. The LPT assesses three major areas, aural/oral, reading, and writing, and utilizes materials and content appropriate for mature students with low-level skills. Nine of the 11 subtests may be administered to small groups. The two subtests that measure lower levels of language functioning require individual administration. The LPT requires 90 minutes but may be administered in several shorter testing sessions.

167

Let's Talk Inventory for Adolescents (LTIA)

The Let's Talk Inventory for Adolescents (Wiig, 1982) is a 40-item verbal test used for probing four communication functions: ritualizing, informing, controlling, and feeling. Designed for use with 9-year-olds to young adults, the LTIA identifies inadequate or delayed social-verbal communication skills. It requires 30 to 45 minutes for administration.

Let's Talk Inventory for Children (LTIC)

The Let's Talk Inventory for Children (Bray & Wiig, 1987) is a downward extension of the Let's Talk Inventory for Adolescents. The LTIC is designed for use with children 4 through 8 years of age and requires 30 minutes for administration.

Merrill Language Screening Test (MLST)

The Merrill Language Screening Test (Mumm, Secord, & Dykstra, 1980), for children 5 through 8 years of age, uses a storytelling format. It assesses five areas: complete sentences, length of words in utterance, subject-verb-tense agreement, elaboration, and general communication competence. Assessment of receptive language is accomplished through use of five Wh-questions.

Metropolitan Achievement Tests
(See chapter 8.)

Miller-Yoder Language Comprehension Test (MYLCT)

The Miller-Yoder Language Comprehension Test (Miller & Yoder, 1984) is a picture book test that taps the child's understanding of short, simple sentences in a variety of grammatical structures. The MYLCT assesses language comprehension ability to determine whether it is similar to that of same-age peers; it is designed for use with children developmentally aged 4 through 8 years.

Multilevel Academic Skills Inventory: Reading Program
(See chapter 9.)

Northwestern Syntax Screening Test (NSST)

The Northwestern Syntax Screening Text (Lee, 1969) is a device used to assess receptive and expressive morphology and syntax, including the following grammatical elements: plurals, verb tenses, pronouns, prepositions, negatives,

168

possessives, passives, subject-verb agreement, Wh-questions, and question-statement differences. The NSST is untimed, requires 15 to 25 minutes to administer, and is for children 3 to 7 years of age.

Patterned Elicitation Syntax Test (PEST)

The Patterned Elicitation Syntax Test (Young & Perachio, 1983) is a multiple-item oral response test designed to assess the child's use of 44 syntactic structures. The PEST is individually administered, requires 20 minutes, and is for children 3 through 7 years of age.

Peabody Individual Achievement Test—Revised
(See chapter 8.)

Peabody Picture Vocabulary Test
(See chapter 7.)

Phonological Process Analysis (PPA)

The Phonological Process Analysis (Weiner, 1979) is designed to assess the rules of phonology inherent in the production of speech. Speech is elicited through the use of drawings provided in the test manual and then analyzed for the child's abilities in using 16 phonological rules. Individually administered, the PPA requires 45 minutes for administration, but the entire analysis need not be administered in one session.

Picture Story Language Test (PSLT)

The Picture Story Language Test (Myklebust, 1965) is designed to assess the student's ability to write a story related to the stimulus picture presented. The factors measured include: number of words written, number of sentences, number of words per sentence, syntax accuracy, and success in expression of meaning. The PSLT requires 20 minutes for administration and is for use with students 7 through 17 years of age.

Porch Index of Communicative Ability (PICA)

The Porch Index of Communicative Ability (Porch, 1981) evaluates the ability of aphasic individuals, 13 years of age or older, to communicate with others. The PICA assesses nine modalities of communication: writing, copying, reading, pantomime, verbal, auditory, visual, gestural, and graphic. Administration takes 30 to 60 minutes and may be used to measure changes in functioning related to time, treatment, or surgery.

169

Porch Index of Communicative Ability in Children (PICAC)

The Porch Index of Communicative Ability in Children (Porch, 1979) is designed to assess three modalities of communication—gestural, verbal, and graphic—in students from 3 to 12 years of age. The Basic Battery tests children 3 through 6 years of age, and the Advanced Battery is for children ages 6 through 12 years. The scoring system employs dimensions of accuracy, responsiveness, completeness, promptness, and efficiency.

Pragmatics Screening Test (PST)

The Pragmatics Screening Test (Prinz & Weiner, 1987) is designed to assess the awareness of and responsiveness to pragmatic aspects of conversation in children from 3½ to 8½ years of age. The PST is composed of three game-like tasks: Absurd Requests, Ghost Trick, and Referential Communication. It requires 15 minutes when administered individually.

Preverbal Assessment Intervention Profile (PAIP)

The Preverbal Assessment Intervention Profile (Connard, 1984) is designed for individuals of all ages whose performance is between the developmental ages of 0 through 9 months. The PAIP is a three-stage observational procedure assessing the sensorimotor domains of auditory, visual, vocal/oral, and motor. It yields an individualized preverbal/motor assessment profile.

Receptive-Expressive Emergent Language Test
(See chapter 7.)

Receptive One-Word Picture Vocabulary Test (ROWPVT)

The Receptive One-Word Picture Vocabulary Test (Gardner, 1985) consists of 100 test plates, each with four illustrations presented horizontally across the page. The child between 2 and 11 years of age identifies the illustration that matches the word presented by the examiner. The ROWPVT requires 20 minutes for administration.

Rhode Island Test of Language Structure (RITLS)

The Rhode Island Test of Language Structure (Engen & Engen, 1983) is used to measure language development in children with normal hearing, 3 through 6 years of age, or for persons from 3 through 20 years of age who have hearing impairments. The RITLS is a 100-item test that presents 20

170

sentence types to measure language structure or syntax. It requires 30 minutes for administration.

SCAN: Screening Test for Auditory Processing Disorders (SCAN)

The Screening Test for Auditory Processing Disorders (Keith, 1986) is designed to identify children with speech perception problems and who may require additional assessment by an audiologist. The test uses familiar, high-frequency words, which the child repeats. The SCAN consists of three subtests: filtered words, auditory figure ground, and competing words. It is intended for children from 3 to 11 years of age and requires 20 minutes for administration.

Screening Test of Adolescent Language (STAL)

The Screening Test of Adolescent Language (Prather, Breecher, Stafford, & Wallace, 1980) is used to determine which students in grade 6 or above require further assessment. The test measures receptive and expressive language through the use of four subtests: vocabulary, auditory memory span, language processing, and proverb explanation. The STAL requires 7 minutes for administration.

Sequenced Inventory of Communication Development—Revised
(See chapter 7.)

Spellmaster Assessment and Teaching System (SATS)

The Spellmaster Assessment and Teaching System (Greenbaum, 1987) consists of diagnostic tests for measuring the spelling of phonetically regular words, irregular words, and homonyms. The SATS is appropriate for school-age students, those in adult basic education classes, and students for whom English is a second language.

SRA Achievement Series
(See chapter 8.)

Stanford Achievement Test
(See chapter 8.)

Temple University Short Syntax Inventory (TUSSI)

The Temple University Short Syntax Inventory (Gerber & Goehl, 1984) is

171

an individually administered measure of early patterns of syntax and morphology. The TUSSI is for children 5 through 7 years of age and requires 15 minutes for administration.

Test for Auditory Comprehension of Language—Revised (TACL-R)

The Test for Auditory Comprehension—Revised (Carrow-Woolfolk, 1985) is designed to measure auditory comprehension of word classes and relations, grammatical morphemes, and elaborated sentence construction. The TACL-R is normed for children from 3 to 10 years of age, requires no verbalization, and takes 20 minutes for administration. The test is published in English and Spanish, and a short version for screening is available.

Test of Adolescent Language—2 (TOAL-2)

The Test of Adolescent Language—2 (Hammill, Brown, Larsen, & Wiederholt, 1987) is designed to assess both spoken and written language. The TOAL-2 yields scores in the following areas: listening, speaking, reading, writing, spoken and written language, vocabulary, grammar, and expressive and receptive language. This instrument requires 1 hour and 45 minutes for administration and is designed for students in grades 6 through 12.

Test of Articulation Performance—Diagnostic (TAP-D)

The Test of Articulation Performance—Diagnostic (Bryant & Bryant, 1983a) is designed to measure the articulation abilities of students from 3 to 12 years of age. The TAP-D examines phonemic errors; speech performance in terms of place, manner, and voice characteristics; phonemic errors in conjunction with other speech sounds; phonemes produced in spoken sentences; phonemes produced in modeled situations; and overall speech adequacy.

Test of Articulation Performance—Screen (TAP-S)

The Test of Articulation Performance—Screen (Bryant & Bryant, 1983b) is a 31-item screening instrument assessing articulation performance in areas similar to that of TAP-D. The TAP-S requires 5 minutes to administer.

Test of Early Language Development
(See chapter 7.)

Test of Early Written Language
(See chapter 7.)

Test of Language Competence— Expanded Edition (TLC-Expanded)

The Test of Language Competence—Expanded Edition (Wiig & Secord, 1988) measures language competence of students at two levels. Level 1 is for children ages 5 to 9; level 2 is for ages 9 to 19. A strategy approach to language is used to evaluate delays in the development of linguistic competence and in the use of semantic, syntactic, and pragmatic strategies. The major emphasis of assessment is on determining the child's ability to perceive, interpret, and respond to conversational demands. Each level yields individual subtest standard scores, and composite scores in expressing intents, interpreting intents, screening composite, and TLC expanded composite. The four subtests (in each level) are: ambiguous sentences, listening comprehension, oral expression, and figurative language.

Test of Language Development—Intermediate (TOLD-2)

The Test of Language Development—Intermediate (Newcomer & Hammill, 1988) is designed to assess the listening, speaking, semantic, and syntactic skills of students 8½ through 13 years of age. The TOLD-2 includes six subtests: sentence combining, vocabulary, word ordering, generals, grammatic comprehension, and mallapropisms. Administration of the TOLD-2 requires 40 minutes.

Test of Language Development—Primary
(See chapter 7.)

Test of Legible Handwriting (TOLH)

The Test of Legible Handwriting (Larsen & Hammill, 1989) is a system of evaluating multiple samples of students' handwriting. Examples of types of handwriting assessed include creative writing, biographical sketches, correspondence, reports, and work samples. The TOLH is normed for students 7½ through 18 years of age.

Test of Pragmatic Skills (TPS)

The Test of Pragmatic Skills (Shulman, 1986) uses four guided-play interactions to assess the child's abilities in language functions such as reasoning,

173

denying, naming, labeling, requesting, and others. The TPS is for use with children from 3 to 8 years of age. Also included is a Language Sampling Supplement (LSS) that assesses the child's ability to use conversational intent to organize discourse. The LSS is to be used only if the child has passed the conversational intent portion of the TPS.

Test of Relational Concepts
 (See chapter 7.)

Test of Written English (TWE)

The Test of Written English (Andersen & Thompson, 1979) is designed to assess four areas of written language: capitalization, punctuation, paragraph writing, and written expression. The examiner may read items to the student so poor readers may be evaluated accurately. The TWE requires 30 minutes for administration, is used with students in grades 1 through 6, and has two forms for pre- and post-testing.

Test of Written Language—2 (TOWL-2)

The Test of Written Language—2 (Hammill & Larsen, 1988) uses spontaneous and contrived formats to assess thematic maturity, word usage, style, spelling vocabulary, and handwriting. The TOWL-2, designed for use with students in grades 2 through 12, is available in English and Spanish.

Test of Written Spelling—2 (TWS-2)

The Test of Written Spelling—2 (Larsen & Hammill, 1986) is designed for students in grades 1 through 12. The TWS-2 assesses the student's ability to spell words that are: readily predictable in sound patterns, not predictable (spelling demons), and a combination of the two types. The TWS-2, which requires 20 minutes for administration, may be used with groups or individuals.

Tree/Bee Test of Auditory Discrimination (T/BTAD)

The Tree/Bee Test of Auditory Discrimination (Fudala, 1978) is designed to measure auditory discrimination in persons from 3 years of age through adulthood. The T/BTAD assesses the discrimination of words, phrases, words-in-story, comprehension, same-different comparisons, letter discrimination, and word pairs. No reading or writing is required during the 10-minute administration time.

Utah Test of Language Development (UTLD)

The Utah Test of Language Development (Mecham & Jones, 1978) contains 51 items to assess the production and comprehension skills of children 1 through 15 years of age. The UTLD requires 30 to 45 minutes for administration.

Wide Range Achievement Test—Revised
(See chapter 8.)

Woodcock-Johnson Psychoeducational Battery—Revised
(See chapter 8.)

Woodcock Language Proficiency Battery (WLPB)

The Woodcock Language Proficiency Battery (Woodcock, 1980) measures oral and written language and reading in either English or Spanish. The WLPB includes the following subtests: picture vocabulary, antonyms and synonyms, analogics, letter-word identification, word attack, passage comprehension, dictation and proofing. The WLPB is for persons ages 3 through adult.

Writing Proficiency Program (WPP)

The Writing Proficiency Program (Bossone, 1979) is a multiple-choice and essay test to measure writing skills. The multiple-choice questions address skills related to sentence fragments, adverbs, adjectives, pronouns, punctuation, sentence sequence, and others. The essay portion measures the student's ability to use persuasive, narrative, and descriptive forms of writing. The WPP requires 50 minutes for administration and is for use with students in grades 6 through 9.

Assessment of Behavior Problems

When teachers express concern about behavior, they usually are not referring to reading behavior or mathematics behavior, although they may have concerns about these and other academic areas. Teachers' concerns regarding behavior may relate to homework not completed or handed in, lack of attention during class, interactions with peers and teachers in class, or other behaviors like these. Additional concerns may have to do with students' behavior outside of class time—for example between classes, during lunch, or at recess.

Teachers' expectations regarding students' behavior centers on what is appropriate for a student of that age and under existing circumstances. Teachers of preschool age children have a different set of expectations than middle school teachers do, and both are different from high school teachers. Teachers in a physical education class have expectations that are different from those of math or English teachers. Again, *teachers' expectations are based on what is considered normal for students of the given age and under existing circumstances.* When students do not meet teacher expectations, they call attention to themselves and teachers frequently express concern regarding their behavior. The assumption that appropriate and adequate progress is being made in the area if behavior (except if there is a noted difference) is not parallel with academic areas in which various types of assessment of progress are routinely conducted. Differences in behavior usually are noted only in cases of an excess or deficit.

Excesses in behavior relate to things such as too much daydreaming, too many fights, too much inappropriate language, and similar behaviors. *Deficits* in behavior refer to an inability to make or keep friends, an inability to think clearly, an inability to complete work on time, and others. The teacher notes excesses or deficits in behavior when they are significantly different from other

177

students in the class. In a very general and indirect manner, this begins the assessment process.

Assessment of behavior problems is multifaceted and includes direct observation, interviews, self-reports, ratings by others such as parents, peers, or teachers, role playing, and other methods. The focus of this chapter is on the various instruments used in assessing behavior problems. A discussion regarding informal observation is followed by descriptions of commercially published assessment instruments. Discussion of the assessment instruments covers both formal and informal instruments. The reader should note that some assessment instruments in the behavioral area may be administered only by licensed psychologists.

Informal Observation

Direct observation assessment instruments may be either locally developed or commercially produced. If observation instruments are locally developed, the process begins with selecting the behaviors that are to be observed. This list of behaviors may be collected from a variety of sources: teachers, other checklists or rating scales, lists of characteristics, and so on. Each of the behaviors on the composite list must be described precisely so little or no ambiguity remains regarding the exact nature of the behavior.

An example of a behavior poorly described is, "Doesn't pay attention." Various persons may interpret this in various ways. Further, it does not describe what the student does. If the student does not "pay attention" because of daydreaming, the problem is different than if the student interferes with others by talking, getting up and walking around, or shouting profanity. The latter information is much more helpful in the total assessment process. When the behaviors are precisely defined, a measurement system can be developed.

The measurement system will relate to the behaviors listed. *Event recording* or *frequency counts* indicate how many times a behavior occurs. A tally next to the listed behavior provides this information. *Duration recording* indicates the length of a behavior—for example, how long a student talks to another or how long a student cries. *Time sampling* is a method of recording the occurrence of a behavior during a specified time—for example, the first 5 minutes of a class period, or between 11:00 and 11:30 each day. These data allow for analysis of frequency and intensity of the behaviors recorded. Running records are attempts to record all events, and, because of the multiplicity of behaviors that may occur during a short amount of time, a coding system usually is used. Whatever the method of measurement, observations should be conducted over several days. Times for observation should be selected on the basis of when the behaviors are likely to occur, and are of sufficient length to provide an adequate sample of behaviors.

When the observations are completed, the data collected are organized into useful material. In general, graphs are used more frequently because they communicate large amounts of information quickly and allow for identification of trends or patterns.

The data collected from locally designed observation instruments comprise only one part of the assessment picture. At times this information leads concerned teachers to conclude that the student's behavior is not significantly different from that of age peers. In other cases this information leads to more inclusive assessment of the student. Comprehensive assessment of a student's behavioral problems would likely include several of the instruments outlined in this chapter. The selection of instruments depends on the information necessary to form a comprehensive picture of the student's behavior, including school behavior, interactions with family members and with peers outside of school, environmental factors that may affect behavior, perceptions of others as (peers, teachers, and parents), and academic performance. The following assessment instruments may be used when student behavior is of concern.

Instruments for Assessing Behavior

AAMD Adaptive Behavior Scale
(See chapter 5.)

Adaptive Behavior Inventory for Children
(See chapter 5.)

Adjective Check List (ACL)

The Adjective Check List (Gough & Heilbrun, 1980) is a 300-adjective list of 37 scales. The ACL scales address attributes such as achievement, dominance, endurance, nurturance, autonomy, aggression, self-control, self-confidence, ideal self, creative personality, and others. The ACL is self-administered, requires approximately 20 minutes, and is for students in 9th grade or above.

Analysis of Coping Style (ACS)

The Analysis of Coping Style (Johnson & Boyd, 1981) is a 20-item test in which the examiner presents pictures of school situations and the students select one of six possible responses. The responses are analyzed for the following

179

patterns of coping styles: externalized attack, internalized attack, avoidance, or denial. Two versions are available, one for elementary-school-age children and one for high-school-age students. The ACS, administered individually, requires 10-20 minutes for administration.

Autism Screening Instrument for Educational Planning (ASIEP)

The Autism Screening Instrument for Educational Planning (Krug, Arick, & Almond, 1980) consists of five subtests, each of which may be administered independently, and which in composite provide a total assessment. The ASIEP, for children 18 months of age through adulthood, may be used with students who are autistic, mentally retarded, deaf and blind, and emotionally disturbed. The subtests include: autism behavior checklist, sample of vocal behavior, interaction assessment, educational assessment, and prognosis of learning rate. The observational methods in all five areas allow students to be "testable." The ASIEP is individually administered and is available in Spanish and English. Time for administration necessarily must vary.

Autistic Behavior Composite Checklist and Profile (ABCCP)

The Autistic Behavior Composite Checklist and Profile (Riley, 1984a) provides an informal evaluation procedure that results in a profile of the student's interfering behaviors, as well as prioritization of areas that require intervention. It also can be used to support a diagnosis of autism. The ABCCP includes 148 items in eight categories: prerequisite learning behaviors; sensory perceptual skills; motor development; prelanguage skills; speech, language, and communication skills; developmental rates and sequences; learning behaviors; and relating skills. It is for use with students ages 4 through 22 years.

Barber Scales of Self-Regard for Preschool Children
(See chapter 7.)

Basic School Skills Inventory—Diagnostic
(See chapter 7.)

Basic School Skills Inventory—Screen
(See chapter 7.)

Behavioral Academic Self-Esteem (BASE)

Designed as an observational rating scale to measure academic self-esteem, the Behavioral Academic Self-Esteem (Coopersmith & Gilberts, 1982) is completed by an adult who has access to sustained observation of the student. The BASE provides ratings in student initiative, social attention, success/failure, social attraction, and self-confidence. This instrument is for children in grades 1 through 8, requires 5 minutes for completion, and may be used in conjunction with the Coopersmith Inventories (1981).

Behavior Dimension Rating Scale (BDRS)

The Behavior Dimension Rating Scale (Bullock & Wilson, 1988) is for students from 5 years of age through adulthood. The BDRS measures behavior in four subscales: Aggressive/Acting Out, Irresponsible/Inattentive, Socially Withdrawn, and Fearful/Anxious. The BDRS consists of 43 items, which are rated by teachers on a 7-point scale. It requires 10 minutes to complete.

Behavior Evaluation Scale (BES)

The Behavior Evaluation Scale (McCarney, Leigh, & Cornbleet, 1983) is an observational inventory that assesses the behavioral problems of students in grades 1 through 12. It may be used with students who have learning disabilities, mental retardation, and physical handicaps. The BES is partially self-administered and partially examiner-administered.

Behavior Problem Checklist—Revised (BPC-R)

The Behavior Problem Checklist—Revised (Quay & Peterson, 1983) is an 85-item paper-and-pencil observational inventory. The BPC-R measures six dimensions of social-emotional functioning in students from grades 1 through 12: conduct disorders, socialized aggression, attention problems—immaturity, anxiety-withdrawal, psychotic behavior, and motor tension—excess. The checklist is administered individually and requires 15 minutes.

Behavior Rating Profile (BRP)

The Behavior Rating Profile (Brown & Hammill, 1983) is a battery of six independent measures: student rating scales—home, school, and peer; teacher rating scale, parent rating scale, and a sociogram. The BRP is designed to identify students with behavior problems, the settings in which the problems seem prominent, and individuals who have different perceptions about the behavior. The BRP has a variable administration time. It is individually administered and may be used with students who are learning disabled.

Burks' Behavior Rating Scales (BBRS)

The Burks' Behavior Rating Scales (Burks, 1977) is an inventory to be used by parents or teachers to rate the following areas of behavioral functioning: anxiety, withdrawal, dependency, sense of persecution, aggressiveness, resistance, ego strength, physical strength, coordination, impulse control, anger control, reality contact, social conformity, and others. The BBRS consists of two versions—grades 1 through 9, and Preschool-Kindergarten. It is individually administered and requires 20 minutes for administration.

California Child Q-Sort Set (CCQSS)

The California Child Q-Sort Set (Block & Block, 1980), an adaptation of the California Q-Sort Deck, consists of a set of 100 descriptive statements divided into 9 categories and designed to obtain an individual's (teacher's or parent's) perception of the child's personality. The descriptive statements are rated from "extremely uncharacteristic" to "extremely characteristic." The CCQSS is untimed, and completion time varies.

California Psychological Inventory—Revised (CPI-R)

The California Psychological Inventory—Revised (Gough, 1987) is a true-false questionnaire that measures socially desirable tendencies. The CPI-R consists of 462 items divided into 20 scales, which address themes such as: dominance, self-acceptance, independence, empathy, responsibility, socialization, self-control, impression, tolerance, well-being, and others. The CPI-R may be administered individually or to groups. It requires an hour for administration and is for ages 13 years through adulthood. The CPI-R is available in English and Spanish.

Child Behavior Checklist for Ages 4-16 (CBC)

The Child Behavior Checklist for Ages 4-16 (Achenbach, 1981) is designed to measure children's competencies and problem areas. It measures behavioral dimensions such as depression, aggression, somatic complaints, hyperactivity, and sexual problems. The checklist may be self-administered or completed by parents. Separate forms are provided for each gender in the following age groups: 4-5, 6-11, and 12-16 years. The instrument may be readministered to measure changes in behavior.

Child Behavior Rating Scale (CBRS)

The Child Behavior Rating Scale (Cassel, 1962) is a 78-item inventory that is completed by someone familiar with the child. The evaluator rates the child on a 6-point scale. The CBRS yields a total personality adjustment score and a profile of the child's adjustment in five areas: self, home, social, school, and physical. It requires 40 minutes for administration and is for preschool through 3rd grade students.

Children's Apperception Test (CAT)

The Children's Apperception Test (Bellak, Bellak, & Haworth, 1980) consists of a series of 10 pictures depicting animals in a variety of situations, and the child makes up a story about each of the pictures. The purpose of the CAT is to understand the child's thoughts, needs, drives, and feelings regarding important relationships, situations, and conflicts the child is experiencing. The CAT is for children from 3 through 10 years of age.

Children's Depression Scale (CDS)

The Children's Depression Scale (Lange & Tisher, 1983) measures six aspects of childhood depression: affective response, social problems, self-esteem, preoccupation with own sickness or death, guilt, and pleasure. The items are presented on cards that the child sorts, according to how he or she feels, into five boxes ranging "very right" to "very wrong." A questionnaire for parents or teachers, which addresses the same items as the child, is included. The CDS is directed at students from 9 to 16 years of age.

Children's Personality Questionnaire (CPQ)

The Children's Personality Questionnaire (Porter & Cattell, 1982) measures 14 traits, such as reserved vs. warmhearted, affected by feelings vs. emotionally stable, undemonstrative vs. excitable, obedient vs. assertive, self-assured vs. apprehensive, relaxed vs. tense, and others. The CPQ includes four forms, each with 140 items. The questionnaire, administered in groups or individually, requires 30 to 60 minutes per form and is for students 8 to 12 years of age.

Classroom Environment Scale (CES)

The Classroom Environment Scale (Moos & Trickett, 1974) is designed to assess the effects of course content, teaching methods, teaching personality, and class characteristics on nine scales. The scales measure involvement, application, teacher support, task orientation, competition, order and organization, rule clarity, teacher control, and innovations. The CES is for use in junior and senior high schools.

Comprehensive Behavior Rating Scale for Children (CBRSC)

The Comprehensive Behavior Rating Scale for Children (Neeper & Lahey, 1988) is designed to measure cognitive, emotional, and behavioral functioning. The CBRSC yields seven scales: inattention/disorganization, linguistic/information processing, conduct disorder, motor hyperactivity, anxiety/depression, sluggish tempo, and social competence. The scale includes 81 descriptive statements, which the teacher rates on a 5-point scale. The CBRSC is for students 6 through 14 years of age.

Conners' Teacher Rating Scale (CTRS)

Designed to measure activity level, the Conners' Teacher Rating Scale (Conners, 1969) is completed by the teacher. The teacher indicates the degree to which the behavior occurs on a scale from "not at all" to "very much." The CTRS measures behaviors such as restlessness, excitability, and inattentiveness, and requires approximately 30 minutes for completion.

Coopersmith Self-Esteem Inventories (CSEI)

The Coopersmith Self-Esteem Inventories (Coopersmith, 1981) have been designed to measure attitudes toward the self in social, academic, and personal contexts. The CSEI School Form (58 items) is for students 8 to 15 years of age, and the Adult Form (25 items) is for persons 15 years of age and older. Both forms are self-administered. The CSEI may be divided into four subscales pertaining to different self-esteem domains: peers, parents, school, and personal interests.

Coping Inventory (CI)

The Coping Inventory (Zeitlin, 1988) has 48 items equally divided into two categories: coping with self, and coping with environment. These two areas are further divided so that the dimensions of productive, active, and flexible coping styles can be further analyzed. The CI is administered by observing students 3 through 16 years of age and is self-rated by persons older than 16 years. The time required for administration varies.

184

Devereux Adolescent Behavior Rating Scale (DABRS)

The Devereux Adolescent Behavior Rating Scale (Spivak, Haimes, & Spotts, 1967) is designed to be used with students 13 through 18 years of age. The DABRS is an 84-item test that provides a profile of 15 behavior dimensions and yields 12 factor scores; among these factors are unethical behavior, defiant-resistive, domineering-sadistic, heterosexual interest, hyperactive, expansive, poor emotional control, need approval and dependency, emotional distance, and others. In addition, the DABRS provides three cluster scores: inability to delay, paranoid thought, and anxious self-blame. The DABRS is completed by someone who lives with the youth.

Devereux Child Behavior Rating Scale (DCBRS)

The Devereux Child Behavior Rating Scale (Spivak, Haimes, & Spotts, 1966) addresses behaviors similar to those of the Devereux Adolescent Behavior Rating Scale. It is for students 8 through 12 years of age.

Devereux Elementary School Behavior Rating Scale (DESBRS)

The Devereux Elementary School Behavior Rating Scale (Spivak & Swift, 1967) is designed to measure problem behaviors that interfere with classroom performance. The teacher rates the student through comparison of the student's behaviors with normal students of the same age. The DESBRS yields scores in areas such as classroom disturbance, impatience, achievement anxiety, inattentive-withdrawn, creative-initiative, and need for closeness with the teacher. Additional scores are obtained in: unable to change, quits easily, and slow work. The scale, for students 6 to 12 years of age, requires 15 minutes to complete.

Direct Observation Form—Revised Edition (DOF-R)

The Direct Observation Form—Revised Edition (Achenbach, 1986) is to be used for observation of a student in the classroom or during a group activity. The DOF-R consists of 10-minute observations, after which the observer writes a narrative description of the child's behavior and a rating of the behaviors that occurred. On-task behavior is also measured at 1-minute intervals. The DOF-R is for use with students 4 to 16 years of age.

Embedded Figures Test (EFT)

The Embedded Figures Test (Witkin, 1971) is a set of 12 colored designs in which the student finds geometric figures. The EFT, available in alternative forms for test-retest situations, is for students 12 years of age through adulthood. The test provides information regarding analytic ability in task performance, social behavior, body concept, preferred defense mechanisms, problem-solving style, and others. The EFT requires 10 to 45 minutes for administration.

Estes Attitude Scales (EAS)

The Estes Attitude Scales (Estes, Estes, Richards, & Roettger, 1981) are designed to measure students' attitudes regarding school subjects. The Elementary Form, for grades 2 through 6, measures attitudes toward math, reading, and science. Reading skills are not required because the examiner reads statements such as, "Reading is fun for me," and the student responds by checking "I agree," "I don't know," or "I disagree." The Secondary Form measures attitudes toward English, math, reading, science, and social studies. Reading skills are required for the Secondary Form, but it has been written at a 6th-grade level. Responses on the Secondary Form are similar to those on the Elementary Form. Attitude scores are calculated for each academic area. Either form requires 20 minutes for administration.

Hahnemann Elementary School Behavior Rating Scale (HESBRS)

The Hahnemann Elementary School Behavior Rating Scale (Spivak & Swift, 1975) rates behaviors such as: originality, independent learning, failure, anxiety, irrelevant talk, social over-involvement, critical competitive approach to the teacher, and others. The HESBRS addresses four positive behaviors and 10 negative behaviors. It is individually administered, requires 15 minutes for administration, and is for students of elementary school age.

Hahnemann High School Behavior Rating Scale (HHSBRS)

The Hahnemann High School Behavior Rating Scale (Spivak & Swift, 1972) is to be completed by the teachers of junior or senior high school age students. The scale consists of descriptive statements that relate to behaviors such as: reasoning ability, verbal interaction, rapport with teacher, poor work habits, dogmatic-inflexible, verbal negativism, expressed inability, and others. The HHSBRS requires 10 minutes for completion.

Index of Personality Characteristics (IPC)

The Index of Personality Characteristics (Brown & Coleman, 1988) is a measure of pervasiveness of personality characteristics in and out of school:

perception of self and others, behavioral manifestations of personality, and students' ability to accept responsibility for their own actions and behaviors. The IPC is for students aged 8 through 18 years, may be administered individually or in groups, and requires 30 minutes for administration.

Inferred Self-Concept Scale

The Inferred Self-Concept Scale (McDaniel, 1973) is designed to evaluate the self-concept of children in grades 1 through 6, based on their behavior in school. This is a 30-item inventory that the teacher uses to rate the student on a 5-point scale ranging from "never" to "always." The scale requires 20 minutes for completion.

Jesness Behavior Check List (JBCL)

The Jesness Behavior Check List (Jesness, 1971) is an 80-item scale that measures 14 behavioral tendencies of students 10 through 18 years of age. The JBCL has two parallel forms: an Observer Form to be completed by teachers, probation officers, therapists, or others, and a Self-Appraisal Form for self-evaluation. Behavioral tendencies measured include: unobtrusiveness, friendliness, responsibility, considerateness, independence, rapport, social control, conformity, and others. The JBCL requires 20 minutes for administration.

Jesness Inventory of Adolescent Personality (JIAP)

A true-false, 155-item questionnaire, the Jesness Inventory of Adolescent Personality (Jesness, 1972) yields scores for the following scales: social maladjustment, value orientation, immaturity, autism, alienation, manifest aggression, withdrawal, social anxiety, repression, denial, and the asocial index. The JIAP, for students ages 8 through 18, requires approximately 30 minutes for administration.

Kohn Problem Checklist, Research Edition (KPC)

The Kohn Problem Checklist (Kohn, 1986a) is designed to assess the presence or absence of behavior problems of preschool- or kindergarten-age children. One or more of the teachers complete a 49-item rating scale that lists observable behaviors relating to behavioral dimensions of angry-defiant and apathetic-withdrawn behavior. Results of the KPC may be combined with the Kohn Social Competence Scale to yield pooled instrument scores.

187

Kohn Social Competence Scale—Research Edition (KSCS)

The Kohn Social Competence Scale (Kohn, 1986b) is designed to assess the social-emotional functioning of preschool- and kindergarten-age children. One or more teachers complete a 73-item scale for children in full-day programs or a 64-item scale for children in half-day programs, measuring dimensions of cooperative-compliant versus angry-defiant, and interest-participation versus apathetic-withdrawn behavior.

Leadership Skills Inventory (LSI)

The Leadership Skills Inventory (Karnes & Chauvin, 1985), designed to assess leadership abilities, is self-administered. It measures abilities in the following categories: fundamentals of leadership, written communication skills, speech communication skills, values clarification, decision making skills, group dynamics skills, problem solving skills, personal development skills, and planning skills. The LSI, for students in grade 4 through 12, requires 45 minutes for administration.

Life Orientation Inventory (LOI)

The Life Orientation Inventory (Kowalchuk & King, 1988) is designed to assess the beliefs that unhappy and potentially suicidal people maintain about themselves and their ability to cope with life. The LOI consists of 113 statements about one's life, half of which are life-affirming and half are pessimistic. A screening form consists of 30 statements following the format of the full form. Both forms assess suicidal orientation as related to gender factors: self-esteem, vulnerability, overinvestment, overdetermined misery, affective domination, alienation, and suicide tenability. The inventory is for students 13 years of age and older. The full inventory requires 30 minutes for administration, and the screening inventory requires 10 minutes.

Martinek-Zaichkowsky Self-Concept Scale for Children

The Martinek-Zaichkowsky Self-Concept Scale for Children (Martinek & Zaichkowsky, 1977) measures global self-concept in children who are in grades 1 through 8. The factors assessed are: satisfaction and happiness, home and family relationships, and circumstances. Ability in games, recreation and sports, personality traits and emotional tendencies, and behavioral and social characteristics in school. The scale requires little or no reading, is culture-free, and requires 10 to 15 minutes for administration.

Minnesota Multiphasic Personality Inventory (MMPI)

The Minnesota Multiphasic Personality Inventory (University of Minnesota, 1967a) is composed of 550 statements to which the respondent indicates "True," "False," or "Cannot Say." The items address factors such as health, education, family, psychosomatic symptoms, sexual and social attitudes; and behavioral manifestations such as delusions, hallucinations, phobias, and others. The MMPI is for students 16 years of age and older and requires 60 minutes for administration. It is individually administered.

Mooney Problem Check Lists (MPCL)

The Mooney Problem Check Lists (Mooney & Gordon, 1950) are designed for students from grade 7 through college. They consist of a series of check lists that the student completes. Areas covered in the check lists vary from form to form according to the age group for which the form is designed. Typical areas include: health and physical development, home and family, boy and girl relations, morals and religion, school or occupation, and social and recreational. Students read examples of problems, underline those that are of some concern, circle the ones of most concern, and write a summary in their own words. This instrument is for students at junior high school level and above and requires 35 minutes for completion.

Peer Acceptance Scale (PAS)

The Peer Acceptance Scale (Bruininks, Rynders, & Gross, 1974) is designed to collect sociometric data. Using a picture scale, each student in the class rates every other student. The picture scale uses stick figures to depict scenes that students mark to indicate whether the student would be a "friend," is "all right," or that they "wouldn't like." The PAS provides data on all the students in the class, not just one specific student.

Perfil de Evaluación del Comportamiento (PEC)

The Perfil de Evaluación del Comportamiento (Brown & Hammill, 1982), in Spanish, provides for an evaluation of the behavior of students in elementary school through high school. The PEC is designed to identify students who have behavior problems, the settings in which the behaviors seem prominent, and individuals who have differing perceptions about the student's behavior. The PEC may be used with students who have learning disabilities. It may be administered individually or in groups.

Piers-Harris Children's Self-Concept Scale

The Piers-Harris Children's Self-Concept Scale (Piers & Harris, 1969) measures self-concept and identifies problem areas in a child's self-confidence. It is for use with students in grades 4 through 12. This scale has 80 items that assess the following aspects of a child's self-esteem, by gender: behavior, intellectual and school status, physical appearance and attributes, anxiety, popularity, and happiness and satisfaction. It is written at a third-grade reading level, may be administered to groups, and requires 20 minutes for administration.

Portland Problem Behavior Checklist—Revised (PPBC-R)

The Portland Problem Behavior Checklist—Revised (Waksman, 1984) is for use with students in kindergarten through 12th grade. Its purpose is to identify students who have conduct, academic, anxiety, peer, and personal problems. For individual use, the PPBC-R requires 10 minutes' administration time.

Process for the Assessment of Effective Student Functioning

The Process for the Assessment of Effective Student Functioning (Lambert, Hartsough, & Bower, 1979) is a rating scale designed for students in kindergarten through grade 7. Ratings are provided by the teacher, the student, and peers. This is a screening instrument requiring 20 minutes for completion by each of the respondents.

Pupil Behavior Inventory (PBI)

The Pupil Behavior Inventory (Vinter, Sarri, Vorwaller, & Schaefer, 1966) is designed for students in grades 7 through 12. The teacher rates the items on a 5-point scale. The PBI addresses the areas of: classroom behavior, academic motivation and performance, social-emotional status, teacher dependence, and personal behavior.

Pupil Behavior Rating Scale (PBRS)

The Pupil Behavior Rating Scale (Lambert, Bower, & Hartsough, 1979) is composed of a teacher-observation screening instrument, a peer-rating, and a self-rating instrument. The teacher-observation scale assesses classroom adaptation, interpersonal skills, and intrapersonal behavior. The peer and self ratings are designed for two levels: kindergarten through grade 3, and grades 3 through 7. A summary chart combines the scores of the teacher, peer, and self-ratings.

The peer and self-ratings for kindergarten through grade 3 are individually administered; the other peer and self-ratings may be administered to a group. Time for administration of the PBRS varies.

Pupil Rating Scale—Revised: Screening for Learning Disabilities (PRS-R)

The Pupil Rating Scale—Revised: Screening for Learning Disabilities (Myklebust, 1981) is designed to assess students' abilities in auditory comprehension, spoken language, orientation, motor coordination, and personal-social behavior. The PRS-R is for children in kindergarten through 6th grade, may be administered to a group, and requires 10 minutes for administration.

Scale of Social Development
(See chapter 7.)

School Behavior Checklist (SBC)

The School Behavior Checklist (Miller, 1977) is designed for students 4 through 13 years of age. It includes both checklists and rating scales. The SBC is completed by the teacher and requires 20 minutes for completion.

Self-Description Questionnaire, I-II-III (SDQ)

The Self-Description Questionnaire (Marsh, 1988) identifies areas of low self-concept. It has three levels, for individuals from 8 years of age through young adults. The SDQ-I is a self-reporting questionnaire for students in grades 2 through 6 and measures areas of self-concept; it requires 20 minutes for administration. The SQD-II is designed to measure the self-concept of students in grades 7 through 11 and requires 25 minutes for administration. The SDQ-III, for persons 16 years of age and older, requires 25 minutes for administration. The SDQ may be used in groups or individually.

Social-Emotional Dimension Scale (SEDS)

The Social-Emotional Dimension Scale (Hutton & Roberts, 1986) is a 32-item scale to be used to identify inappropriate behaviors of students. Six areas are assessed: physical/fear reaction, depressive reaction, avoidance of peer interaction, avoidance of teacher interaction, aggressive interaction, and inappropriate behaviors. The SEDS is for individual administration with students 5½ through 18½ years of age.

Teacher's Report Form (TRF)

The Teacher's Report Form (Achenbach & Edelbrock, 1980) is a modified form of the Child Behavior Checklist. Items from the Child Behavior Checklist which are inapplicable for teacher rating are omitted; teacher ratable items are substituted. Separate scoring profiles are available for each sex and at the 4 to 11 and 12 to 16 year age levels. Scores for Internalizing and Externalizing problem dimensions and Total Problem Scores are provided.

Tennessee Self-Concept Scale (TSCS)

The Tennessee Self-Concept Scale (Fitts, 1965) is available in two forms. Form C includes scales for eight areas: identity, self-satisfaction, behavior, physical self, moral-ethical self, personal self, family self, and social self. The Clinical and Research Form (C & R) addresses the same issues as Form C plus defensive position, general maladjustment, psychosis, personality disorder, neurosis, and personality integration. Written at a 6th-grade reading level, the TSCS is self-administered and is for students from 12 years of age through adulthood. It requires 20 minutes for completion.

Test of Early Socio-Emotional Development
(See chapter 7.)

Thematic Apperception Test (TAT)

The Thematic Apperception Test (Murray, 1943) consists of 19 cards containing vague pictures in black and white and one blank card. The child is to make up a story to fit the picture for those cards with pictures. The child imagines a picture on the blank card and describes it. The stories are evaluated in relation to the child's aggression, affiliation and achievement, and perceived environmental forces such as receiving affection, being criticized, exposure to physical danger, and others. Administration time varies. The TAT is for students 14 years of age and older.

Waksman Social Skills Rating Scale (WSSRS)

Designed for students in kindergarten through 12th grade, the Waksman Social Skills Rating Scale (Waksman, 1984) is a checklist of 21 items used to screen children and adolescents with suspected social skill deficits. Teachers rate students on a 4-point scale (0—never exhibited, to 3—usually exhibited), which is translated into a total score. Descriptors on the WSSRS range from an aggressive domain to a passive domain. The scale requires 15 minutes for completion.

Walker-McConnell Scale of Social Competence and School Adjustment

The Walker-McConnell Scale of Social Competence and School Adjustment (Walker & McConnell, 1988) is a 43-item teacher rating scale of social skills. Areas measured include teacher-preferred social behavior, and peer-preferred social behavior, both of which relate to peer interactions and school adjustment, focusing on adjustment to the behavioral demands of the classroom. The scale is for students in kindergarten through 6th grade, is completed by the teacher, and requires 5 minutes for completion.

Walker Problem Behavior Identification Checklist (WPBIC)

The Walker Problem Behavior Identification Checklist (Walker, 1983) is for use with students in preschool through grade 6. It consists of a 50-item checklist of behavioral statements, which the teacher indicates as true or false with respect to the student being rated. The WPBIC provides a cut-off score for classifying students as disturbed, and scores for five scales: acting-out, withdrawal, distractibility, disturbed peer relations, and immaturity. This checklist requires 5 minutes for completion.

Assessment of Sensory Abilities, Perceptual Abilities, and Motor Skills

When a student has educational difficulties, accurate information about his or her visual and auditory abilities is vital. Most schools have screening programs to determine if further assessment of visual or auditory acuity is necessary, but students may miss out on these screening programs or develop problems after the screening process. Therefore, a review of records is essential, to determine whether further assessment in either of these areas is required.

Visual and auditory perception and discrimination are also important to success in school. These areas are not regularly screened in the schools, but they may require specific attention if other information indicates possible problems. Basic motor abilities are also important, and if students are significantly delayed in this area, special training and adapted programming may be indicated. Finally, integration of these various skills is important for normal learning. Visual-motor skills, perceptual-motor skills, and other, related abilities may become a proper target for assessment in many instances.

Although most assessment, beyond the screening level, of hearing and vision ordinarily will be carried out by professionals other than educators, educators have to be informed about the nature of the assessment and how assessment results are reported, in order to be able to effectively use this sort of information in overall planning for students. Assessment in these areas will be discussed in this chapter.

Assessment of Auditory Abilities

Assessment of possible hearing impairment is usually conducted by an audiologist. The results of an audiometric assessment typically includes an audiogram (a chart showing the degree of hearing loss, if any, in each ear) and a discussion of the probable effects of any existing auditory loss. The numbers on the left side of an audiogram (see Figure 13.1) indicate the intensity of sound (in decibels) required for the individual to hear at various frequencies. The 0 near the top of the scale indicates the degree of loudness necessary for a person with normal hearing to hear sound. The larger the number (of decibels) indicated, the greater is the hearing loss. The profile for both ears will be recorded on one audiogram.

An audiogram provides the results of testing at frequencies of 125, 250, 500, 1000, 2000, 4000, and 8000 hertz. The sounds that are more important fall between the 500- and 2000-hertz range. One system of classifying the severity of loss is:

mild	27-40 dB
moderate	41-55 dB
moderately severe	56-70 dB
severe	71-90 dB
profound	91 + dB

Although audiometric assessments provide relatively precise results, caution must be exercised in making interpretations based on this, or any, system of classification. Factors such as age of onset of hearing loss, frequencies at which the losses occur, quality of past educational programs, the student's cognitive ability, and others may have a great influence on the actual negative effects of a loss, regardless of severity in decibels. A specialist in hearing must evaluate all of these factors and provide a comprehensive summary evaluation.

Assessment of Visual Abilities

Assessment of visual ability normally is conducted by an ophthalmologist or optometrist, but initial screening-level assessment takes place in the schools. Most teachers are familiar with the *Snellen chart,* which has large letters (or symbols, for younger children) at the top, and progressively smaller letters lower on the chart.

The classification system used with the Snellen chart is one of ratios: 20/20, 20/60, and so on. The first number is the distance in feet at which the test is made; the second is the size of symbols or letters on the chart expressed in terms of the distance at which a person with normal vision can comfortably

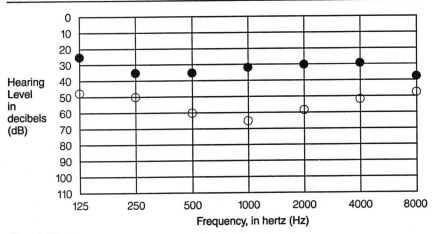

Figure 13.1
A Sample Audiogram

read them. Therefore, if at 20 feet an individual can read the "20-foot" letter or symbol, his or her distance visual acuity is 20/20, or normal. If an individual can read only the letter or symbol that is a "60-foot" letter or symbol, distance visual acuity is 20/60. This information relates only to distance vision; near-point vision may be considerably different.

Near-point vision is just one of several aspects of vision that must be assessed (in addition to distance-vision), to rule out visual problems as a possible cause of educational difficulties. Various visual problems—for example, near-point vision, muscle imbalance, fusion, color perception, degree of vision—may be diagnosed through the use of specialized testing equipment. Teacher observations are an additional, important part of the informal assessment that should take place with respect to vision. If students appear to lose their place regularly while reading, show unusual eye discomfort, hold reading material at unusual distances, exhibit light sensitivity or similar characteristics, referral to an eye specialist is essential.

Other visual acuity screening devices have been designed specifically for use with handicapped children. The *Washer Visual Acuity Screening Technique* (Washer, 1984) is typical of these instruments. This technique was developed specifically for use with severely handicapped students but is also of value with younger, nonhandicapped children. It measures both near and distance

197

vision and may be administered by teachers or by trained volunteers. It involves a preliminary conditioning process to familiarize subjects with the symbols, matching skills, and eye occlusion required in the assessment. This test may be completed with no verbal skills and very few perceptual or motor skills. The WVAST is for use with individuals of 2.5 mental age and up.

Assessment of Perception and Perceptual-Motor Skills

An individual can have normal sensory acuity (can receive visual, auditory, and other sensory information normally) but be unable to interpret and use sensory information in the same manner as other individuals do. This ability to interpret and use information, which involves relating it to other information that is stored in memory, is called perception. It is an active process, recognized as essential to normal learning, but precisely how it works, and what to do to improve poorly developed perceptual abilities, is a matter of continuing debate.

This section is devoted to a review of measures of perceptual abilities. It focuses primarily upon auditory and visual perception because that is where assessment efforts historically have been directed. In most cases tests of perception require some type of perceptual-motor integration (for example, copying designs to test visual perception requires visual-motor integration), and thus many are called perceptual-motor tests.

Some perceptual-motor tests, and the intervention programs to which they sometimes have led, have received considerable negative comment. For example, Witt, Elliott, Gresham, and Kramer (1988) believe that perceptual-motor tests "are among the most frequently used, abused, and misused measures in school settings" (p. 286). But they have not received as much negative comment when used at the early childhood/preschool level.

In addition to their use as direct measures of discrimination, perception, and integration of perceptual and motor abilities, the results of some of these tests have been used to infer things such as a brain dysfunction or brain injury. With tests in which such use is relatively common, it will be noted in the review. A discussion of perceptual-motor and motor tests follows.

Perceptual-Motor Tests

Auditory Discrimination Test—Revised
  (See chapter 11.)

Bender Visual Motor Gestalt Test for Children (BVMGT-C)

The Bender Visual Motor Gestalt Test (Bender, 1951) was first used to attempt to differentiate brain-injured and non brain-injured adults. The Bender Visual Motor Gestalt Test for Children (Bender & Clawson, 1962) provides an interpretation of the same test items, for children ages 7 to 11. Both Bender tests have been used, primarily by clinical psychologists, for a wide variety of purposes including attempts to distinguish between individuals who are brain-injured, perceptually handicapped (but not brain-injured), or emotionally disturbed. Additional uses have related to determining the existence of psychoses or maturational lags.

The BVMGT-C consists of nine geometric designs, which the student copies on paper. Interpretation of the test relates to placement of the designs on the page, accuracy of the designs, and overall organization.

Developmental Test of Visual-Motor Integration (VMI)

The Developmental Test of Visual-Motor Integration (Beery & Buktenica, 1982) has a short form for children ages 2 to 8 (15 geometric figures) and a long form for individuals 2 to 18 years of age (24 geometric figures). The long form can be used with adults of all ages; however, it would likely be used only with developmentally delayed adults. Test items, which the subjects copy, are arranged in order of increasing difficulty. The long form VMI requires about 15 minutes, can be administered individually or in small groups, and is easily scored on a pass-fail basis. The VMI measures visual perception and motor coordination.

Developmental Test of Visual Perception
(See Frostig Developmental Test of Visual Perception, p. 199.)

Frostig Developmental Test of Visual Perception (DTVP)

The Frostig Developmental Test of Visual Perception, also called the Developmental Test of Visual Perception (Frostig, Lefever, & Whittlesey, 1966) is for students ages 3 to 8 years, and is designed to measure five perceptual skills: eye-hand coordination, figure-ground perception, form constancy, position in space, and spatial relations. The DTVP was designed for group administration, and raw scores for each subtest can be converted to Perceptual Age scores.

Goldman-Fristoe-Woodcock Test of Auditory Discrimination

The Goldman-Fristoe-Woodcock Test of Auditory Discrimination (Goldman, Fristoe, & Woodcock, 1970) is an individually administered test of a student's ability to discriminate speech sounds. It is for subjects ages 3 and older. Through the use of an audiocassette, discrimination is assessed in a quiet background and against a background of noise. Administration requires 20 to 30 minutes. Standard scores and percentile ranks are provided.

Jordan Left-Right Reversal Test—Revised

The Jordan Left-Right Reversal Test—Revised (Jordan, 1980) is a screening device, for either group or individual administration by classroom teachers. For use with students ages 5 to 12 years, it assesses the extent to which the individual reverses letters, numbers, or words. This paper-and-pencil test includes two parts: level 1 assesses reversals of capital letters and numerals; level 2 assesses reversed lowercase letters within words and whole-word reversals within sentences. The test requires 15 to 20 minutes to complete and provides percentile and developmental age scores.

Memory for Designs Test (MFD)

The Memory for Designs Test (Graham & Kendall, 1960) was developed to help identify persons with brain injury. The MFD is an individual test for persons 8.5 to 60 years of age. It provides a 15-item measure of the subject's ability to draw various designs from memory. Subjects are shown each design for just 5 seconds and then must reproduce the design. Though untimed, the test usually requires about 10 minutes.

Minnesota Spatial Relations Test—Revised (MSRT-R)

The Minnesota Spatial Relations Test—Revised (American Guidance Service, 1979) assesses spatial visualization ability and the ability to manipulate three-dimensional objects. The MSRT-R involves transferring blocks from one board to another, fitting the blocks into cut-outs. Designed for use with subjects ages 16 years and older, it is administered individually and provides standard scores and percentile ranks.

Motor-Free Visual Perception Test (MVPT)

The Motor-Free Visual Perception Test (Colorusso & Hammill, 1972) is a

36-item, point-and-tell test in which the subject matches a line drawing to one of a multiple-choice set of other drawings. Developed for use with students ages 4 to 8, it may be used with older individuals who have motor problems. The MVPT is untimed, usually requiring about 10 minutes. It is individually administered and is most often used with persons who are physically handicapped, mentally retarded, or learning disabled. The MVPT provides perceptual age scores and perceptual quotients.

Preverbal Assessment Intervention Profile
(See chapter 11.)

Primary Visual Motor Test (PVMT)

The Primary Visual Motor Test (Haworth, 1970) was developed for use with individuals having mental ages of 4 to 8. It is a nonverbal test in which the examiner provides 16 designs for the student to copy in designated spaces on the test sheet. Its primary use is to assess visual-motor functioning, but it may provide an indication of intellectual performance in students who are speech handicapped or hearing impaired. The PVMT can be administered to individuals or small groups.

Purdue Perceptual-Motor Survey (PPMS)

The Purdue Perceptual-Motor Survey (Roach & Kephart, 1966) is a 22-item assessment instrument designed to measure laterality, directionality, and perceptual-motor matching skills. The PPMS has 11 subtests: walking board, jumping, identification of body parts, imitation of movement, obstacle course, chalkboard, test of physical fitness, angels-in-the-snow, ocular pursuit movement, developmental drawing, and rhythmic writing. Test norms provide information on average performance for children ages 6-10.

Quick Neurological Screening Test (QNST)

The Quick Neurological Screening Test (Mutti, Sterling, & Spalding, 1978) assesses 15 areas of neurological integration. The pattern of scores obtained may be used to suggest further diagnostic assessment needs. The QNST is scored simultaneously with administration. Areas assessed are maturity of motor development, large and small muscle skill and control, motor planning and sequencing, sense of rate and rhythm, spatial organization, visual and auditory perceptual abilities, balance and cerebellar-vertibular function, and attentional difficulties. Intended for use with students ages 5 to 18 years, the QNST is untimed but typically requires about 20 minutes to administer.

Screening Test for Auditory Perception (STAP)

The Screening Test for Auditory Perception (Kimmell & Wahl, 1981) assesses the inability to discriminate between long and short vowels, single versus blend initial consonants, rhyming versus nonrhyming words, same versus different rhythmic patterns, and same versus different words. The STAP specifically screens for weaknesses rather than assessing strengths. It requires approximately 45 minutes to administer and score. Raw scores can be converted to grade equivalents, age equivalents, or percentiles. The STAP can be individually or group administered, and a cassette tape form is available for uniform administration. It is appropriate for use with students in grades 1-6 and older remedial students.

Sensory Integration and Praxis Tests (SIPT)

The Sensory Integration and Praxis Tests (Ayres, 1987), for students 4 to 8 years old, constitute a revision of the Southern California Sensory Integration Tests (Ayres, 1979). They include 17 separate tests: space visualization, figure-ground perception, standing and walking balance, design copying, postural praxis, motor accuracy, kinesthesia, manual form perception, finger identification, graphesthesia, localization of tactile stimuli, sequencing praxis, oral praxis, praxis on verbal command, constructional praxis, postrotary nystagmus, and bilateral motor coordination.

The SIPT may be used as a total battery, or selected tests may be administered. It is computer-scored only, and time required for administration varies. The SIPT measures visual, tactile, and kinesthetic perception and motor performance. Its primary use is to determine the degree and type of disorder experienced by students who have perceptual motor difficulties associated with learning disabilities, emotional disorders, or minimal brain dysfunction.

Tree/Bee Test of Auditory Discrimination
(See chapter 11.)

Visual Aural Digit Span Test (VADS)

The Visual Aural Digit Span Test (Koppitz, 1978) provides an assessment of intersensory integration and short-term memory. The four VADS subtests provide scores that are combined to form 11 scores that identify the level of intersensory integration across the various input-output modalities. These 11 scores are: aural-oral, visual-oral, aural-written, visual-written, aural input, visual input, oral expression, written expression, intrasensory integration, intersensory integration, and total. The VADS includes digit sequences on 26 test cards, which are reproduced from memory, first orally, then in writing after oral presentation. Finally, they must be reproduced as a separate series, visually.

The VADS may be used to diagnose learning styles, or to plan interventions for learning disabled students. For students ages 5½ to 12 years, the VADS may be used individually or in small groups and is available in English and Spanish.

Visual Memory Test (VMT)

The Visual Memory Test (Wepman, Morency, & Seidl, 1975) assesses a student's ability to remember nonalphabetical visual forms. The VMT is a 16-item test, requiring 10 to 15 minutes, in which the student chooses a design from four designs on a response page to match the design shown by the examiner. This individually administered test has norms for ages 5, 6, 7, and 8. If the student does not reach the "adequacy threshold" for his or her age, further evaluation is indicated.

Motor Tests

The assessment instruments just outlined measure motor ability, but primarily with respect to perceptual ability or to perceptual-motor integration. Some tests measure motor skills alone. Two of them are described below.

Bruininks-Oseretsky Test of Motor Proficiency (BOTMP)

The Bruininks-Oseretsky Test of Motor Proficiency (Bruininks, 1978) measures performance in gross, fine, and general motor development. It is available in a comprehensive or short form. The complete battery encompasses 46 items and requires 45 to 60 minutes for administration. The short form has 14 items, requires 15 to 20 minutes to administer, and is intended as a quick screening device. Areas tested include: running speed and agility, balance, bilateral coordination, strength, upper-limb coordination, response speed, visual-motor control, and upper-limb speed and dexterity. Separate scores for fine, gross, and general motor development are provided.

Test of Motor Impairment—Henderson Revision (TOMI)

The Test of Motor Impairment (Stott, Moyes, & Henderson, 1984) measures four dimensions of motor performance: manual dexterity, ball skills, static balance, and dynamic balance. TOMI tasks are provided in five age bands, with eight tasks in each band. Students who fail at their own age level can be tested at a lower age level. TOMI tasks are play-type activities such as jumping in squares, tossing a beanbag, threading beads, and the like. As part of the TOMI assessment, three checklists—faults of coping style, faults of motor control, and concurrent observations—may provide insight into the factors that are causing motor difficulties. The TOMI, individually administered, is used with students ages 4 years through adulthood. Total testing time ranges from 20 to 45 minutes.

Career, Vocational, and Transition-Related Assessment

According to many experts, career education and vocational education should begin at elementary school levels. The Career Education Incentive Act of 1977 (Public Law 95-207) was passed to provide incentive funds to state and local school districts to promote this concept. Accordingly, some school districts have developed K-12 programs (Gaylord-Ross, 1988). But the emphasis has evolved into a "lifelong career development approach," characterized by a model based on 12 specific propositions about career development (Berkell & Brown, 1989; Brolin, 1973, 1983, 1988).

This model emphasizes the development of basic academic skills and career and self-awareness at the elementary levels, but most nonacademic assessment that is directed specifically toward assisting students to make meaningful career choices and obtaining meaningful, lasting employment takes place at the secondary level. This assessment may relate to career/vocational aptitude and skills, or simply awareness and interests. Each of these is important if we are to aid students in making meaningful career/vocational choices and then follow through with appropriate preparation for these careers or vocations.

The concept of transition may be considered in relation to transition from home to school, or from one school level to another, but it is more frequently discussed with respect to transition from school to adulthood and employment (Berkell & Brown, 1989; Chadsey-Rusch, Hanley-Maxwell, Phelps, & Rusch, 1986; Clark & Knowlton, 1987). Concern has been growing about the realization that the schools have not really been preparing American youth for employment—and particular concern with respect to persons with handicapping conditions. Berkell and Brown (1989) have said, "The transition from school to work encompasses a period that includes high school, graduation, postsecondary education or adult services, and the initial years of employment" (p. 3).

As for assessment related to transition (school to adulthood), they suggest that information in six areas should be considered:

1. Academic.
2. Psychological.
3. Psychomotor.
4. Medical.
5. Social.
6. Vocational.

Berkell and Brown list 92 tests, categorized into six areas—ability, achievement, aptitude, interest, personality, and social—as potentially applicable to transition-related assessment. Of these 92 tests, over half are aptitude tests or interest inventories. Many tests in the other four areas already have been reviewed in other chapters. Aptitude tests, interest inventories, and measures of social and daily living skills are discussed in this chapter. In addition, we consider assessment tools such as work samples as they apply at this age level and for these purposes.

Measures of Vocational Aptitude

Vocational aptitude may be assessed in a variety of ways. In this section we review a number of assessment instruments that measure specific skills that are important to success in various vocations. In the past, tests designed to measure single, specific skills (or perhaps two or three highly related skills) were in very common use. More recently, there has been a move toward greater use of test batteries that assess a wide variety of skills and aptitudes. The tests described here provide a representative sample of both single-purpose tests and comprehensive test batteries.

Bennett Mechanical Comprehension Test (BMCT)

The Bennett Mechanical Comprehension Test (Bennett, 1970) was designed to assess perception and understanding of mechanical elements and physical forces in practical situations. The content of the BMCT primarily consists of pictures of mechanisms or objects whose functions require comprehension (understanding)—for example, a series of gears and the question, "Which will make the most turns per minute?" This 68-item test is for use with high school age students or adults, has a 30-minute administration time limit, and may be administered individually or in small groups. Norms are provided for six different industrial groups, and the test is available in English and Spanish.

Crawford Small Parts Dexterity Test (CSPDT)

The Crawford Small Parts Dexterity Test (Crawford & Crawford, 1956) measures fine eye-hand coordination, which may be pertinent to skills such as those required to assemble small electronic or electrical devices or to repair a clock. In one part of the CSPDT, the examinee must use tweezers to pick up pins and then insert them in small holes in a metal plate. In a second part, he or she must pick up a screw and start it in a threaded hole. Then the screw must be screwed through the metal plate with a screw driver. The CSPDT is for high school age students and adults and provides two scores, one for "pins and collars" and another for "screws."

Differential Aptitude Tests (DAT)

The Differential Aptitude Tests (Bennett, Seashore, & Wesman, 1981) provide an integrated battery of eight aptitude tests for use in educational/vocational guidance of junior and senior high age students. The DAT also may be used with adults in various vocational and career planning situations. The areas assessed are: verbal reasoning, numerical ability, abstract reasoning, clerical speed and accuracy, mechanical reasoning, space relations, and spelling and language usage. The DAT usually requires about 3 hours' working time. It may be hand-scored or machine-scored, and percentile ranks and stanines are provided separately for males and females. A "Computerized Adaptive Edition" of the DAT may be computer-administered and computer-scored.

General Aptitude Test Battery (GATB)

The General Aptitude Test Battery (U.S. Dept. of Labor, 1970) was developed for use by the U.S. Employment Service. It measures nine aptitude areas: general learning ability, verbal aptitude, numerical aptitude, spatial aptitude, form perception, clerical perception, motor coordination, finger dexterity, and manual dexterity. The GATB is administered to high school age or adult examinees, takes 2½ hours, and may be machine- or hand-scored. It is available in English or Spanish.

Minnesota Clerical Test—Revised (MCT-R)

The Minnesota Clerical Test (Ryan, 1979) assesses perceptual speed and accuracy as related to traditional clerical tasks. The MCT-R has two subtests—one relating to number comparison, the other to name comparison. It requires the examinee to find and check similar pairs (of numbers or names). The MCT-R, which may be administered individually or in small groups, requires 15 minutes.

Minnesota Rate of Manipulation Tests (MRMT)

The Minnesota Rate of Manipulation Tests (University of Minnesota, 1967b) assess manual dexterity through the use of two test boards, and tasks requiring finger movement and hand and arm movement. The MRMT has five tests: placing, turning, displacing, one-hand turning and placing, and two-hand turning and placing. These tests were designed for adolescents and adults and require 30 to 50 minutes for administration.

OASIS Aptitude Survey (OASIS-AS)

The OASIS Aptitude Survey (Parker, 1983a) is one half of the Occupational Aptitude Survey and Interest Schedule (OASIS). (The OASIS Interest Schedule is reviewed later in this chapter.) The OASIS-AS measures six of the aptitude factors derived from the GATB: general ability, verbal aptitude, numerical aptitude, spatial aptitude, perceptual aptitude, and manual dexterity. It is hand-scored, requires 30 to 40 minutes to administer, and may be administered to individuals or groups.

Pennsylvania Bi-Manual Worksample

The Pennsylvania Bi-Manual Worksample (Roberts, 1969) provides a measure of ability to integrate gross and fine motor movements in a work setting. No reading is required, and the instrument may be used with students who are deaf or mentally handicapped. In addition, special administration procedures for use with blind students may be obtained from the publisher. Developed for persons age 16 years and older, the sample takes 12 minutes to administer.

Interest Inventories

Interest inventories were developed as a result of evidence suggesting that most individuals in various occupational groups appeared to have similar likes and dislikes with respect to things such as hobbies, sports, types of play, social interests, and "type of person" (tall, short, quiet, talkative, aggressive, shy, etc.). In addition, it was discovered that the pattern of likes and dislikes of persons in each occupational group was different from the patterns in other groups. Thus, an "inventory" could be developed to determine an individual's interests. These patterns of interest then could be compared to those of persons successfully engaged in various occupations.

Several interest inventories are outlined in the following sections. A few have assessment components that relate to "personality need"—a factor that also appears to be related to vocational success. Some require a fair degree of verbal ability and knowledge in the world of work, and therefore must be selected carefully. In the following sections, inventories requiring near normal reading ability and knowledge of the world of work, and others, developed primarily for use with handicapped students, are described.

Gordon Occupational Check List II (Gordon)

The Gordon Occupational Check List (Gordon, 1981) assesses occupational interests in nonprofessional areas such as business, outdoor, arts, technology, and service areas. The list may be read to students who cannot read at the 6th-grade level, and it requires 20 to 25 minutes for administration. Designed for high school age students and adults, it is hand-scored. The Gordon is used for initiating counseling discussions and may provide a basis for further testing.

Hall Occupational Orientation Inventory—Revised (HALL-R)

The Hall Occupational Orientation Inventory (Hall & Tarrier, 1987) focuses on 22 occupational and personality characteristics. These are: creativity/independence, risk, information/knowledge, belongingness, security, aspiration, esteem, self-actualization, personal satisfaction, routine-dependence, data orientation, things orientation, people orientation, location concern, aptitude concern, monetary concern, physical abilities concern, environment concern, co-worker concern, qualifications concern, time concern, and defensiveness.

The HALL is available at three levels: intermediate, for grades 3-7; young adult/college, for high school and college students; and adult basic, for adults with reading handicaps. Intermediate HALL contains school-focused items that may complement awareness programs; Young Adult/College HALL focuses on jobs and occupations; Adult Basic HALL is a world-of-work test. All three HALL inventories relate to interests and personality orientation. The HALL inventories may be self-administered and self-scored, and they require 30 to 45 minutes to complete.

209

Kuder General Interest Survey (Kuder)

The Kuder General Interest Survey (Kuder, 1987) measures interests in 10 interest areas: outdoor, mechanical, scientific, computational, persuasive, artistic, literary, musical, social service, and clerical, and relates them to vocational areas. Students respond to questions in which they indicate which of three activities they most prefer and which they least prefer. The Kuder provides a comparison for each student, with both male and female norms, and offers teachers and counselors a basis for vocational counseling. The Kuder is used in grades 6 through 12 and can be machine- or hand-scored.

OASIS Interest Schedule (OASIS-IS)

The OASIS Interest Schedule (Parker, 1983b) is one half of the Occupational Aptitude Survey and Interest Schedule (OASIS). (The other half, the Aptitude Survey, was reviewed earlier in this chapter.) The OASIS-IS contains 240 items to which the student indicates "Like," "Neutral," or "Dislike." It measures 12 interest factors: artistic, scientific, nature, protective, mechanical, industrial, business detail, selling, accommodating, humanitarian, leading-influencing, and physical performing. The OASIS measures were designed for use with students in grades 8-12.

Reading-Free Vocational Interest Inventory—Revised (RFVII)

The Reading-Free Vocational Interest Inventory—Revised (Becker, 1981) was normed on students and adults with learning disabilities and mental retardation from vocational training centers and sheltered workshops. It consists of 55 sets of three pictures each; from each set the subject picks the picture that represents the work he or she likes most, by making a large circle on the picture. The RFVII can be given individually or in small groups. It results in a profile indicating relative interest in 11 areas: automotive, building trades, clerical, animal care, food service, patient care, horticulture, housekeeping, personal service, laundry service, and materials handling.

Self Directed Search (SDS)

The Self Directed Search (Holland, 1985) is a comprehensive occupational interest survey that is self-administered, self-scored, and self-interpreted. It surveys aspirations, activities, competencies, occupations, and self-estimates of abilities of persons between ages 15 and 70 who are in need of occupational guidance. The SDS provides scores in six areas: realistic, investigative, artistic, social, enterprising, and conventional. Through use of the Occupations Finder, the SDS provides a directory of over 1,000 occupations that are coded with respect to these six areas.

In addition to the standard SDS, an SDS Form E(asy) is available for those with reading skills at 4th grade level and below. The directory for SDS Form E is limited to 500 occupations, and a simplified code system is utilized to search for these occupations.

Strong Interest Inventory

Strong-Campbell Interest Inventory (SCII)

The Strong-Campbell Interest Inventory (Strong, Hansen, & Campbell, 1985) is a revision of the Strong Interest Inventory. The SCII requires a considerable degree of verbal ability and is composed of over 300 items, grouped into seven parts. The first five parts require the subject to mark "like," "indifferent," or "dislike" with respect to categories on occupations, school subjects, activities, amusements, and feelings about various types of people. The last two parts require an expression of preference between paired items, and a set of self-descriptive statements. The Strong is scored only by computer through designated scoring centers. Scoring is in several dimensions, including six General Occupational Themes (realistic, investigative, artistic, social, enterprising, and conventional), and according to a variety of occupational scales.

Wide Range Interest-Opinion Test (WRIOT)

The Wide Range Interest-Opinion Test (Jastak & Jastak, 1979) requires no reading or writing. It consists of 150 sets of three pictures each, to which the respondent must indicate his or her choice by marking on a separate answer sheet. The WRIOT provides both a vocational profile and a personal attitude profile. The vocational areas (clusters) include art, literature, music, drama, sales, management, office work, personal service, protective service, social service, social science, biological science, physical science, numbers, mechanics, machine operation, outdoor, and athletics. The personal attitude areas include sedentariness, risk, ambition, chosen skill level, sex stereotype, agreement, negative bias, and positive bias. The WRIOT can be scored by hand or by computer.

Social and Daily Living Skills

As an adult interacts with other adults, certain minimum social skills appear to be essential for success in employment or in daily living. In a discussion of the ecology of the work place, Chadsey-Rusch and Rusch (1988) conclude,

211

"It is clear that social ecological variables can have an effect on matches between workers and their jobs. If workers display inappropriate social skills, for example, there is a strong likelihood they will be fired" (p. 249). Their analysis relates primarily to individuals with handicapping conditions, but it applies to all persons in the work place.

Assessment instruments reviewed next were designed to assess social and daily living skills, skills related to interviewing for employment, and similar skills. If the transition from school to adult life and the work place is to be facilitated, results of assessment of social and daily living skills of adolescents and young adults must be evaluated in conjunction with information about vocational interests and aptitudes.

Analysis of Coping Style
(See chapter 12.)

Brigance Diagnostic Inventory of Essential Skills (BDIES)

The Brigance Diagnostic Inventory of Essential Skills (Brigance, 1980) was designed to measure skills essential to success as a citizen, consumer, worker, and family member. This inventory includes measures of ability in reading, language arts, and math, and applied skills such as in health and attitude, responsibility and self-discipline, job interview skills, auto safety, communication, and telephone skills. In addition, levels of competency in money and finance, food and clothing, and travel and communication are assessed.

Untimed, the BDIES may be used from grade 6 through adulthood. Its primary purpose is to provide a basis for additional educational efforts, but it also gives a profile of strengths and weaknesses, which may be used for transition planning.

Comprehensive Test of Adaptive Behavior
(See chapter 5.)

Coopersmith Self-Esteem Inventories
(See chapter 12.)

Devereux Adolescent Behavior Rating Scale
(See chapter 12.)

Hahnemann High School Behavior Rating Scale
(See chapter 12.)

Scales of Independent Behavior
(See chapter 5.)

Social and Prevocational Information Battery—Revised (SPIB-R)

The Revised Social and Prevocational Information Battery (Halpern, Raffeld, Irvin, Link, & Munkres, 1986) provides information regarding the student's knowledge/understanding of budgeting, banks, purchasing habits, and home management. It also assesses knowledge of health care, grooming, and acceptable job-related behavior. It was designed for use with the educable mentally handicapped and some trainable mentally retarded, ages 12 through approximately 20 years. The SPIB-R is orally administered and may be considered a general measure of knowledge related to community adjustment.

Tennessee Self-Concept Scale
(See chapter 12.)

Test of Practical Knowledge (TPK)

The Test of Practical Knowledge (Wiederholt & Larsen, 1983) contains 100 items, grouped into three factors: personal knowledge, social knowledge, and occupational knowledge. It may be considered a measure of both adaptive behavior and prevocational knowledge. The TPK may be group-administered, and it is hand-scored. Results of the TPK can be profiled in percentiles or stanines, and the total percentile score may be converted to the Practical Knowledge Quotient.

Tests for Everyday Living (TEL)

The Tests for Everyday Living (Halpern, Irvin, & Landman, 1979) provide scores in purchasing habits, banking, budgeting, health care, home management, job search skills, and job-related behavior. The TEL is a competency-based instrument in which 209 of the 245 items require no reading skill. It is for secondary school age students and adults and is hand-scored.

Weller-Strawser Scales of Adaptive Behavior
(See chapter 5.)

Work Samples

Work samples are designed to assess students' skills and attitudes as they complete tasks that are similar to those they might perform in various types of employment. Formal (commercially designed and standardized) work samples are related to selected vocations as defined by the *Dictionary of Occupational Titles*, published by the U.S. Department of Labor. In addition, teachers often design informal work samples that relate to local work situations into which students may be placed in training programs, or that experience indicates are popular employment options.

Whether formal or informal, the purpose of assessment using work samples is to determine whether the student has the skills, the attitudes, and the interest required for various vocational options. Three widely accepted work sample assessment tools are described next, followed by some suggestions for teachers or others to follow if they are developing or designing informal work samples themselves.

JEVS Work Sample Evaluation System (JEVS)

The JEVS Work Sample Evaluation System (Jewish Employment & Vocational Service, 1976) (also known as the Philadelphia J.E.V.S. Work Sample Battery) was developed for use with high school age students and adults. JEVS provides work activities for evaluation of performance, interest, and work behavior. It has 28 separate tests, including nut-bolt-washer assembly, rubber stamping, washer threading, sign making, tile sorting, nut packing, metal square fabrication, belt assembly, proofreading, lock assembly, filing by letters, payroll computation, pipe assembly, blouse making, computing postage, and others.

The JEVS provides a time and quality rating for each test: 1 (lowest 40%), 2 (middle 20%), 3 (highest 40%). It also provides 27 ratings by the evaluator: 5 in behavior in interpersonal relations, 9 in worker characteristics, 6 in learning and comprehension, 5 in manipulative skills, and 2 in significant worker characteristics.

Singer Vocational Evaluation System (VES)

The Singer Vocational Evaluation System (Singer Systems, 1982) provides a set of 27 work samples, covering areas such as plumbing and pipe fitting, drafting, masonry, sheet metal, cosmetology, medical services, filing, electronics assembly, and others. Administration of samples has no prescribed order, and all samples need not be administered. Students record their interests on the Work-Activity Ratings Form, which becomes a partial guide as to which work samples to utilize. Evaluators record their observations on the Task Observation Form. After an activity is completed, students rate their interest in a given job for the second time, and the evaluator reviews student performance. The VES may be used to establish interest, aptitude, ability, or a combination of these three, and is for high school age students and adults.

Wide Range Employability Sample Test (WREST)

The Wide Range Employability Sample Test (Jastak & Jastak, 1980) provides an evaluation of technical work skills and productivity through the use of 10 concrete tasks. These are: folding, stapling, packaging, measuring, stringing, gluing, collating, color matching, pattern matching, and assembling. Students also are rated with respect to appearance, attendance, punctuality, perseverance, organization of work, relations with co-workers, relations with supervisor, flexibility, safety practices, and conformity to rules. The WREST, for high school age students and adults, may require up to 2 hours to administer.

Informal (Self-Developed) Work Sample Assessment

Informal work samples may be developed to provide a basis for instruction/ training during the last two or three years in school, to provide information about certain specific skills in which a student is deficient or to prepare students for specific job placements. In each case, the first question is: "What skills should be assessed?" If the purpose is, for example, preparation for a specific local job market, educators will find it advantageous to observe the job setting in question and interview the employer in some detail. After these observations and interviews, a description of work skill areas, similar to those in Table 14.1, can be generated. In addition, as part of the work sample assessment process, the following work-related social skills should be rated:
— has positive attitude about work
— accepts direction from supervisor (teacher)
— follows oral and written directions
— remains at job station
— uses appropriate language
— completes assigned tasks
— accepts criticism
— works alone or in groups
— attends regularly and exhibits punctuality.
(Scott, Ebbert, & Price, 1986, p. 3)

Certain steps should be taken in developing work samples for local use. These include:
1. Examining commercially produced work sample systems to become familiar with the procedures and activities commonly used.
2. Developing a statement of the specific purpose for the assessment.

Table 14.1

**Informal Work Sample Assessment: General Work Skills and
Teacher-Developed Work Sample Activities**

General Work Skill Area	Work Sample Activities
Assembling	Assembling nuts, bolts, and washers
Disassembling	Assembling ink pens (Disassembly)
Packaging; Counting	Placing specified amount of beans, wooden pegs, bottle caps, etc. into egg carton sections
	Placing specified number of pieces of styrofoam packing material into Ziploc bag and seal
	Bundling 15 drinking straws with rubber bands
Sorting, Matching, Discriminating	Fitting lids on small plastic containers of various sizes
	Reproducing card designs using parquetry blocks, wooden cubes, beads and string
	Sorting and matching fabric swatches by texture, design, color, etc.
	Matching wallpaper patterns
	Categorizing various items by physical properties: size, shape, color, composition, etc.
Measuring	Measuring string, oaktag, or posterboard strips, wood dowels, etc.
	Weighing bird seed, mail, food-stuffs, etc.
Sequencing	Filing name cards, functional word cards, etc.
	Sorting cancelled checks, invoices, etc., by date, number, etc.
	Using telephone directories to locate information
	Following step-by-step instructions in assembly tasks
Using Tools, Materials, and Processes	Using adding machine or calculator to total groceries
	Using typewriter, computer, etc.
	Using hand tools in production activities
Homemaking	Setting a table following picture diagram
	Using needle and thread to sew on buttons

From M. Scott, A. Ebbert, and D. Price (1986), "Assessing and Teaching Employability Skills with Prevocational Work Samples," *Directive Teacher*, 8(1),4. © 1986, NCEMMH, Ohio State University. Used by permission.

3. Observing and interviewing individuals involved in work similar to that targeted in the statement of purpose.
4. Developing and field-testing instruments.

After modifications are made as a result of field-testing, the resulting work sample should provide unique insights that are unavailable in standardized, mass-produced work samples.

Special Areas of Concern in Assessment

This final chapter covers a number of assessment topics and concerns that, while overlapping with topics in preceding chapters, seem different enough to merit consideration in a separate chapter. These include assessment of giftedness, talent, and creativity; computer applications in assessment; assessment relating to transition from special to regular classroom settings; various other, special-purpose assessment instruments and techniques; assessment of the "difficult child"; and assessment reports. We first consider assessment related to giftedness, talent, and creativity.

Assessment Relating to Giftedness, Talent, and Creativity

Most of this text relates to assessment designed to provide insight into the needs of students who are not performing satisfactorily in the schools. The problem may be primarily academic, primarily behavioral, or some combination of these two areas, but the students have been identified as requiring assistance. Assessment relating to the gifted/talented or creative most often focuses on discovering gifted, talented, and creative students. In some ways this is similar to our focus with students who have handicaps or disabilities, but it also has significant differences. Some gifted, talented, or creative students are quickly recognized, but many are not until they have been in school for several years and valuable time has been wasted. Some never cause problems in the school or call undue attention to themselves, and their unusual abilities are never recognized.

In a few states, programs for the gifted/talented are greatly encouraged, but there are not the same type of mandates, backed by state regulations and carried out under the threat of litigation, as is the case with students who have handicaps or disabilities. Therefore, assessment of gifted/talented and creative students has received much less attention and emphasis than assessment of students with handicaps or disabilities.

The problem of identification-related assessment of gifted/talented and creative students is aptly summarized by the following words from the Foreword to the Los Angeles Unified School District (1985) Guide to its *Screening Program for Gifted and Talented: Grades 1 and 2*:

> "Screening for Gifted/Talented Pupils in Grades 1 and 2 is an organized screening program to observe, assess, and nurture potentially gifted/talented students in grades 1 and 2 where early labeling of children is difficult because there may be insufficient data for processing, because the child's length of time in school may have been too short for observation of characteristics, and because test results are not always reliable. (p. iii)

Teachers are encouraged to identify potentially gifted or talented students and are provided a specific screening program that represents the most logical first step in assessment of gifted/talented students. Los Angeles screening methods include both informal observation and structured observation.

Parents are asked if they want their child to participate in the screening program. If they do, they are asked to complete a 19-item inventory in which they rate their child, compared to other children of their age, with respect to a number of statements such as "remembers more details of past experiences," "likes to talk more about what has been read," and "shows less patience in activities that are routine or too easy." (This parent inventory is available in English, Cantonese, Korean, and Spanish.) Teachers complete a similar scale, as well as a summary analysis worksheet designed to help them decide whether to refer the child for further evaluation to the school psychologist.

The Los Angeles program provides an example of the extent to which some cities may go in attempts to identify and provide programs for gifted/talented students. In contrast, some areas of the nation make essentially no attempts to identify gifted/talented students. Nevertheless, we may make the following generalizations about assessment and identification procedures for gifted/ talented and creative students, in areas where they do exist. Assessment/identification procedures are likely to involve some combination of:

— screening
— teacher nomination

— parent nomination
— peer or self nomination
— scores on tests of cognitive ability/intelligence
— scores on achievement tests
— scores on tests of creativity
— expert opinion (relating to talent in art, music, etc.).

Because we have already reviewed cognitive ability tests (chapter 5) and achievement tests (chapter 8), the one major assessment area mentioned above that we have not considered is that of creativity. Creative potential is assessed as a factor separate from giftedness and talent, but few school programs exist for creative students, as separate from students who are gifted or have unusual talent. More often, creativity is assessed as one component of giftedness or talent.

Though many existing tests of creativity have been seriously questioned with respect to both validity and reliability, feasible alternatives have not been offered. Creativity may be among the more elusive characteristics that we may attempt to measure. The tests outlined next provide a sample of existing attempts to measure it.

Tests of Creativity

Cornell Critical Thinking Tests (CCTT)

The Cornell Critical Thinking Tests (Ennis & Millman, 1985) are provided as two separate tests. Level X, for students in grades 5-14, includes sections on induction, credibility, deduction, and identification of assumptions; students are asked to think critically about problems in a science fiction story, selecting answers from a multiple-choice format. Level Z is for advanced secondary students or adults; sections include deduction, semantics, credibility, induction, prediction in planning experiments, definition, and identification of assumptions. This level involves a series of problem situations that test-takers must analyze.

Creative Reasoning Test (CRT)

The Creative Reasoning Test (Doolittle, 1989) is a problem-solving instrument involving a set of riddles. Students generate solutions in a variety of categories, evaluating those solutions in relation to information provided in the problems until they arrive at a satisfactory answer. The CRT was developed at two levels of difficulty—Level A, for pre-secondary students, and Level B, for secondary students.

Creativity Tests for Children (CTC)

The Creativity Tests for Children (Guilford, 1971) consist of a series of 10 tests designed to measure various aspects of divergent production. The subtests are:

Names for Stories—A series of stories is presented; the subject must think of names for the stories.

What to Do With It—Names of objects are listed along with those objects' common use; subjects are to think of different, unusual uses of these objects.

Similar Meanings—Words are given, and the subject must think of another word for each that means about the same.

Writing Sentences—Five words are listed; subjects must write sentences in which they use at least two of these words and are to construct as many sentences as they can, using all of the five words as often as possible.

Kinds of People—A series of "signs" (for example, a sign that is the picture of a book in a circle) is presented; subjects are to think of the kind of person who might be related to each sign, or the kind of activity that sign suggests.

Make Something Out of It—Figures are presented; subjects are to visualize various things they can "make out of it" and name the thing they visualize.

Different Letter Groups—A group of letters is presented, and subjects look for ways in which the letters are similar.

Making Objects—A group of geometric shapes or "pieces" is given; the subject must put together the pieces to make real objects.

Hidden Letters—A figure is presented with many intersecting lines contained within the outer perimeter; subjects must find letters "hidden" in it.

Adding Decorations—Students view very plain, outlined figures representing real objects; they use lines to "decorate" these objects.

The CTC is for 4th grade and older students; 100 minutes are required for administration of the total battery.

Screening Assessment for Gifted Elementary Students (SAGES)

The Screening Assessment for Gifted Elementary Students (Johnsen & Corn, 1987) is for students ages 7 to 12 years. Its three subtests sample aspects of aptitude, achievement, and creativity. The Aptitude subtest involves solving new problems by identifying relationships among pictures and figures. Achievement is measured by assessing science, social studies, and math. Creativity is measured by an assessment of divergent production. The first two subtests

222

may be administered individually or in small groups. The Creativity subtest must be administered individually. The entire test requires 30 to 50 minutes for administration.

Thinking Creatively in Action and Movement (TCAM)

Thinking Creatively in Action and Movement (Torrance, 1981) includes norms for ages 3 through 8. The four subparts, called activities, are:

How Many Ways—is scored for fluency and originality with respect to the ways the child "invents" to move across the floor. The fluency score is a simple count of the number of ways and combinations of ways. The originality score is the total of scores in a system that rates responses from 0 to 3 for originality. (Example: Simple crawling is a 0, jogging is a 1, duck walking is a 2, and goosestepping is a 3.)

Can You Move Like?—is scored for one category, imagination. One sample question is, "Can you move like a tree in the wind? Imagine you are a tree and the wind is blowing very hard." Children are asked to show the examiner how many ways they can move like a tree in the wind. This subpart has six questions, with a provision for the examiner to rate responses on a scale from 1 to 5.

What Other Ways?—involves the child's putting a paper cup into a wastebasket in a variety of ways. It is scored for fluency and originality.

What Might It Be?—asks the child to think of ways in which he or she might play with paper cups. He or she is provided many cups, with the suggestion to imagine they are something else. Scored for fluency and originality.

Torrance Tests of Creative Thinking (TTCT)

The Torrance Tests of Creative Thinking (Torrance, 1966, 1980) target four mental characteristics: fluency, flexibility, originality, and elaboration. The Verbal TTCT tests utilize word-based exercises that can be administered orally to students in kindergarten through grade 3. Verbal tests involve activities such as guessing causes, guessing consequences, product improvement, unusual uses (for common objects), "just suppose," and others. The Figural TTCT utilizes activities in which the student is to draw pictures that "tell an exciting story" or that are unusual in some way. The TTCT provides percentiles (local and national), a creativity index, and a computer-generated narrative for each student.

Watson-Glaser Critical Thinking Appraisal (WGCTA)

The Watson-Glaser Critical Thinking Appraisal (Watson & Glaser, 1980)

223

measures aspects of creativity and critical thinking. Test exercises include problems, statements, arguments, and information similar to that which might be found in newspapers, magazines, and everyday adult life. Controversial political, economic, and social issues are raised to measure the degree to which strong feelings or bias may influence critical thinking ability. The WGCTA contains 80 items that measure inferences, recognition of assumptions, deductive ability, interpretations, and ability to evaluate arguments. It can be administered to individuals or to small groups, is designed for use with students in grades 9-12 and adults, and requires 50 to 60 minutes to administer.

Computer Applications in Assessment

Some of the assessment tools reviewed in this text can be scored by computer; some can be scored *only* by computer. Computer scoring may include a profile prepared for each student, or a narrative analysis, providing a discussion that relates specifically to the student under consideration. Computers are of great value in providing local school district normative data or local school data. A computer program can be used in a variety of ways to integrate and analyze information relating to any one student, providing unique information for purposes of diagnosis and classification. One such system is reviewed in the following paragraphs.

McDermott Multidimensional Assessment of Children (M-MAC)

The McDermott Multidimensional Assessment of Children (McDermott & Watkins, 1985) has two major levels: Classification and Program Design. It provides for the integration and analysis of information from over 30 possible sources, including intelligence tests, achievement tests, adaptive behavior scales, professional judgments of specialists from pertinent disciplines, teacher rating scales, parent rating scales, criterion-referenced tests, special language and cultural features, environmental and educational background, health status, and others.

The classification level of M-MAC generates the following multidimensional classifications: exceptional talent, normal intellectual functioning, mental retardation, intellectual retardation, educational retardation, commensurate achievement, specific learning disability, developmental learning disorder, possible academic overcompensation, possible communication disorder, possible visual-motor problem, good social-emotional adjustment, adequate social-emotional adjustment, conduct disorder, anxiety-withdrawal disorder, attention deficit disorder, and disturbance of emotions and conduct.

The program design level provides behavioral objectives to be used with

IEPs, or for other educational planning purposes. This latter information may be used for students who are not identified as having handicaps.

Assessment Relating to Transition from Special to Regular Classes

A great deal of assessment, following specific guidelines, is required before a student is placed in a special class or a special program for students with handicapping conditions or disabilities. The same laws and regulations that dictate this assessment indicate that students should return to less restrictive settings and programs as soon as possible, given their unique educational needs. Their return should be based on a variety of assessment results, with considerable emphasis on informal assessment. The results of the informal assessments, coupled with information regarding the skills necessary for successful functioning in the regular classroom, can provide the basis for special teaching efforts, targeting the most essential skills for reentry into the mainstream.

One way to summarize the skills required for successful functioning in various mainstream settings, and compare these requirements with the skills the student possesses, is through use of the Transition Checklist (Wood and Miederhoff, 1988). In this checklist the teacher first observes and evaluates/rates the mainstream setting according to various characteristics, under three categories: classroom, interpersonal/social relations, and related environments.

Classroom includes variables such as grouping for instruction, use of homework assignments, evaluation techniques (how tests are given, etc.), teaching techniques, and others. *Interpersonal social relations* includes characteristics such as the type of student interaction (cooperative, competitive, etc.), dress code or appearance standards, and others. *Related environments* encompasses things such as requirements to function in the school cafeteria, in physical education, and others. In each area the teacher determines the skills or abilities required for success, and then the degree to which the student has acquired them. This is to be used as a guide for further teaching/learning activities and provides a preliminary assessment of the likelihood of success in the mainstream setting.

Other Assessment Instruments

The tests/assessment instruments reviewed in this section represent a variety of special-purpose assessment tools. In addition to the brief description of each of these instruments, we will comment on its uniqueness.

Analytic Learning Disability Assessment (ALDA)

The Analytic Learning Disability Assessment (Gnagey & Gnagey, 1982) measures 72 skills that are believed to be important to success in basic school subjects, with particular focus on reading, spelling, writing, and mathematics. It is for use with students ages 8 through 14 and, though untimed, usually requires 75 to 80 minutes for administration.

Its authors indicate that it is not appropriate for use unless a dysfunction is suspected. The ALDA's uniqueness lies in the fact that it attempts to match strengths and weaknesses, as assessed by the ALDA, with teaching methods believed to be appropriate given the individual's strengths and weaknesses. This matching is done with 11 reading methods, 23 spelling methods, 6 methods of mathematics computation, and 8 handwriting methods.

Carolina Picture Vocabulary Test (CPVT)

The Carolina Picture Vocabulary Test (Layton & Holmes, 1985) is a receptive sign vocabulary test for deaf and hearing impaired children ages 4 to 11½. This 130-item individual test requires 10 to 15 minutes to administer. The CPVT is unique with respect to the population of students for whom it is appropriate, and the manual signing skills required by the examiner.

Dvorine Color Vision Test (DCVT)

The Dvorine Color Vision Test (Dvorine, 1958), for use with subjects from preschool age through adulthood, requires 2 to 3 minutes for administration. It utilizes a bound set of color plates in which a numeral or design made up of colored dots is presented against a background of contrasting dots. Incorrect responses indicate both the type and degree of color blindless. The DCVT is unique in that it measures a very specific visual ability, and interpretation is absolute rather than normative.

Meadow-Kendall Social-Emotional Assessment Inventory for Deaf and Hearing Impaired Students (SEAI)

The Meadow-Kendall Social-Emotional Assessment Inventory for Deaf and Hearing Impaired Students (Meadow, Getson, Lee, & Stamper, 1983—preschool level; Meadow, Karchmer, Peterson, & Rudner, 1983—school-age) was designed to assess the social and emotional development of a specific population—individuals who are deaf or hearing impaired. At the preschool level, scores are obtained in sociable/communicative behaviors, impulsive dominating behaviors, developmental lags, anxious/compulsive behaviors, and special areas. At the school-age level, scores are obtained in social adjustment, self-image, and emotional adjustment.

Peer Attitudes Toward the Handicapped Scale (PATHS)

The Peer Attitudes Toward the Handicapped Scale (Bagley & Greene, 1981) is designed to measure the attitudes of nonhandicapped students toward the handicapped in general, not any particular student. PATHS contains 30 statements, each describing a handicapped student and problems that student experiences. The examinee reads the description and indicates where the handicapped student should work—that is, work with me in my group, work in another group, work with no students, work outside of class, or stay at home. PATHS includes subscales for persons with physical, learning, and behavioral handicaps. Scores are converted into a range of attitudes score, from "very positive" to "very negative." PATHS is for students in grades 4 through 8 and requires 15 minutes to administer. It is unique in that it assesses attitudes toward a very small, special population.

Slingerland Screening Tests for Identifying Children with Specific Language Disability (Slingerland Tests)

The Slingerland Screening Tests for Identifying Children with Specific Language Disability (Slingerland, 1970, 1974) are provided in four levels: Form A (end of first or beginning of second grade), Form B (end of second or beginning of third grade), Form C (end of third grade or beginning of fourth grade), and Form D (grades 5 and 6). The Slingerland tests have eight subtests for Forms A, B, & C, and an additional subtest for Form D. These subtests are: copying from a wall chart; copying words in isolation; recalling words, numbers, and letters; matching words to sample; drawing from memory; writing letters, numbers, and words from memory; writing the initial and ending letter in words; recalling words, letters, and numbers; and the additional Form D test, writing answers to questions. In addition, optional, auditory ability subtests are available. The Slingerland is a group test (except for the optional, auditory subtests).

Study of Children's Learning Styles, Research Edition (SCLS)

Study of Children's Learning Styles, Research Edition (Stott, McDermott, Green, & Francis, 1987) is a questionnaire, completed by the classroom teacher, that provides a preliminary assessment of how a child may perform academically, based on learning patterns. The SCLS yields scores in three dimensions of learning style: avoidant, inattentive, and overly independent. Approximately

2 minutes per child are required for the teacher to complete the SCLS question-naire. Through the identification of patterns of learning-related behaviors and problem solving, this instrument provides useful information for teaching and intervention planning.

System of Multicultural Pluralistic Assessment (SOMPA)

The System of Multicultural Pluralistic Assessment (Mercer & Lewis, 1977) is a multiple assessment system encompassing assessment of cognitive abilities, perceptual-motor behavior, and adaptive behavior. Its basic premise is that linguistic and cultural differences must be evaluated when assessing a child's performance. The two major components in the SOMPA consist of parent interview-based information and student assessment-based information. Parent interview-based information includes the Adaptive Behavior Inventory for Chil-dren (see chapter 5), Sociocultural Scales, and Health History Inventories. Student assessment information includes physical dexterity task performance, weight by height, visual acuity and auditory information, Bender Visual Motor Gestalt Test information (see chapter 13), and WISC-R or WIPPSI information (see chapter 5).

The SOMPA is for students 5 through 11 years of age, and norms are provided for Black, Hispanic, and Anglo children. This system is unique in the manner in which it utilizes the results of several other standardized tests and the manner in which it takes into account sociocultural and health factors.

Your Style of Learning and Thinking (SOLAT)

Your Style of Learning and Thinking (Torrance, McCarthy, & Kolesinski, 1987) is a self-administered, self-scored assessment designed to determine an individual's learning strategy and brain hemisphere preference. Though it assesses with respect to brain hemisphericity, it is deliberately designed to promote understanding and use of a whole-brain approach to learning. That is, it is designed as both a teaching tool and an assessment tool.

Assessment of the "Difficult" Child

Assessment of children who are resistant or uncooperative provides a major challenge, especially to assessment personnel who have limited experience. If those administering the assessment cannot gain the desired degree of cooper-ation but elect to continue the assessment anyway, this must be noted on the assessment report to inform those who read the report that the results may have been influenced by resistance and lack of cooperation. The best procedure, however, is to find a way to gain cooperation.

Assessment personnel should do everything possible to eliminate distractions and to not exceed the limits of the child's attention span, but many other factors may be involved in the lack of cooperation of "difficult" children. Some are shy, unresponsive, or uncommunicative. Some are argumentative. Still others are frightened by the assessment setting, and others may be highly distractible or hyperactive. Whatever the difficulties, those conducting the assessment must attempt to structure the situation so that meaningful assessment can take place.

Ulrey and Biasini (1989) suggest that some of the potential difficulties can be prevented during the assessment preliminaries. Things such as how initial introductions are carried out, time taken to talk with both the parents and the child, and how the child views the tone of interactions between parents and assessment personnel can make a big difference. With younger children, the question of whether the parents are to be present during evaluation and, perhaps even more important, how this question is approached and resolved can be significant. (For additional information regarding assessment of very young children, see chapter 7.)

How the child is approached in an attempt to encourage him or her to feel that the evaluation session will be interesting is also quite important. This is highly dependent upon age, but, for example, with younger children, suggesting that it will be "fun" may be much less effective than saying there are some games and puzzles to try (Ulrey & Biasini, 1989). Perhaps the most important thing for assessment personnel to remember is that although they should remain in charge of the situation, confrontations in assessment are not situations that they can "win." Students at times will be resistive or uncooperative in the assessment setting, just as they are in their homes and in the classroom. Adults must use all their possible ingenuity to structure the situation so that the student will cooperate because it seems to be the better alternative.

Assessment Reports

How assessment results should be reported remains an open question, with, apparently, considerable variation in practice. The question is further complicated by the fact that assessment has a number of purposes in addition to that of basic problem solving/decision making. One type of assessment, screening, requires a very simple reporting process. Its purpose is to make a preliminary determination as to whether further assessment should take place. One guideline for reporting screening assessment results is very obvious: Results should be very clearly identified as the results of screening so that no misinterpretation will occur in the future. If this is not done, preliminary results that indicate the possibility of learning disabilities, for example, might be later mistakenly interpreted as actual identification of the existence of learning disabilities.

In addition to screening, assessment has at least three major purposes:
1. To establish eligibility for special education services (classification).
2. To provide information that is of maximum value in planning initial intervention.
3. To provide information that can serve as a basis for ongoing instructional/program effectiveness decisions.

In general we might say that each of these types of assessment report "collects and condenses pertinent information about the pupil, both past and present data, and preserves it for other teachers and specialists who are or will be involved in the delivery of educational services to the child" (Reed, 1980, p. 190). An additional essential guideline in preparing the reports is that they be unambiguous and easily understood by the parents.

Various school districts have established assessment summary forms that appear to satisfy the purposes of that district. Some have developed unique summary formats for specific handicapping conditions, with behavior disorders/emotional disturbance apparently the most often targeted for such a special summary. In any case, a basic question with respect to which type of assessment report will be used relates to whether the report should reflect information relating to "process" or "product." If a decision is made to require a process-oriented report, this also dictates a number of quite different assessment procedures and may require one type of assessment for classification purposes and another for instructional planning purposes.

Hoy and Retish (1984) conducted an investigation of the perceived value in educational programming of two types of assessment reports. The first, the Standard Psychological Report (SPR), contained primarily norm-referenced data (the results of various assessment instruments). The alternative assessment reports were based on Feuerstein's Learning Potential Assessment Device (LPAD) (Feuerstein, Rand, Hoffman, & Miller, 1980), which has been suggested as a valuable alternative to Standard Psychological Reports. In general, the LPAD fits the concept of assessment of various cognitive functions and determination of the effectiveness of various types of mediation.

In using the LPAD, the examiner functions as a teacher, attempting to discover how the student accomplishes various learning tasks. Unfortunately, the results of the Hoy and Retish study were inconclusive with respect to any clear-cut superiority of either the traditional Standard Psychological Report or process-oriented LPAD. Teachers who evaluated these reports were divided in their opinions of their value and applicability in the practical educational setting. Perhaps the only clear concensus with regard to assessment reports relates to the need to remember that they are modes of communication in which report writers must continue to strive for clarity and understandability.

References

Abbott, D. A., & Meredith, W. H. (1986). Strengths of parents with retarded children. *Family Relations, 40,* 371-375.

Abidin, R. R. (1986). *Parenting stress index* (2nd ed.). Charlottesville, VA: Pediatric Psychology Press.

Achenbach, T. M. (1981). *Child behavior checklist for ages 4-16.* Burlington: University of Vermont.

Achenbach, T. M. (1986). *Child behavior checklist for ages 2-3.* Burlington: University of Vermont.

Achenbach, T. M. (1986). *Direct observation form—Revised edition.* Burlington: University of Vermont.

Achenbach, T. M., & Edelbrock, C. (1980). *Teacher's report form.* Burlington: University of Vermont.

Adams, G. (1984a). *Comprehensive test of adaptive behavior.* San Antonio, TX: Psychological Corp.

Adams, G. (1984b). *Normative adaptive behavior checklist.* San Antonio, TX: Psychological Corp.

Adams, S. (1979) *Adston mathematics skill series: Common fractions.* Baton Rouge, LA: Adston Educational Enterprises.

Adams, S., & Ellis, L. (1979). *Adston mathematics skill series: Working with whole numbers.* Baton Rouge, LA: Adston Educational Enterprises.

Adams, S., & Sauls, C. (1979). *Adston mathematics skill series: Readiness for operations.* Baton Rouge, LA: Adston Educational Enterprises.

Adams, W., Erb, L., & Sheslow, D. (1988). *Test of academic progress.* San Antonio, TX: Psychological Corp.

Alpern, G., Boll, T., & Shearer, M. (1980). *Developmental profile II*. Aspen, CO: Psychological Development Publications.

American Educational Research Association, American Psychological Association, & National Council on Measurement in Education (joint committee). (1985). *Standards for educational and psychological testing. Washington, D.C.: American Psychological Association.*

American Guidance Service/Test Division. *(1979). Minnesota spatial relations test.* Circle Pines, MN: American Guidance Service.

American Psychological Association. (1981). Ethical principles of psychologists. *American Psychologist, 36,* 633-638.

Anastasi, A. (1982). *Psychological testing*. New York: Macmillan.

Anderhalter, O. F. (1989). *School readiness test*. Bensenville, IL: Scholastic Testing Service.

Andersen, V., & Thompson, K. (1979). *Test of written English*. Novato, CA: Academic Therapy Publications.

Apgar, V. (1953). APGAR rating scale: A proposal for a new method of resolution of the newborn infant. *Current Research in Anesthesia & Analgesia, 32,* 260-267.

Arena, J. (1982). *Diagnostic spelling potential test*. Novato, CA: Academic Therapy Publications.

Armenia, J. W., Kamp, D., McDonald, D., & Von Kuster, L. (1975). *Wisconsin design for math skill development*. Minneapolis: National Computer Systems.

Ayres, J. (1972). *Southern California sensory integration tests*. Los Angeles: Western Psychological Services.

Ayres, J. (1987). *Sensory integration and PRAXIS tests*. Los Angeles: Western Psychological Services.

Bader, L. (1983). *Bader language and reading inventory*. New York: Macmillan.

Bagley, M. T., & Greene, J. F. (1981). *Peer attitudes toward the handicapped scale*. Austin, TX: Pro-Ed.

Bailey, D. B., Jr., & Simeonsson, R. J. (1988a). *Family assessment in early intervention*. Columbus, OH: Charles E. Merrill.

Bailey, D. B., Jr., & Simeonsson, R. J. (1988b). In S. L. Odom & M. B. Karnes (Eds.), *Early intervention for infants and children with handicaps: An empirical base*. Baltimore: Paul H. Brookes.

Bailey, D. B., Simeonsson, R. J., Winton, P. J., Huntington, G. S., Comfort, M., Isbell, P., O'Donnell, K. J., & Helm, J. M. (1986). Family-focused intervention: A functional model for planning, implementing, and evaluating individualized family services in early intervention. Journal of the Division for Early Childhood, 10, 156-171.

Bankson, N. W. (1977). *Bankson language screening test*. Austin, TX: Pro-Ed.

Barber, L. (1975). *The Barber scales of self-regard for preschool children.* Schenectady, NY: Union College.

Bassler, O. C., Beers, M. I., Richardson, L. I., & Thurman, R. L. (1979). Peabody mathematics readiness test. Bensenville, IL: Scholastic Testing Service.

Bayley, N. (1984). *Bayley scales of infant development.* San Antonio, TX: Psychological Corp.

Beatty, L. S., Madden, R., Gardner, E. F., & Karlsen, B. (1984). *Stanford diagnostic mathematics test.* San Antonio, TX: Psychological Corp.

Becker, R. C. (1981). *Reading-free vocational interest inventory—Revised.* Columbus, OH: Elbern Publications.

Beery, K., & Buktenica, N. (1982). *Developmental test of visual-motor integration.* Chicago: Follett.

Beeson, B., & Pellegrin, L. (1979). *Adston mathematics skill series: Decimal numbers.* Baton Rouge, LA: Adston Educational Enterprises.

Bellak, L., Bellak, S. S., & Haworth, M. R. (1980). *Children's apperception test.* Larchmont, NY: CPS, Inc.

Bender, L. (1951). *Bender-gestalt test.* New York: Grune & Stratton.

Bender, L., & Clawson, A. (1962). *Bender visual motor gestalt test for children.* Los Angeles: Western Psychological Services.

Bennett, G. K., Seashore, H. G., & Wesman, A. G. (1981). *Differential aptitude tests.* San Antonio, TX: Psychological Corp.

Bennett, G. W. (1970). *Bennett mechanical comprehension test.* San Antonio, TX: Psychological Corp.

Berkell, D. E., & Brown, J. M. (1989). *Transition from school to work for persons with disabilities.* New York: Longman.

Bernstein, D., & Tiegerman, E. (1985). *Language and communication disorders.* Columbus, OH: Charles Merrill.

Blankenship, C. S. (1985). Using curriculum-based assessment data to make instructional decisions. *Exceptional Children, 52,* 233-238.

Bliss, L. S., & Allen, D. V. (1983). *Screening kit of language development.* East Aurora, NY: Slosson Educational Publications.

Block, J., & Block, J. (1980). *California child Q-sort set.* Palo Alto, CA: Consulting Psychologists Press.

Boder, E., & Jarrico, S. (1982). *Boder test of reading-spelling patterns.* New York: Grune & Stratton.

Boehm, A. (1986). *Boehm test of basic concepts—Revised.* San Antonio, TX: Psychological Corp.

Boehm, A. (1986). *Boehm test of basic concepts—Preschool version.* San Antonio, TX: Psychological Corp.

Bossone, R. M. (1979). *Writing proficiency program.* Monterey, CA: CTB/McGraw-Hill.

Botel, M. (1978). *Botel reading inventory.* Chicago: Follett.

Bracken, B. (1984). *Bracken basic concept scale.* San Antonio, TX: Psychological Corp.

Bradley-Johnson, S. (1987). *Cognitive abilities scale.* Austin, TX: Pro-Ed.

Bray, C. M., & Wiig, E. H. (1987). *Let's talk inventory for children.* San Antonio, TX: Psychological Corp.

Brazelton, T. B. (1973). *Neonatal behavior assessment scale.* Philadelphia: J.B. Lippincott.

Bricker, D., Bailey, E., & Gentry, D. (1985). *The evaluation and programming system for infants and young children.* Eugene: University of Oregon.

Brigance, A. H. (1977). *Brigance diagnostic inventory of basic skills.* North Billerica, MA: Curriculum Associates.

Brigance, A. H. (1978). *Brigance diagnostic inventory of early development.* North Billerica, MA: Curriculum Associates.

Brigance, A. H. (1980). *Brigance diagnostic inventory of essential skills.* North Billerica, MA: Curriculum Associates.

Brigance, A. H. (1983). *Brigance diagnostic comprehensive inventory of basic skills.* North Billerica, MA: Curriculum Associates.

Britton, J. (1970). *Language and learning.* Harmondsworth, Middlesex, England: Penguin.

Brolin, D. (Ed.). (1973, 1983, 1988). *Life-centered career education: A competency based approach* (1st, 2nd, 3rd eds.). Reston, VA: Council for Exceptional Children.

Bromwich, R. (1981). *Working with parents and infants: An interactional approach.* Baltimore: University Park Press.

Brown, L., & Coleman, M. C. (1988). *Index of personality characteristics.* Austin, TX: Pro-Ed.

Brown, L., & Hammill, D. (1982). *Perfil de evaluación del comportamiento.* Austin, TX: Pro-Ed.

Brown, L., & Hammill, D. (1983). *Behavior rating profile.* Austin, TX: Pro-Ed.

Brown, L., & Leigh, J. E. (1983). *Adaptive behavior inventory.* Austin, TX: Pro-Ed.

Brown, L., Sherbenou, R. J., & Dollar, S. K. (1982). *Test of nonverbal intelligence.* Austin, TX: Pro-Ed.

Brown, V., Hammill, D., & Weiderholt, J. L. (1986). Test of reading comprehension. Austin, TX: Pro-Ed.

Brown, V., & McEntire, E. (1984). *Test of mathematical abilities.* Austin, TX: Pro-Ed.

Brueckner, L. J. (1955). *Diagnostic tests and self-helps in arithmetic.* Monterey, CA: CTB/McGraw-Hill.

Bruininks, R. H. (1978). *Bruininks-Oseretsky test of motor proficiency.* Circle Pines, MN: American Guidance Service.

Bruininks, R. H., Rynders, J. E., & Gross, J. C. (1974). Social acceptance of mildly retarded pupils in resource rooms and regular classes. *American Journal of Mental Deficiency, 78,* 377-383.

Bruininks, R. H., Woodcock, R., Weatherman, R., & Hill, B. (1984). *Scales of independent behavior.* Allen, TX: DLM Teaching Resources.

Bryant, B. R., & Bryant, D. L. (1983a). *Test of articulation performance—Diagnostic.* Austin, TX: Pro-Ed.

Bryant, B. R., & Bryant, D. L. (1983b). *Test of articulation performance—Screen.* Austin, TX: Pro-Ed.

Bullock, L. M., & Wilson, M. J. (1988). *Behavior dimension rating scale.* Allen, TX: DLM Teaching Resources.

Burgemeister, B. B., Blum, L. H., & Lorge, I. (1972). *Columbia mental maturity scale* (3rd ed.). San Antonio, TX: Psychological Corp.

Burks, H. F. (1977). *Burks' behavior rating scales.* Los Angeles: Western Psychological Services.

Burns, P., & Roe, B. (1980). *Informal reading assessment.* Boston: Houghton-Mifflin.

Buswell, G., & Johns, L. (1925). *Fundamental processes in arithmetic.* Muncie, IN: Allen House.

Bzock, K., & League, R. (1971). *Receptive-expressive emergent language scale.* Baltimore: University Park Press.

Caldwell & Bradley (1979). *Home observation for the measurement of environment.* Little Rock, Arkansas: University of Arkansas at Little Rock

Campione, J. C. (1989). Assisted assessment: A taxonomy of approaches and an outline of strengths and weaknesses. *Journal of Learning Disabilities, 22,* 151-165.

Carrow, E. (1974). *Carrow elicited language inventory.* Austin, TX: Learning Concepts.

Carrow-Woolfolk, E. (1985). *Test for auditory comprehension of language-revised.* Allen, TX: DLM Teaching Resources.

Cassel, R. N. (1962). *Child behavior rating scale.* Los Angeles: Western Psychological Services.

Cattell, P. (1969). *Cattell infant intelligence scale.* San Antonio, TX: Psychological Corp.

Chadsey-Rusch, J., Hanley-Maxwell, H. C., Phelps, L. A., & Rusch, F. (1986). *School-to-work transition issues and models.* Champaign, IL: U.S. Dept. of Education.

Chadsey-Rusch, J., & Rusch, F. (1988). Ecology of the work place. In R. Gaylord-Ross, *Vocational education for persons with handicaps.* Mountain View, CA: Mayfield Publications.

Clark, G. M., & Knowlton, H. E. (Eds.). (1987). Transition from school to adult life. *Exceptional Children, 53*(6) (entire special issue), 487-563.

Clark, J. B., & Madison, C. L. (1986). *Clark-Madison test of oral language.* Tigard, OR: C.C. Publications.

Clary, L. (1976). Tips for testing reading informally in the content areas. *Journal of Reading, 20,* 156-157.

Collier, C. (1985). A comparison of acculturation and education characteristics of referred and nonreferred culturally and linguistically different children. *Dissertation Abstracts, 46,* 2993A.

Collier, C. (1988). *Assessing minority students with learning and behavior problems.* Lindale, TX: Hamilton Publications.

Colarusso, R. P., & Hammill, D. D. (1972). *Motor-free visual perception test.* San Rafael, CA: Academic Therapy Publications.

Cone, J. D. (1984). *The pyramid scales.* Austin, TX: Pro-Ed.

Connally, A. (1988). *Key math—Revised: A diagnostic inventory of essential mathematics.* Circle Pines, MN: American Guidance Service.

Connard, P. (1984). *The pre-verbal assessment-intervention profile.* Portland, OR: ASIEP Education Co.

Conners, C. K. (1969). A teacher rating scale. *American Journal of Psychiatry, 126,* 884-888.

Cooper, A., & School, B. A. (1982). *Language inventory for teachers.* Novato, CA: Academic Therapy Publications.

Coopersmith, S. (1981). *Coopersmith self-esteem inventory.* Palo Alto, CA: Consulting Psychologists Press.

Coopersmith, S., & Gilberts, R. (1982). *Behavioral academic self-esteem.* Palo Alto, CA: Consulting Psychologists Press.

Coplan, J. (1987). *Early language milestone scale.* Austin, TX: Pro-Ed.

Council for Exceptional Children. (1983). Code of ethics and standards for professional practice. *Exceptional Children, 50,* 205-209.

Crawford, J. E., & Crawford, D. M. (1956). *Crawford small parts dexterity test.* San Antonio, TX: Psychological Corp.

Critchlow, D. E. (1974). *Dos amigos verbal language scales.* East Aurora, NY: United Educational Services.

CTB/McGraw-Hill. (1972). *Prescriptive reading inventory.* Monterey, CA: CTB/McGraw-Hill.

CTB/McGraw-Hill. (1983). *DMI mathematics systems.* Monterey, CA: CTB/McGraw-Hill.

Deno, S., & Fuchs, L. (1987). Developing curriculum-based measurement systems for data-based special education problem solving. *Focus on Exceptional Children, 19*(6), 1-16.

Doll, E. (1966). *Preschool attainment record.* Circle Pines, MN: American Guidance Service.

Doolittle, J. H. (1989). *Creative reasoning test.* Pacific Grove, CA: Midwest Publications.

Doren, M. (1973). *Doren diagnostic reading list of word recognition skills* (2nd ed.). Circle Pines, MN: American Guidance Service.

DuBose, R. F., & Langley, M. B. (1984). *Developmental activities screening inventory.* Austin, TX: Pro-Ed.

Dunn, L. M. (1981). *Peabody picture vocabulary test—Revised edition.* Circle Pines, MN: American Guidance Service.

Dunn, L. M., & Markwardt, F. C. (1989). *Peabody individual achievement test—Revised.* Circle Pines, MN: American Guidance Service.

Dunst, C. J., & Leet, H. E. (1987). Measuring the adequacy of resources in households with young children. *Child: Care, Health, & Development, 13,* 111-125.

Durrell, D. D., & Catterson, J. H. (1980). *Durrell analysis of reading difficulty* (3rd ed.). San Antonio, TX: Psychological Corp.

Dvorine, I. (1958). *Dvorine color vision test.* San Antonio, TX: Psychological Corp.

Edmonston, N. K., & Thane, N. L. (1988). *Test of relational concepts.* Austin, TX: Pro-Ed.

Eisenson, J. (1954). *Examining for aphasia* (2nd ed.). San Antonio, TX: Psychological Corp.

Ekwall, E. (1979). *Ekwall reading inventory.* Boston: Allyn & Bacon.

Elliott, C. D. (1989). *Differential ability scales.* San Antonio, TX: Psychological Corp.

Engen, E., & Engen, T. (1983). *Rhode Island test of language structure.* Austin, TX: Pro-Ed.

Ennis, R. H., & Millman, J. (1985). *Cornell critical thinking tests, levels X and Z.* Pacific Grove, CA: Midwest Publications.

Enright, B. E. (1983). *The Enright diagnostic inventory of basic arithmetic skills.* North Billerica, MA: Curriculum Associates.

Estes, T. H., Estes, J. J., Richards, H. C., & Roettger, D. (1981). *Estes attitude scales.* Austin, TX: Pro-Ed.

Farran, D. C., Kasari, C., Yoder, P., Harber, L., Huntington, G. S., & Comfort-Smith, M. (1987). Rating mother-child interactions in handicapped and at-risk infants. In T. Tamir (Ed.), *Stimulation and intervention in infant development.* London: Freund Publishing House.

Feuerstein, R. (1979). *The dynamic assessment of retarded performers: The learning potential assessment device, theory, instruments, and techniques.* Baltimore: University Park Press.

Feuerstein, R., Rand, Y., Hoffman, M. B., & Miller, R. (1980). *Instrumental enrichment: An intervention program for cognitive modifiability.* Baltimore: University Park Press.

Finn, J. (1982). Patterns in special education placement as revealed by OCR surveys. In K. A. Heller, W. H. Holzman, & S. Messick (Eds.), *Placing children in special education: A strategy for equity* (pp. 322-381). Washington, D.C.: National Academy Press.

Fitts, W. H. (1965). Tennessee Self Concept Scale. Los Angeles: Western Psychological Services.

Folio, M., & Fewell, R. (1983). *Peabody developmental scales.* Allen, TX: DLM Teaching Resources.

Foster, R., Giddan, J., & Stark, J. (1973). *Assessment of children's language comprehension.* Palo Alto, CA: Consulting Psychologists Press.

Fountain Valley Teacher Support System in Mathematics. (1976). Huntington Beach, CA: Zweig Associates.

Frankenburg, W., Dodds, J., & Fandal, A. (1981). *Denver developmental screening tests—Revised.* Denver: Denver Developmental Materials.

Frostig, M., Lefever, W., & Whittlesey, R. B. (1966). *Developmental test of visual perception.* Palo Alto, CA: Consulting Psychologists Press.

Fudala, J. B. (1978). *Tree/bee test of auditory discrimination.* East Aurora, NY: United Educational Services.

Fudala, J. B., Kunze, L. H., & Ross, J. D. (1974). *Auditory pointing test.* East Aurora, NY: United Educational Services.

Furuno, S., O'Reilly, K., Hosaka, C., Inatsuka, T., Aleman, T., & Zeisloft, B. (1979). *Hawaii early learning profile.* Palo Alto, CA: Vort Corp.

Gallagher, J. J., Scharfman, W., & Bristol, M. (1984). The division of responsibilities in families with preschool handicapped and nonhandicapped children. *Journal of the Division for Early Childhood, 8,* 3-12.

Gardner, M. F. (1979). *The expressive one-word picture vocabulary test.* Novato, CA: Academic Therapy Publications.

Gardner, M. F. (1985). *Receptive one-word picture vocabulary test.* Novato, CA: Academic Therapy Publications.

Gates, A. I., McKillop, A. S., & Horowitz, E. C. (1981). *Gates-McKillop-Horowitz reading diagnostic tests.* New York: Teachers College Press.

Gauthier, S. V., & Madison, C. L. (1983). *Kindergarten language screening test.* Tigard, OR: C.C. Publications.

Gaylord-Ross, R. (1988). *Vocational education for persons with handicaps.* Mountain View, CA: Mayfield Publishing.

Gearheart, B., & Gearheart C. (1989). *Learning disabilities: Educational strategies* (5th ed.). Columbus, OH: Charles Merrill.

Geers, A., & Lane, H. (1984). *CID preschool performance scale.* Chicago: Stoelting Co.

Gelb, F. (1978). *Steenburgen diagnostic-prescriptive math program and quick math screening test.* Novato, CA: Academic Therapy Publications.

Gerald, J. E., & Weinstock, G. (1981). *Language proficiency test.* Novato, CA: Academic Therapy Publications.

Gerber, A., & Goehl, H. (1984). *Temple University short syntax inventory.* East Aurora, NY: Slosson Educational Publications.

Gessell, J. (1977). *Diagnostic mathematics inventory.* Monterey, CA: CTB/McGraw-Hill.

Gickling, E., & Thompson, V. (1985). A personal view of curriculum-based assessment. *Exceptional Children, 52,* 205-218.

Gilmore, J. V., & Gilmore, E. C. (1968). *Gilmore oral reading test.* San Antonio, TX: Psychological Corp.

Ginsburg, H., & Baroody, A. J. (1983). *Test of early mathematics ability.* Austin, TX: Pro-Ed.

Ginsburg, H. P., & Mathews, S. C. (1984). *Diagnostic test of arithmetic strategies.* Austin, TX: Pro-Ed.

Giordana, G. (1986). *Informal writing inventory.* Bensenville, IL: Scholastic Testing Service.

Giordana, G. (1988). *Reading comprehension inventory.* Bensenville, IL: Scholastic Testing Service.

Gnagey, T. D. (1979). *Diagnostic screening test: Spelling* (3rd ed.). East Aurora, NY: Slosson Educational Publications.

Gnagey, T. D. (1980). *Diagnostic screening test: Math* (3rd ed.). East Aurora, NY: Slosson Educational Publications.

Gnagey, T. D., & Gnagey, P. D. (1982). *Analytic learning disability assessment.* East Aurora, NY: Slosson Educational Publications.

Goldman, R., & Fristoe, M. (1972). *Goldman-Fristoe test of articulation.* Circle Pines, MN: American Guidance Service.

Goldman, R., Fristoe, M., & Woodcock, R. (1970). *Goldman-Fristoe-Woodcock test of auditory discrimination.* Circle Pines, MN: American Guidance Service.

Goodman, J. (1981). *Goodman lock box.* Chicago: Stoelting Co.

Goodman, K. (Ed.). (1973). *Miscue analysis: Applications to reading instruction.* Urbana, IL: National Council of Teachers of English.

Goodman, Y., & Burke, C. (1972). *Reading miscue inventory.* New York: Macmillan.

Gordon, L. V. (1981). *Gordon occupational checklist.* San Antonio, TX: Psychological Corp.

Gough, H. G. (1987). *California psychological inventory—Revised*. San Antonio, TX: Psychological Corp.

Gough, H. G., & Heilbrun, A. B. (1980). *The adjective check list*. Palo Alto, CA: Consulting Psychologists Press.

Graden, J., Casey, A., & Christenson, S. (1985). Implementing a prereferral intervention system: Part 1. The model. *Exceptional Children, 51,* 377-384.

Graham, F. K., & Kendall, B. S. (1960). *Memory for designs test*. Missoula, MT: Psychological Test Specialists.

Greenbaum, C. R. (1987). *The spellmaster assessment and teaching system*. Austin, TX: Pro-Ed.

Guerin, G. R., & Maier, A. S. (1983). *Informal assessment in education*. Palo Alto, CA: Mayfield Publishing.

Guilford, J. P. (1971). *Creativity tests for children*. Beverly Hills, CA: Sheridan Psychological Services.

Hall, L. G., & Tarrier, R. B. (1987). *Hall occupational orientation inventory—Revised*. Bensenville, IL: Scholastic Testing Service.

Halpern, A., Irvin, L., & Landman, J. (1979). *Tests for everyday living*. Monterey, CA: CTB/McGraw-Hill.

Halpern, A., Raffeld, P., Irvin, L. K., Link, R., & Munkres, A. (1986). *Social and prevocational information battery—Revised*. Monterey, CA: CTB/McGraw-Hill.

Hammill, D. D. (1985). *Detroit tests of learning aptitude—2*. Austin, TX: Pro-Ed.

Hammill, D. D., Brown, V. L., Larsen, S. C., & Wiederholt, J. L. (1987). *Test of adolescent language—2*. Austin, TX: Pro-Ed.

Hammill, D. D., & Bryant, B. R. (1983, 1986). *Detroit tests of learning aptitude—primary*. Austin, TX: Pro-Ed.

Hammill, D. D., & Larsen, S. C. (1988). *Test of written language—2*. Austin, TX: Pro-Ed.

Hammill, D. D., & Leigh, J. E. (1983a). *Basic school skills inventory—Diagnostic*. Austin, TX: Pro-Ed.

Hammill, D. D., & Leigh, J. E. (1983b). *Basic school skills inventory screen*. Austin, TX: Pro-Ed.

Hargrove, L. J., & Poteet, J. A. (1984). *Assessment in special education: The education evaluation*. Englewood Cliffs, NJ: Prentice-Hall.

Harrington, R., & Gibson, E. (1986). Preassessment procedures for learning disabled children: Are they effective? *Journal of Learning Disabilities, 19,* 548-541.

Haworth, M. R. (1970). *Primary visual motor test*. New York: Grune & Stratton.

Hedrick, D. D., Prather, E. M., & Tobin, A. R. (1984). *Sequenced inventory of communication development* (rev.). Seattle: University of Washington Press.

Heward, W. L., & Orlansky, M. D. (1988). *Exceptional children* (3rd ed.). Columbus, OH: Charles Merrill.

Hiskey, M. S. (1976). *Hiskey-Nebraska test of learning aptitude.* Lincoln, NE: Marshall Hiskey.

Holland, J. L. (1985). *Self directed search.* Odessa, FL: Psychological Assessment Resources.

Hollands, R. (1983). *Progress tests in math.* Hampshire, England: Macmillan Education.

Holroyd, J. (1974). The questionnaire on resources and stress: An instrument to measure family response to a handicapped member. *Journal of Community Psychology, 2,* 92-94.

Holroyd, J. (1986). *Questionnaire on resources and stress for families with a chronically ill or handicapped member, Manual.* Brandon, VT: Clinical Psychology Publishing.

House, L., & Rogerson, B. S. (1984). *Comprehensive screening tool for determining optimal communication mode.* East Aurora, NY: United Educational Services.

Howell, K. W., & Morehead, M. K. (1987). *Curriculum-based evaluation for special and remedial education.* Columbus, OH: Charles Merrill.

Howell, K. W., Zucker, S. H., & Morehead, M. K. (1982a). *Multilevel academic skills inventory: Math program.* San Antonio, TX: Psychological Corp.

Howell, K. W., Zucker, S. H., & Morehead, M. K. (1982b). *Multilevel academic skills inventory: Reading program.* San Antonio, TX: Psychological Corp.

Howell, K. W., Zucker, S. H., & Morehead, M. K. (1982c). *Multilevel academic survey test.* San Antonio, TX: Psychological Corp.

Hoy, M. P., & Retish, P. M. (1984). A comparison of two types of assessment reports. *Exceptional Children, 51,* 225-229.

Hresko, W. P. (1988). *Test of early written language.* Austin, TX: Pro-Ed.

Hresko, W. P., & Brown, L. (1984). *Test of early socioemotional development.* Austin, TX: Pro-Ed.

Hresko, W. P., Reid, D. K., & Hammill, D. D. (1981). *Test of early language development.* Austin, TX: Pro-Ed.

Hresko, W. P., Reid, D. K., Hammill, D. D., Ginsburg, H. P., & Baroody, A. J. (1988). *Screening children for related early educational needs.* Austin, TX: Pro-Ed.

Hudson, F., Colson, S., Welch, D., Banikowski, A., & Mehring, T. (1988). *Hudson education skills inventory.* Austin, TX: Pro-Ed.

Hutton, J. B., & Roberts, T. G. (1986). *Social-emotional dimension scale.* Austin, TX: Pro-Ed.

Ireton, H., & Thwing, E. (1979). *Minnesota child development inventory.* Minneapolis: Behavior Systems.

Jastak, J., & Jastak, S. (1979). *Wide range interest-opinion test.* Wilmington, DE: Jastak Associates.

Jastak, J., & Jastak, S. (1980). *Wide range employability sample test.* Wilmington, DE: Jastak Associates.

Jastak, S., & Wilkinson, G. S. (1984). *Wide range achievement test—Revised.* Wilmington, DE: Jastak Assessment Systems.

Jesness, C. F. (1971). *Jesness behavior check list.* Palo Alto, CA: Consulting Psychologists Press.

Jesness, C. F. (1972). *Jesness inventory of adolescent personality.* Palo Alto, CA: Consulting Psychologists Press.

Jewish Employment and Vocational Service (1976). *JEVS work sample evaluation system.* Philadelphia: Author.

Johns, J. (1982). *Advanced reading inventory.* Dubuque, IA: Kendall-Hunt.

Johnsen, S. K., & Corn, A. (1987). *Screening assessment for gifted elementary students.* Austin, TX: Pro-Ed.

Johnson, O. G., & Boyd, H. F. (1981). *Analysis of coping style.* San Antonio, TX: Psychological Corp.

Jordan, B. T. (1980). *Jordan left-right reversal test—Revised.* San Rafael, CA: Academic Therapy Publications.

Jordan, J. B., Gallagher, J. J., Hutinger, P. L., & Karnes, M. B. (1988). *Early childhood special education: Birth to three.* Reston, VA: Council for Exceptional Children.

Kamm, K., Miles, P., Van Blaricon, V., Harris, M., & Stewart, D. (1972). *Wisconsin tests of reading skill development.* Minneapolis: National Computer Systems.

Karlin, R. (1973). Evaluation for diagnostic teaching. In W. MacGinitie (Ed.), *Assessment problems in reading.* Newark, DE: International Reading Association.

Karlsen, B., & Gardner, E. F. (1984). *Stanford diagnostic reading test* (3rd ed.). San Antonio, TX: Psychological Corp.

Karnes, F. A., & Chauvin, J. (1985). *Leadership skills inventory.* East Aurora, NY: DOK Publishers.

Kaufman, A. S., & Kaufman, N. L. (1983). *Kaufman assessment battery for children.* Circle Pines, MN: American Guidance Service.

Kaufman, A. S., & Kaufman, N. L. (1985). *Kaufman test of educational achievement.* Circle Pines, MN: American Guidance Service.

Keith, R. W. (1986). *SCAN: A Screening test for auditory processing disorders.* San Antonio, TX: Psychological Corp.

Kimmell, G. M., & Wahl, J. (1981). *Screening test for auditory perception—Revised.* Novato, CA: Academic Therapy Publications.

Kingston, N. D. (1985). *Test of computational processes.* Allen, TX: DLM Teaching Resources.

Kinzler, M. C., & Johnson, C. C. (1983). *The Joliet 3-minute speech and language screen.* Tucson, AZ: Communication Skill Builders.

Kirk, S., McCarthy, J., & Kirk, W. (1978). *Illinois test of psycholinguistic abilities.* Baltimore: University Park Press.

Knoblach, H., Stevens, F., & Malone, A. (1980). *The revised Gesell developmental schedules.* Hagerstown, MD: Harper & Row.

Koenig, C., & Kunzelmann, H. (1980). *Classroom learning screening manual.* San Antonio, TX: Psychological Corp.

Kohn, M. (1986a). *Kohn problem checklist—Research edition.* San Antonio, TX: Psychological Corp.

Kohn, M. (1986b). *Kohn social competence scale—Research edition.* San Antonio, TX: Psychological Corp.

Koppitz, E. M. (1978). *Visual aural digit span test.* New York: Grune & Stratton.

Kowalchuk, B., & King, D. (1988). *Life orientation inventory.* Austin, TX: Pro-Ed.

Krug, D. A., Arick, J. R., & Almond, P. J. (1980). *Autism screening instrument for educational planning.* Portland, OR: ASIEP Education Co.

Kuder, G. (1987). *Kuder general interest survey.* Chicago: Science Research Associates.

Lambert, N. M., Hartsough, C.S., & Bower, E.M. (1979). *Process for the Assessment of Effective Student Functiong.* Monterey, CA: CTB/McGraw-Hill.

Lambert, N. M., Bower, E. M., & Hartsough, C. S. (1979). *Pupil behavior rating scale.* Monterey, CA: CTB/McGraw-Hill.

Lambert, N., Windmiller, M., Tharinger, D., & Cole, L. (1981). *AAMD adaptive behavior scale—School edition.* Monterey, CA: CTB/McGraw-Hill.

Lange, M., & Tisher, M. (1983). *Children's depression scale.* Hawthorn, Victoria, Australia: Australian Council for Educational Research, Ltd.

Larsen, S., & Hammill, D. (1986). *Test of written spelling—2.* Austin, TX: Pro-Ed.

Larsen, S., & Hammill, D. (1989). *Test of legible handwriting.* Austin, TX: Pro-Ed.

Layton, T. L., & Holmes, D.W. (1985). *Carolina picture vocabulary test.* Tulsa, OK: Modern Education Corp.

Lee, L. (1969). *Northwestern syntax screening test.* Evanston, IL: Northwestern University Press.

Leiter, R. G., & Arthur, G. (1955). *Leiter international performance scale.* Chicago: Stoelting Co.

Leland, H., Shoace, M., McElwain, D., & Christie, R. (1980). *Adaptive behavior scale for infants and early childhood.* Columbus, OH: Ohio State University, Nisonger Center.

LeMay, D., Griffin, P., & Sanford, A. (1981). *Learning accomplishment profile: Diagnostic edition* (rev.). Lewisville, NC: Kaplan School Supply.

Lewis, M., & Michalson, L. (1983). *Scales of socio-emotional development.* New York: Plenum Press.

Lillie, D., & Harbin, G. (1975). *Carolina developmental profile.* Lewisville, NC: Kaplan Co.

Los Angeles Unified School District. (1985). *Screening program for gifted and talented, grades 1 and 2* (Publication No. EC-5789). Los Angeles: Author.

Lundell, K.,Brown, W., & Evans, J. (1976). *Criterion test of basic skills.* Novato, CA: Academic Therapy Publications.

MacGinitie, W. (1978). *Gates-MacGinitie reading tests* (2nd ed.). Chicago: Riverside Publishing.

Mahoney, G., Finger, I., & Powell, A. (1985). Relationship of maternal behavioral style to the development of organically impaired mentally retarded infants. *American Journal of Mental Deficiency, 90,* 296-302.

Mardell-Czudnowski, C., & Goldenberg, D. (1983). *Developmental indicators for the assessment of learning—Revised.* Edison, NJ: Childcraft Education Corp.

Marsh, H. W. (1988). *Self-description questionnaire: Research edition.* San Antonio, TX: Psychological Corp.

Martinek, T., & Zaichkowsky, L. D. (1977). *Martinek-Zaichkowsky self-concept scale for children.* Creve Coeur, MO: Psychologists & Educators, Inc.

McCarney, S. B., Leigh, J. E., & Cornbleet, J. A. (1983). *Behavior evaluation scale.* Austin, TX: Pro-Ed.

McCarthy, D. (1972a). *McCarthy scales of children's abilities.* San Antonio, TX: Psychological Corp.

McCarthy, D. (1972b). *McCarthy Screening test.* San Antonio, TX: Psychological Corp.

McCarthy, J., Bos, C., Lund, K., Glattke, J., & Vaughn, S. (1985). *Arizona basic assessment and curriculum utilization system for young handicapped children.* Denver: Love Publishing.

McCollum, J. A., & Stayton, V. D. (1985). Infant/parent interaction: Studies and intervention guidelines based on the SIAI model. *Journal of the Division for Early Childhood, 9*(2), 125-135.

McCullough, C. M. (1963). *McCullough word analysis test.* Boston: Ginn.

McDaniel, E. L. (1973). *Inferred self-concept scale.* Los Angeles: Western Psychological Services.

McDermott, P. A., & Watkins, M. W. (1985). *The McDermott multidimensional assessment of children.* San Antonio, TX: Psychological Corp.

McGonigal, M. J., & Garland, C. W. (1988). The individualized family service plan and the early intervention team: Team and family issues and recommended practices. *Infants & Young Children, 1*(1), 10-21.

McLoughlin, J. A., & Lewis, R. B. (1986). *Assessing special students*. Second edition. Columbus, OH: Charles Merrill.

McLoughlin, J. A., & Lewis, R. B. (1990). *Assessing special students*. Third edition. Columbus, OH: Charles Merrill.

Meadow, K. P., Getson, P., Lee, C.K., & Stamper, L. (1983). *Meadow-Kendall social-emotional assessment inventory for deaf and hearing impaired students (school-age level)*. Washington, D.C.: Outreach Gallaudet College.

Meadow, K. P., Karchmer, M. A., Peterson, L. M., & Rudner, L. (1983). *Meadow-Kendall social-emotional assessment inventory for deaf and hearing impaired students*. Washington, D.C.: Outreach Gallaudet College.

Mecham, M. J., & Jones, D. (1978). *Utah test of language development*. Austin, TX: Pro-Ed.

Meisels, S., & Wiske, M. (1983). *Early screening inventory*. New York: Teachers College Press.

Mercer, J., & Lewis, J. (1977). *System of multicultural pluralistic assessment*. San Antonio, TX: Psychological Corp.

Mercer, J., & Lewis, J. (1978). *Adaptive behavior inventory for children*. San Antonio, TX: Psychological Corp.

Milani-Comparetti, A., & Gidoni, E. A. (1977). *Milani-Comparetti developmental scale*. Omaha, NE: Meyers Children's Rehabilitation Institute.

Miller, J. F., & Yoder, D. (1984). *Miller-Yoder language comprehension test*. Austin, TX: Pro-Ed.

Miller, L. C. (1977). *School behavior checklist*. Los Angeles: Western Psychological Services.

Miller, L. J. (1982). *Miller assessment for preschoolers*. San Antonio, TX: Psychological Corp.

Mooney, R. L., & Gordon, L. V. (1950). The Mooney problem check lists (rev.). San Antonio, TX: Psychological Corp.

Moos, R. H., & Trickett, E. J. (1974). *Classroom environment scale*. Palo Alto, CA: Consulting Psychologists Press.

Morgan, D. A., & Guilford, A. M. (1984). *Adolescent language screening test*. Tulsa, OK: Modern Education Corp.

Mumm, M., Secord, W., & Dykstra, K. (1980). *Merrill language screening test*. San Antonio, TX: Psychological Corp.

Murray, H. A. (1943). *Thematic apperception test*. Cambridge, MA: Harvard University Press.

Mutti, M., Sterling, H. M., & Spalding, N. V. (1978). *Quick neurological test—Revised*. San Rafael, CA: Academic Therapy Publications.

Myers, C. E., Mink, I., & Nihira, K. (1977). *Home qualilty rating scale*. Pomona, CA: UCLD/Neuropsychiatric Institute, Pacific State Hospital Research Group.

Myklebust, H. R. (1965). *The picture story language test*. New York: Grune & Stratton.

Myklebust, H. R. (1981). *Pupil rating scale (revised): Screening for Learning Disabilities*. Los Angeles: Western Psychological Services.

Neeper, R., & Lahey, B. B. (1988). *Comprehensive behavior rating scale for children*. San Antonio, TX: Psychological Corp.

Newborg, J., Stock, J., Wnek, L., Guidubaldi, J., & Suinicki, J. (1984). *Battelle developmental inventory*. Allen, TX: DLM Teaching Resources.

Newborg, J., Stock, J., Wnek, L., Guidubaldi, J., & Suinicki, J. (1988). *Battelle developmental inventory screening test*. Allen, TX: DLM Teaching Resources.

Newcomer, P., & Bryant, B. (1986). *Diagnostic achievement test for adolescents*. Austin, TX: Pro-Ed.

Newcomer, P., & Curtis, D. (1984). *Diagnostic achievement battery*. Austin, TX: Pro-Ed.

Newcomer, P., & Hammill, D. D. (1988). *Test of language development—2, primary*. Austin, TX: Pro-Ed.

Olswang, L. B., Stoel-Gammon, C., Coggins, T. E., & Carpenter, R. L. (1987). *Assessing linguistic behaviors*. Tucson, AZ: Communication Skill Builders.

Parker, R. M. (1983a). *OASIS aptitude survey*. Austin, TX: Pro-Ed.

Parker, R. M. (1983b). *OASIS interest schedule*. Austin, TX: Pro-Ed.

Peterson, N. L. (1987). *Early intervention for handicapped and at-risk children*. Denver: Love Publishing.

Piaget, J. (1965). *The child's concept of number*. New York: Norton.

Piers, E. V., & Harris, D.B. (1969). *Piers-Harris children's self-concept scale*. Los Angeles: Western Psychological Services.

Pollner, M., & McDonald-Wiler, L. (1985). The social construction of unreality: A case study of a family's attribution of competence to a severely retarded child. *Family Process, 24,* 241-254.

Porch, B. E. (1979). *Porch index of communicative ability in children*. Palo Alto, CA: Consulting Psychologists Press.

Porch, B. E. (1981). *Porch index of communicative ability*. Palo Alto, CA: Consulting Psychologists Press.

Porter, R. B., & Cattell, R. B. (1982). *Children's personality questionnaire*. Champaign, IL: Institute for Personality & Ability Testing.

Prather, E. M., Breecher, S., Stafford, M. L., & Wallace, E. (1980). *Screening test of adolescent language*. Seattle: University of Washington Press.

Prinz, M., & Weiner, F. F. (1987). *Pragmatics screening test*. San Antonio, TX: Psychological Corp.

Project RHISE. (1979). *Rockford infant developmental evaluation scales*. Bensenville, IL: Scholastic Testing Service.

Quay, H. C., & Peterson, D. R. (1983). *The behavior problem checklist—Revised.* Coral Gables, FL: Herbert C. Quay.

Raven, J. C. (1938, 1947, 1976). *Raven progressive matrices.* London: H.K. Lewis.

Reed, V. (1980). Writing pupil assessment reports. In B. R. Gearheart & E. P. Willenberg, *Application of pupil assessment information.* Denver: Love Publishing.

Regional Resource Center. (1971). *Diagnostic math inventories* (Project No. 472917, Contract No. OEC-0-9-472-917-4591 [608]). Eugene: University of Oregon.

Regional Resource Center. (1971). *Diagnostic reading inventory* (Project No. 472917, Contract No. OEC-0-9-472917-4591 [608]). Eugene: University of Oregon.

Reid, D. K., Hresko, W. P., & Hammill, D. D. (1981). *Test of early reading ability.* Austin, TX: Pro-Ed.

Reid, K. (1988). *Teaching the learning disabled: A cognitive developmental approach.* Boston: Allyn & Bacon.

Reisman, F. (1978). *A guide to the diagnostic teaching of arithmetic* (2nd ed.). Columbus, OH: Charles E. Merrill.

Reisman, F. (1985). *Sequential assessment of mathematics inventory.* San Antonio, TX: Psychological Corp.

Richmond, B. O., & Kicklighter, R. H. (1980). *Children's adaptive behavior scale.* Atlanta: Humanics.

Riley, A. M. (1984a). *Autistic behavior composite checklist and profile.* Tucson, AZ: Communication Skill Builders.

Riley, A. M. (1984b). *Evaluating acquired skills in communication.* Tucson, AZ: Communication Skill Builders.

Roach, E. G., & Kephart, N. C. (1966) *Purdue perceptual-motor survey.* San Antonio, TX: Psychological Corp.

Roberts, J. R. (1969). *Pennsylvania bi-manual worksample.* Circle Pines, MN: American Guidance Service.

Robinson, E. A., & Eyberg, S. M. (1981). The dyadic parent-child interaction coding system: Standardization and validation. *Journal of Consulting & Clinical Psychology, 49,* 245-250.

Rosenberg, S., Robinson, C., & Beckman, P. (1984). Teaching skills inventory: a measure of parent performance. *Journal of the Division for Early Childhood, 8,* 107-113.

Ryan, M. (1979). *Minnesota clerical test.* Austin, TX: Psychological Corp.

Salvia, J., & Ysseldyke, J. E. (1988). *Assessment in special and remedial education.* Boston: Houghton Mifflin.

249

Samuda, R. J. (1976). Problems and issues in assessment of minority group children. In R. L. Jones (Ed.), *Mainstreaming and the minority child*. Reston, VA: Council for Exceptional Children.

Sanford, A. (1981). *Learning accomplishment profile for infants*. Lewisville, NC: Kaplan School Supply.

Schafer, D. S., & Moersch, M. S. (Eds.). (1981). *Developmental programming for infants and young children*. Ann Arbor: University of Michigan Press.

Scott, M., Ebbert, A., & Price, D. (1986). Assessing and teaching employability skills with prevocational work samples. *Directive Teacher, 8*(1). (NCEMMH, Ohio State University).

Semel, E., & Wiig, E. (1987). *Clinical evaluation of language functions—Diagnostic battery*. San Antonio, TX: Psychological Corp.

Shames, G. H., & Wiig, E. H. (Eds.) (1986). *Human communication disorders: An introduction*. Columbus, OH: Charles Merrill.

Shearer, D. E., Billingsley, J., Froham, A., Hilliard, J., Johnson, F., & Shearer, M. (1976). *Portage guide to early education—Revised*. Portage, WI: Portage Project.

Shub, A. N., Carlin, J. A., Friedman, R. L., Kaplan, J. M., & Katien, J. C. (1973). *Diagnosis: An instructional aid: Reading*. Chicago: Science Research Associates.

Shulman, B. (1986). *Test of pragmatic skills*. Tucson, AZ: Communication Skill Builders.

Silvaroli, N. J. (1986). *Classroom reading inventory* (5th ed.). Dubuque, IA: Wm. C. Brown Co.

Simon, C. S. (1987). *Evaluating communicative competence*. Tucson, AZ: Communication Skill Builders.

Singer Systems. (1982). *Singer Vocational Evaluation System*. Rochester, NY: Singer Co.

Slingerland, B. (1970, 1974). *Slingerland screening tests for identifying children with specific language disability*. Cambridge, MA: Educators Publishing Service.

Slosson, R. L. (1963). *Slosson oral reading test*. East Aurora, NY: Slosson Educational Publications.

Slosson, R. L. (1983). *Slosson intelligence test*. East Aurora, NY: Slosson Educational Publications.

Sonnenschein, J. (1983). *Basic achievement skills individual screener*. San Antonio, TX: Psychological Corp.

Spache, G. D. (1981). *Diagnostic reading scales—Revised*. Monterey, CA: CTB/McGraw-Hill.

Spadafore, G. J. (1983). Spadafore diagnostic reading test. Novato, CA: Academic Therapy Publications.

Spanier, G. B. (1976). Measuring dyadic adjustment: New scales for assessing the quality of marriage and similar dyads. *Journal of Marriage & the Family, 38*, 15-28.

250

Sparrow, S. S., Balla, D. A., & Cicchetti, D. V. (1984). *Vineland adaptive behavior scales*. Circle Pines, MN: American Guidance Service.

Spivak, G., Haimes, P., & Spotts, J. (1966). *Devereux child behavior rating scale*. Devon, PA: Devereux Foundation.

Spivak, G., Haimes, P., & Spotts, J. (1967). *Devereux adolescent behavior rating scale*. Devon, PA: Devereux Foundation.

Spivak, G., & Swift, M. (1967). *Devereux elementary school behavior rating scale*. Devon, PA: Devereux Foundation.

Spivak, G., & Swift, M. (1972). *Hahnemann high school behavior rating scale*. Philadelphia: George Spivak & Marshall Swift.

Spivak, G., & Swift, M. (1975). *Hahnemann elementary school behavior rating scale*. Philadelphia: George Spivak & Marshall Swift.

Stott, D. H., McDermott, P. A., Green, L. F., & Francis, J. (1987). *Study of children's learning styles: Research edition*. San Antonio, TX: Psychological Corp.

Stott, D. H., Moyes, F. A., & Henderson, S. E. (1984). *Test of motor impairment—Henderson revision*. San Antonio, TX: Psychological Corp.

Strom, R. D. (1984). *Parent as a teacher inventory*. Bensenville, IL: Scholastic Testing Service.

Strong, E. R., Hansen, J. C., & Campbell, D. P. (1985). *Strong-Campbell interest inventory*. Stanford, CA: Stanford University Press.

Strotman, D. E., & Steen, M. T. (1977). *Individualized criterion referenced testing—Mathematics*. Tulsa, OK: Educational Development Corp.

Sucher, F., & Allred, R. A. (1981). *The new Sucher-Allred reading placement inventory*. Oklahoma City: Economy Co.

Taylor, R. L. (1985). Measuring adaptive behavior: Issues and instruments. *Focus on Exceptional Children, 18*(2), 1-8.

Temple, C., & Gillet, J. W. (1984). *Language arts: Learning processes and teaching practices*. Boston: Little, Brown.

Terman, L., & Merrill, M. (1972). *Stanford-Binet intelligence scale* (3rd ed.). Boston: Houghton-Mifflin.

Thorndike, R. L., Hagen, E. P., & Sattler, J. M. (1986). *Stanford-Binet intelligence scale* (4th ed.). Chicago: Riverside Publishing Co.

Toronto, A., Leverman, C., Hanna, C., Rosengweis, P., & Maldonado, A. (1975). *Del Rio language screening test, English/Spanish*. Austin, TX: National Educational Laboratory Publishers.

Torrance, E. P. (1966, 1980). *Torrance tests of creative thinking*. Bensenville, IL: Scholastic Testing Services.

Torrance, E. P. (1981). *Thinking creatively in action and movement*. Bensenville, IL: Scholastic Testing Services.

Torrance, E. P., McCarthy, B., & Kolesinski, M. (1987). *Your style of learning and thinking*. Bensenville, IL: Scholastic Testing Services.

Tucker, J. A. (1985). Curriculum-based assessment: An introduction. *Exceptional Children, 52,* 199-204.

Turnbull, A. P., & Turnbull, H. R. (1985). *Parents speak out: Then and now.* Columbus, OH: Charles Merrill.

Turnbull, A. P., & Turnbull, H. R. (1986). *Families, professionals, and exceptionality: A special partnership.* Columbus, OH: Charles Merrill.

Ulrey, G., & Rogers, S. (1982). *Psychological assessment of handicapped infants and young children.* New York: Thieme-Stratton.

Ulrey, J. R., & Biasini, F. J. (1989). Evaluating the difficult child. *Teaching Exceptional Children, 21*(3), 10-13.

Underhill, R. G., Uprichard, A. E., & Heddens, J. W. (1980). *Diagnosing mathematical difficulties.* Columbus, OH: Charles Merrill.

University of Minnesota. (1967a). *Minnesota multiphasic personality inventory.* San Antonio, TX: Psychological Corp.

University of Minnesota. (1967b). *Minnesota rate of manipulation tests.* Minneapolis: University of Minnesota.

U.S. Department of Labor. (1970). *General aptitude test battery.* Washington, D.C.: U.S. Government Printing Office.

Uzgiris, I., & Hunt, J. M. (1975). *Assessment in infancy: Original scales of psychological development.* Urbana: University of Illinois Press.

Venn, J. J., Serwatka, T. S., & Anthony, A. (1987). *Scale of social development.* Austin, TX: Pro-Ed.

Vinter, R., Sarri, R., Vorwaller, D., & Schaefer, W. (1966). *Pupil behavior inventory.* Ann Arbor, MI: Campus Publishers.

Waksman, S. (1984). *The Portland problem behavior checklist—Revised.* Portland, OR: ASIEP Education Co.

Waksman, S. A. (1984). *Waksman social skills rating scale.* Portland, OR: ASIEP Education Co.

Walker, H. M. (1983). *Walker problem behavior identification checklist—Revised.* Los Angeles: Western Psychological Services.

Walker, H. M., & McConnell, S. (1988). *Walker-McConnell scale of social competence and school adjustment.* Austin, TX: Pro-Ed.

Washer, R. W. (1984). *Washer visual acuity screening technique.* Bensenville, IL: Scholastic Testing Service.

Watson, G., & Glaser, E. M. (1980). *Watson-Glaser critical thinking appraisal.* San Antonio, TX: Psychological Corp.

Wechsler, D. (1967). *Wechsler preschool and primary scales of intelligence.* San Antonio, TX: Psychological Corp.

Wechsler, D. (1974). *Wechsler intelligence scale for children—Revised*. San Antonio, TX: Psychological Corp.

Weiner, F. (1979). *Phonological process analysis*. Baltimore: University Park Press.

Weller, C., & Strawser, S. (1981). *Weller-Strawser scales of adaptive behavior: For the learning disabled*. Novato, CA: Academic Therapy Publications.

Wepman, J. M. (1973). *Auditory discrimination test* (rev.). Chicago: Language Research Associates.

Wepman, J. M., Morency, A., & Seidl, M. (1975). *Visual memory test*. Los Angeles: Western Psychological Services.

White, O., Edgar, E., Haring, N., Afflect, J., Hayden, A., & Bendersky, M. (1981). *Uniform assessment system*. San Antonio, TX: Psychological Corp.

Wiederholt, J. L. (1985). *Formal reading inventory*. Austin, TX: Pro-Ed.

Wiederholt, J. L., & Bryant, B. R. (1986). *Gray oral reading tests—Revised*. Austin, TX: Pro-Ed.

Wiederholt, J. L., & Larsen, S. C. (1983). *Test of practical knowledge*. Austin, TX: Pro-Ed.

Wiig, E. H. (1982). *Let's talk inventory for adolescents*. San Antonio, TX: Psychological Corp.

Wiig, E., & Secord, W. (1988). *Test of language competence—Expanded edition*. San Antonio, TX: Psychological Corp.

Williams, M. R., & Somerwill, H. (1982). *Early mathematical language*. Hampshire, England: Macmillan.

Witkin, H. A. (1971). *Embedded figures test*. Palo Alto, CA: Consulting Psychologists Press.

Witt, J. C., Elliott, S. N., Gresham, F. M., & Kramer, J. J. (1988). *Assessment of special children*. Boston: Scott, Foresman/Little Brown.

Wood, F. H., Johnson, J. L., & Jenkins, J. R. (1986). The Lora case: Nonbiased referral, assessment, and placement procedures. *Exceptional Children, 52*, 323-331.

Wood, J. W., & Miederhoff, J. W. (1988). Bridging the gap. *Teaching Exceptional Children, 21*(2), 66-70.

Woodcock, R. W., (1980). *Woodcock language proficiency battery*. Allen, TX: DLM Teaching Resources.

Woodcock, R. W., (1982) (Spanish version). *Woodcock language proficiency battery*. Allen, TX: DLM Teaching Resources.

Woodcock, R. W. (1987). *Woodcock reading mastery tests—Revised*. Circle Pines, MN: American Guidance Service.

Woodcock, R. W., & Johnson, M. B. (1977). *Woodcock-Johnson psycho-educational battery*. Allen, TX: DLM Teaching Resources.

Woods, M. L., & Moe, A. J. (1989). *Analytic reading inventory* (2nd ed.). San Antonio, TX: Psychological Corp.

Young, E. C., & Perachio, J. J. (1983). *The patterned elicitation syntax test*. Tucson, AZ: Communication Skill Builders.

Zehrback, R. R. (1987). *Comprehensive identification process*. Bensenville, IL: Scholastic Testing Service.

Zeitlin, S. (1988). *Coping inventory*. Bensenville, IL: Scholastic Testing Service.

Zimmerman, I., Steiner, V., & Pond, R. (1979). *Preschool language scale*. San Antonio, TX: Psychological Corp.

Zweig, R. (1971). *Fountain Valley teacher support system in reading*. Huntington Beach, CA: Richard Zweig Associates.

Appendix A:
Rules and Regulations Regarding
Least Restrictive Environment,
Public Law 94-142

T he regulations below are highly important in that they must be considered, along with assessment results, in determining educational interventions and placements.

General

Each public agency shall insure:

That to the maximum extent appropriate, handicapped children, including children in public or private institutions or other care facilities, are educated with children who are not handicapped, and

That special classes, separate schooling or other removal of handicapped children from the regular educational environment occurs only when the nature or severity of the handicap is such that education in regular classes with the use of supplementary aids and services cannot be achieved satisfactorily.

From *Federal Register,* 1977, 42(163), p. 42497.

Continuum of alternative placements

Each public agency shall insure that a continuum of alternative placements is available to meet the needs of handicapped children for special education and related services.

The continuum required under the first paragraph of this section must:

(1) Include the alternative placements listed in the definition of special education (instruction in regular classes, special classes, special schools, home instruction, and instruction in hospitals and institutions), and

(2) Make provision for supplementary services (such as resource room or itinerant instruction) to be provided in conjunction with regular class placement.

Placements

Each public agency shall insure that:

(a) Each handicapped child's educational placement

(1) Is determined at least annually.

(2) Is based on his or her individualized education program, and

(3) Is as close as possible to the child's home.

(b) The various alternative placements included are available to the extent necessary to implement the individualized education program for each handicapped child;

(c) Unless a handicapped child's individualized education program requires some other arrangement, the child is educated in the school which he or she would attend if not handicapped; and

(d) In selecting the least restrictive environment, consideration is given to any potential harmful effect on the child or on the quality of services which he or she needs.

Appendix B:
Test Publishers in This Text

Academic Therapy Publications, 20 Commercial Blvd., Novato, CA 94947

Allen House, 1119 W. Bethel Ave., Muncie, IN 47303

Allyn and Bacon, 470 Atlantic Ave., Boston, MA 02210

American Association on Mental Deficiency, 5101 Wisconsin Ave. NW, Washington, D C 20016

American College Testing Program, P.O. Box 168, Iowa City, IA 52240

American Guidance Service, Publishers' Building, P.O. Box 99, Circle Pines, MN 55014

American Orthopsychiatric Association, 1775 Broadway, New York, NY 10019

American Printing House for the Blind, 1839 Frankfort Ave., P.O. Box 6085, Louisville, KY 40206

American Psychological Association, 1200-17th St. NW, Washington, D C 20036

ASIEP Education Co., 3216 N.E. 27th, Portland, OR 97212

Barnell-Loft, Ltd., 958 Church St., Baldwin, NY 11510

Bausch & Lomb, Rochester, NY 14602

Ber-Sil Co., 3412 Seaglen Dr., Rancho Palos Verdes, CA 90274

Campus Publishers, 713 W. Ellsworth Rd., Ann Arbor, MI 48104

Childcraft Education Corp., 20 Kilmer Rd., Edison, NJ 08818

Common Market Press, P.O. Box 45628, Dallas, TX 75245

Communication Skill Builders, 3830 E. Bellevue, P.O. Box 42050-E, Tucson, AZ 85733

Consulting Psychologists Press, 577 College Ave., P.O. Box 11636, Palo Alto, CA 94306

Cooperative Educational Agency, CESA-12, Box 564, Portage, WI 53901
Counselor Recordings and Tests, Box 6184, Acklen Station, Nashville, TN 37212
C.P.S., Box 83, Larchmont, NY 10538
CTB/McGraw-Hill, 2500 Garden Rd., Monterey, CA 93940
Curriculum Associates, 5 Esquire Rd., North Billerica, MA 01862
Denver Developmental Materials, P.O. Box 6919, Denver, CO 80206
Devereux Foundation Press, 19 S. Waterloo Rd., Box 400, Devon, PA 19333
DLM Teaching Resources, P.O. Box 4000, One DLM Park, Allen, TX 75002
Early Education Intervention Systems, Pawtucket, RI 02860
Edmark Associates, P.O. Box 3903, Bellevue, WA 98009
Education Associates, 8 Crab Orchard Rd., P.O. Box Y, Frankfort, KY 40602
Educational and Industrial Testing Service, P.O. Box 7234, San Diego, CA 92107
Educational Services, P.O. Box 1835, Columbia, MO 65205
Educational Testing Service, Rosedale Rd., Princeton, NJ 08541
Educators Publishing Service, 75 Moulton St., Cambridge, MA 02238
Elbern Publications, 3120 Elbern Ave., P.O. Box 09497, Columbus, OH 43209
Evaluation Systems, 640 N. LaSalle St., Suite 698, Chicago, IL 60610
Follett Publishing Co., 1010 W. Washington Blvd., Chicago, IL 60607
Foreworks Publications, Box 9747, North Hollywood, CA 91609
Gallaudet College, Box 114, Washington, D C 20002
Ginn & Co., 191 Spring St., Lexington, MA 02173
Grune & Stratton, 111 Fifth Ave., New York, NY 10003
Hahnemann University, Preventive Intervention Research Center, 1505 Race St.,
    Bellet Bldg., Philadelphia, PA 19102
Harcourt Brace Jovanovich, Orlando, FL 32887
Harper & Row, 10 E. 53rd St., New York, NY 10022
Harvard University Press, 79 Garden St., Cambridge, MA 02138
Hiskey, M. S., 5640 Baldwin, Lincoln, NE 68507
Houghton Mifflin, One Beacon St., Boston, MA 02108
ICD Rehabilitation & Research Center, 340 E. 24th St., New York, NY 10018
Institute for Personality and Ability Testing, 1602 Coronado Dr., P.O. Box 188,
    Champaign, IL 61820
Jastak Associates, 1526 Gilpin Ave., Wilmington, DE 19806
Kaplan School Supply, 1310 Lewisville-Clemmons Rd., Lewisville, NC 27023
Ladoca Publishing Foundation, East 51st Ave. & Lincoln St., Denver, CO 80216
Language Research Associates, 175 E. Delaware Place, Chicago, IL 60611
Learning Concepts, 2501 N. Lamar, Austin, TX 78705
Linguametrics Group, P.O. Box 3495, San Rafael, CA 94912
J. B. Lippincott Co., East Washington Square, Philadelphia, PA 19105
Love Publishing, 1777 S. Bellaire St., Denver, CO 80222
Macmillan Publishing Co., 866 Third Ave., New York, NY 10022
Charles E. Merrill Publishing, 1300 Alum Creek Dr., Columbus, OH 43216

Midwest Publications, P.O. Box 448, Dept. 17, Pacific Grove, CA 93950

Modern Curriculum Press, 13900 Prospect Rd., Cleveland, OH 44136

Modern Education Corp., P.O. Box 721, Tulsa, OK 74101

T. Ernest Newland, 1004 Ross Dr., Champaign, IL 61820

Nisonger Center/Ohio State University, 1580 Cannon Dr., Columbus, OH 43210

Northwestern University Press, 1735 Benson Ave., Evanston, IL 60201

Personnel Press, 20 Nassau St., Princeton, NJ 08540

Prep Inc., 1007 Whitehead Rd., Trenton, NJ 08638

Pro-Ed., 5341 Industrial Oaks Blvd., Austin, TX 78735

Psychological Assessment Resources, P.O. Box 998, Odessa, FL 33556

Psychological Corp., 555 Academic Ct., P.O. Box 839954, San Antonio, TX 78283

Psychological Development Publications, P.O. Box 3198, Aspen, CO 81612

Psychological Test Specialists, Box 9229, Missoula, MT 59807

Psychologists and Educators Press, 211 W. State St., Jacksonville, IL 62650

Riverside Publishing, 8420 Bryn Mawr Ave., Chicago, IL 60631

Scholastic Testing Service, 480 Meyer Rd., P.O. Box 1056, Bensenville, IL 60106

Science Research Associates, 155 N. Wacker Dr., Chicago, IL 60606

Singer Company Career Systems, 80 Commerce Dr., Rochester, NY 14623

Slosson Educational Publications, 140 Pine St., P.O. Box 280, East Aurora, NY 14052

Stoelting Co., 1350 S. Kostner Ave., Chicago, IL 60623

Teachers College Press, 1234 Amsterdam Ave., New York, NY 10027

Teaching Resources Corp., 50 Pond Park Rd., Hingham, MA 02043

United Educational Services, P.O. Box 357, East Aurora, NY 10452

University of Illinois Press, 54 E. Gregory Dr., Box 5081, Station A., Champaign, IL 61820

University of Iowa, Bureau of Educational Research and Service, Iowa City, IA 52242

University of Miami, Box 248074, Coral Gables, FL 33124

University Park Press, 233 E. Redwood St., Baltimore, MD 21202

Valpar Corp., 3801 E. 34th St., Suite 105, Tucson, AZ 85713

Vocational Research Institute, 2100-12 Arch St., 6th Floor, Philadelphia, PA 19103

VORT Corporation, P.O. Box 60880, Palo Alto, CA 94306

Western Psychological Services, 12031 Wilshire Blvd., Los Angeles, CA 90025

Wm. C. Brown Publishers, 2460 Kerper Blvd., Dubuque, IA 92001

Zaner-Bloser, 2300 W. Fifth Ave., P.O. Box 16764, Columbus, OH 43216

Richard L. Zweig Associates, 20800 Beach Blvd., Huntington Beach, CA 92648

Test Index

A

AAMD Adaptive Behavior Scale—School Edition, 76-77

Adaptive Behavior Inventory, 78

Adaptive Behavior Inventory for Children, 78

Adaptive Behavior Scale for Infants and Early Childhood, 108

Adjective Check List, 179

Adolescent Language Screening Test, 161

Adston Mathematics Skill Series: Common Fractions, 151

Adston Mathematics Skill Series: Decimal Numbers, 151

Adston Mathematics Skill Series: Readiness for Operations, 151

Adston Mathematiccs Skill Series: Working With Whole Numbers, 151

Advanced Reading Inventory, 138

American School Achievement Test, 129

Analysis of Coping Style, 179-180

Analytic Learning Disability Assessment, 226

Analytic Reading Inventory, 138

APGAR Rating Scale, 108

Arizona Basic and Assessment Utilization System for Young Handicapped Children, 115

Assessing Linguistic Behaviors, 108

Assessment of Children's Language Comprehension, 161-162

Auditory Discrimination Test—Revised, 162

Auditory Pointing Test, 162

Autism Screening Instrument for Educational Planning, 180

Autistic Behavior Composite Checklist and Profile, 180

B

Bader Language and Reading Inventory, 138-139

Bankson Language Screening Test, 162

Barber Scales of Self-Regard for Preschool Children, 115

Basic Achievement Skills Individual Screener, 133-134

Basic School Skills Inventory—Diagnostic, 115

Basic School Skills Inventory—Screen, 116

Battelle Developmental Inventory, 108

Battelle Developmental Inventory Screening Test, 109

Bayley Scales of Infant Development, 109

Behavior Dimension Rating Scale, 181

Behavior Evaluation Scale, 181

Behavior Problem Checklist—Revised, 181

Behavior Rating Profile, 181

Behavioral Academic Self-Esteem, 180-181

Bender Visual Motor Gestalt Test, 199

Bennett Mechanical Comprehension Test, 206-207

Boder Test of Reading-Spelling Patterns, 139

Boehm Test of Basic Concepts—Preschool, 116

Boehm Test of Basic Concepts—Revised, 163

Botel Reading Inventory, 139

Bracken Basic Concept Scale, 116

Brigance Diagnostic Comprehensive Inventory of Basic Skills, 139-140

Brigance Diagnostic Inventory of Basic Skills, 140

Brigance Diagnostic Inventory of Early Development, 109

Brigance Diagnostic Inventory of Essential Skills, 212

Bruininks—Oseretsky Test of Motor Proficiency, 203

Burks' Behavior Rating Scales, 182

C

California Achievement Tests, 129

California Child Q-Sort Set, 182

California Psychological Inventory—Revised, 182

Carolina Developmental Profile, 116-117

Carolina Picture Vocabulary Test, 226

Carrow Elicited Language Inventory, 163

Cattell Infant Intelligence Scale, 109

Child Behavior Checklist for Ages 2-3, 109-110

Child Behavior Checklist for Ages 4-16, 182

Child Behavior Rating Scale, 183

Children's Adaptive Behavior Scale, 78-79

Children's Apperception Test, 183

Children's Depression Scale, 183

Children's Personality Questionnaire, 183

CID Preschool Performance Scale, 117

Clark-Madison Test of Oral Language, 163-164

Classroom Environment Scale, 183-184

Classroom Learning Screening Manual, 152

Classroom Reading Inventory, 141

Clinical Evaluation of Language Functions: Diagnostic Battery, 164

Cloze Procedure, 141

Cognitive Abilities Scale, 110

Columbia Mental Maturity Scale, 72

Comprehensive Behavior Rating Scale for Children, 184

Comprehensive Identification Process, 117

Comprehensive Screening Tool for Determining Optimal Communication Mode, 164

Comprehensive Test of Adaptive Behavior, 79

Comprehensive Tests of Basic Skills, 129

Conner's Teacher Rating Scale, 184

Coopersmith Self-Esteem Inventories, 184

Coping Inventory, 184

Cornell Critical Thinking Tests, 221

Crawford Small Parts Dexterity Test, 207

Creative Reasoning Test, 221

Creativity Tests For Children, 222

Criterion Test of Basic Skills, 152

Critical Events Checklist, 99-102

D

Del Rio Language Screening Test, 118

Denver Developmental Screening Test—Revised, 110

Detroit Tests of Learning Aptitude—Primary, 118

Detroit Tests of Learning Aptitude 2, 72-73

Developmental Activities Screening Inventory—Revised, 110

Developmental Indicators for the Assessment of Learning—Revised, 118

Developmental Profile II, 110

Developmental Test of Visual Motor Integration, 199

Developmental Test of Visual Perception, 199-200

Devereux Adolescent Behavior Rating Scale, 185

Devereux Child Behavior Rating Scale, 185

Devereux Elementary School Behavior Rating Scale, 185

Diagnosis: An Instructional Aid, 141

Diagnostic Achievement Battery, 134

Diagnostic Achievement Test for Adolescents, 134

Diagnostic Mathematics Inventory, 153

Diagnostic Reading Scales—Revised, 142

Diagnostic Screening Test: Math, 153

Diagnostic Screening Test: Spelling, 164

Diagnostic Spelling Potential Test, 165

Diagnostic Test of Arithmetic Strategies, 153
Diagnostic Tests and Self-Helps in Arithmetic, 153
Differential Ability Scales, 73
Differential Aptitude Tests, 207
Direct Observation Form—Revised Edition, 185
DMI Mathematics System, 153-154
Doren Diagnostic Test of Word Recognition, 142
Dos Amigos Verbal Language Scales, 165
Durrell Analysis of Reading Difficulty, 142
Dvorine Color Vision Test, 226
Dyadic Adjustment Scale, 102
Dyadic Parent-Child Interaction Coding System, 102

E
Early Intervention Developmental Profile, 110-111
Early Language Milestone Scale, 111
Early Learning Accomplishment Profile, 111
Early Mathematical Language, 154
Early Screening Inventory, 119
Educational Development Series, 129
Ekwall Reading Inventory, 142-143
Embedded Figures Test, 185-186
Enright Diagnostic Inventory of Basic Arithmetic Skills, 154
Estes Attitude Scales, 186
Evaluating Acquired Skills in Communication, 165
Evaluating Communicative Competence, 165
Evaluation and Programming System for Infants and Young Children, 119
Examining for Aphasia, 166
Expressive One-Word Picture Vocabulary Test, 166

F
Family Adjustment Survey, 102
Family Information Preferences Inventory, 102-103
Family Needs Survey, 103
Family Resource Scale, 103
Family Roles Scale, 103
Formal Reading Inventory, 143
Fountain Valley Teachers Support System in Mathematics, 154

Fountain Valley Teachers Support System in Reading, 143
Frostig Developmental Test of Visual Perception, 199-200
Fundamental Processes in Arithmetic, 154

G
Gates-MacGinitie Reading Tests, 143
Gates-McKillop-Horowitz Reading Diagnostic Tests, 143-144
General Aptitude Test Battery, 207
Gilmore Oral Reading Test, 144
Goldman-Fristoe Test of Articulation, 166
Goldman-Fristoe-Woodcock Test of Auditory Discrimination, 200
Goodman Lock Box, 119
Gordon Occupational Check List II, 209
Gray Oral Reading Test—Revised, 144

H
Hahnemann Elementary School Behavior Rating Scale, 186
Hahnemann High School Behavior Rating Scale, 186
Hall Occupational Orientation Inventory, 209
Hawaii Early Learning Profile, 111
Hiskey-Nebraska Test of Learning Aptitude, 73
Home Observation for the Measurement of Environment, 103
Home Quality Rating Scale, 104
Hudson Educational Skills Inventory, 155

I
Illinois Test of Psycholinguistic Abilities, 120
Index of Personality Characteristics, 186-187
Individualized Criterion Referenced Testing—Mathematics, 155
Inferred Self-Concept Scale, 187
Informal Reading Assessment, 144
Informal Writing Inventory, 166
Iowa Tests of Basic Skills, 129
Iowa Tests of Educational Development, 129

J
Jesness Behavior Check List, 187
Jesness Inventory of Adolescent Personality, 187

JEVS Work Sample Evaluation System, 214
Joliet 3-Minute Speech and Language Screen, 167
Jordan Left-Right Reversal Test—Revised, 200

K
Kaufman Assessment Battery for Children, 69-71, 130
Kaufman Test of Educational Achievement, 130-131
Key Math—Revised, 155
Kindergarten Language Screening Test, 167
Kohn Problem Checklist, 187
Kohn Social Competence Scale, 188
Kuder General Interest Survey, 210

L
Language Inventory for Teachers, 167
Language Proficiency Test, 167
Leadership Skills Inventory, 188
Learning Accomplishment Profile— Revised, 120
Leiter International Performance Scale, 73-74
Let's Talk Inventory for Adolescents, 167
Let's Talk Inventory for Children, 167
Life Orientation Inventory, 188

M
Martinek-Zaichkowsky Self-Concept Scale for Children, 188
Maternal Behavior Rating Scale, 104
McCarthy Scales of Children's Abilities, 74
McCarthy Screening Test, 120-121
McCullough Word Analysis Tests, 144
McDermott Multidimensional Assessment of Children, 224-225
Meadow-Kendall Social-Emotional Assessment Inventory for Deaf and Hearing Impaired Students, 226-227
Memory for Designs Test, 200
Merrill Language Screening Test, 168
Metropolitan Achievement Tests, 129
Milani-Comparetti Developmental Scale, 111
Miller Assessment for Preschoolers, 121
Miller-Yoder Language Comprehension Test, 168
Minnesota Child Development Inventory, 111

Minnesota Clerical Test—Revised, 207-208
Minnesota Multiphasic Personality Inventory, 12
Minnesota Rate of Manipulation Test, 208
Minnesota Spatial Relations Test, 200
Mooney Problem Check Lists, 189
Motor-Free Visual Perception Test, 200-201
Multilevel Academic Skills Inventory: Reading Program, 145
Multilevel Academic Skills Inventory: Math Program, 156
Multilevel Academic Survey Test, 145

N
Neonatal Behavior Assessment Scale, 112
New Sucher-Allred Reading Placement Inventory, 145
Normative Adaptive Behavior Checklist, 79
Northwestern Syntax Screening Test, 12

O
Oasis Aptitude Survey, 208
Oasis Interest Schedule, 210

P
Parent as a Teacher Inventory, 104
Parent Behavior Progression, 104
Parent/Caregiver Involvement Scale, 104-105
Parenting Stress Index, 105
Patterned Elicitation Syntax Test, 169
Peabody Developmental Motor Scales, 112
Peabody Individual Achievement Test— Revised, 131-132
Peabody Mathematics Readiness Test, 156
Peabody Picture Vocabulary Test— Revised, 121
Peer Acceptance Scale, 189
Peer Attitudes Toward the Handicapped Scale, 227
Pennsylvania Bi-Manual Work Sample, 208
Perfil de Evaluacion del Comportamiento, 189
Phonological Process Analysis, 169
Picture Story Language Test, 169
Piers-Harris Children's Self-Concept Scale, 190

Portland Problem Behavior Checklist—
Revised, 190
Porch Index of Communicative Ability,
169
Porch Index of Communicative Ability in
Children, 170
Portage Guide to Early Education, 112
Pragmatics Screening Test, 170
Preschool Attainment Record, 112
Preschool Language Scale, 112
Prescriptive Reading Inventory, 146
Preverbal Assessment Intervention Profile,
170
Primary Visual Motor Test, 201
Process for the Assessment of Effective
Student Functioning, 190
Progress Tests in Maths, 156
Pupil Behavior Inventory, 190
Pupil Behavior Rating Scale, 190-191
Pupil Behavior Rating Scale—Revised:
Screening for Learning Disabilities, 191
Purdue Perceptual-Motor Survey, 201
Pyramid Scales, 80

Q
Questionnaire on Resources and Stress,
105
Quick Neurological Screening Test, 201

R
Raven Progressive Matrices, 74
Reading Comprehension Inventory, 146
Reading-Free Vocational Interest
Inventory—Revised, 210
Reading Miscue Analysis, 146
Receptive-Expressive Emergent
Language Scale, 113
Receptive One-Word Picture Vocabulary
Test, 170
Regional Resource Center Diagnostic Math
Inventories, 156-157
Regional Resource Center Diagnostic
Reading Inventory, 146
Revised Gesell Developmental Schedules,
113
Rhode Island Test of Language Structure,
170-171
Rockford Infant Developmental
Evaluation Scales, 113

S
Scale of Social Development, 113

Scales of Independent Behavior, 79
Scales of Socio-Emotional Development,
113
SCAN: Screening Test for Auditory
Processing Disorders, 171
School Behavior Checklist, 191
School Readiness Test, 122
Screening Assessment for Gifted
Elementary Children, 222-223
Screening Children for Related Early
Educational Needs, 123
Screening Test for Auditory Perception,
202
Screening Test for Auditory Processing
Disorders, 171
Screening Test of Adolescent Language,
171
Screen Kit of Language Development, 122
Self-Description Questionnaire, 191
Self Directed Search, 210-211
Sensory Integration and Praxis Tests, 202
Sequenced Inventory of Communication
Development—Revised, 114
Sequential Assessment of Mathematics
Inventory, 157
Sequential Tests of Educational Progress,
129
Singer Vocational Evaluation System, 214
Slingerland Screening Tests for Identifying
Children with Specific Language
Disability, 227
Slosson Intelligence Test, 74-75
Slosson Oral Reading Test, 146-147
Snellen Eye Chart, 196-197
Social and Prevocational Information
Battery—Revised, 213
Social-Emotional Dimension Scale, 191
Social Interaction Assessment/
Intervention, 105-106
Spadafore Diagnostic Reading Test, 147
Spellmaster Assessment and Teaching
System, 171
SRA Achievement Series, 129
Stanford Achievement Test Series, 129
Stanford-Binet Intelligence Scale, 64-67
Stanford Diagnostic Reading Test—Third
Edition, 147
Stanford Diagnostic Mathematics Test, 157
Streenburgen Diagnostic-Prescriptive
Math Program and Quick Math
Screening Test, 157
Strong-Campbell Interest Inventory, 211

Strong Interest Inventory, 211
Study of Children's Learning Styles: Research Edition, 227-228
System of Multicultural Pluralistic Assessment, 228

T
Teacher's Report Form, 192
Teaching Skills Inventory, 106
Temple University Short Syntax Inventory, 171-172
Tennessee Self-Concept Scale, 192
Test for Auditory Comprehension of Language—Revised, 172
Test of Academic Progress, 134-135
Test of Adolescent Language—2, 172
Test of Articulation Performance—Diagnostic, 172
Test of Articulation Performance—Screen, 172
Test of Computational Processes, 158
Test of Early Language Development, 123
Test of Early Mathematics Ability, 123
Test of Early Reading Ability, 124
Test of Early Socioemotional Development, 124
Test of Early Written Language, 124
Test of Language Competence—Expanded Edition, 173
Test of Language Development—2 Primary, 124
Test of Language Development—2 Intermediate, 173
Test of Legible Handwriting, 173
Test of Mathematical Abilities, 158
Test of Motor Impairment, 203
Test of Nonverbal Intelligence, 75
Test of Practical Knowledge, 213
Test of Pragmatic Skills, 173-174
Test of Reading Comprehension, 147
Test of Relational Concepts, 124-125
Test of Written English, 174
Test of Written Language—2, 174
Test of Written Spelling—2, 174
Test for Everyday Living, 213
The Pyramid Scales, 80
Thematic Apperception Test, 192
Thinking Creatively in Action and Movement, 223
Torrance Tests of Creative Thinking, 223
Transition Checklist, 225
Tree/Bee Test of Auditory Discrimination, 174

U
Uniform Performance Assessment System, 114
Utah Test of Language Development, 175
Uzgiris-Hunt Ordinal Scales of Psychological Development, 114

V
Vineland Adaptive Behavior Scales, 80
Visual Aural Digit Span Test, 202-203
Visual Memory Test, 203

W
Waksman Social Skills Rating Scale, 192-193
Walker-McConnell Scale of Social Competence and Social Adjustment, 193
Walker Problem Behavior Identification Checklist, 193
Washer Visual Acuity Screening Technique, 197-198
Watson-Glaser Critical Thinking Appraisal, 223-224
Wechsler Adult Intelligence Scale—Revised, 67
Wechsler Intelligence Scale for Children—Revised, 67-69
Wechsler Preschool and Primary Scale of Intelligence, 67, 125
Weller-Strawser Scales of Adaptive Behavior, 80
Wide Range Achievement Test—Revised, 133
Wide Range Employability Sample Test, 215
Wide Range Interest-Opinion Test, 211
Wisconsin Design for Math Skill Development, 158
Wisconsin Tests of Reading Skill Development, 148
Woodcock-Johnson Psychoeducational Battery—Revised, 71-72, 132
Woodcock Language Proficiency Battery, 175
Woodcock Reading Mastery Tests—Revised, 148
Writing Proficiency Program, 175

Y
Your Style of Learning and Thinking, 15

Subject Index

A

AAMD (now AAMR), 15, 63
Academic achievement tests, 127-130
Acculturation, 56
Adaptive behavior, 75-76
Advocacy groups, influence in assessment, 14, 15
American Association on Mental Deficiency (Retardation), 15, 63
American Educational Research Association, 19, 50
American Psychological Association, 15, 19, 50
"Anglocentric" bias in tests, 51-52
Annual goals (in IEP), 47
Assessment
    auditory abilities, 196-198
    criterion referenced, 7
    cultural diversity in, 51
    definition of, 3
    diagnostic, 5
    early childhood, 95-98
    ecological, 7
    ethical principles in, 50-51
    factors influencing, 11-15
    family, 97-98
    formative, 5-6
    norm-referenced, 6-7
    purposes of, 5-6
    readiness-related, 5
    reports, 229
    sequence of, 12-13
    single purpose, 10
    sociocultural factors in, 54-57
    summative, 6
    types of, 4-5
    visual abilities, 196-198
Assessment process, chart of, 42-43
Audiogram, 197
Auditory abilities, assessment of, 196

B

Behavior problems, 177-178
Behavioral theories, 95
Bias in assessment, 51-52

C

Career development, 205
Career Education Incentive Act of 1977 (PL 95-207), 205
Central tendency, measures of, 24
Checklists, 86-87
Chronolog, 85
Cognitive ability, 63, 64
Cognitive learning styles, 56-57
Communication, definition and nature of, 159-160
Composition, categories of, 161
Computational skills, 150
Computer applications in assessment, 224

Correlation, 31-32
Council for Exceptional Children, 15
Creativity, 219-221
Criterion-referenced assessment, 7-8
Cultural background, influence on test results, 55
Cultural diversity, relation to assessment, 51-54
Curriculum-based assessment, 82-84

D
Daily living skills, 211-212
Deciles, 28-29
Diagnostic assessment, 5
Diagnostic probes, 92-93
Diagnostic teaching, 92-93
Direct observation, 84-85
Distance vision, 197

E
Early childhood assessment, 95-98
Ecological assessment, 7
Error analysis, 87-88
Ethical principles, in assessment, 50-51
Experiential background, influence on assessment, 55-56

F
Factors influencing assessment, 11-15
    chart of, 14
Family assessment, 97-98
Formative assessment, 5-6
Frequency recording, 85

G
Giftedness, 219-221
Grade equivalent, 32-33

H
Head Start programs, 95-96

I
IEP, 46-48
    format of, 46
    table of components, 47
Individualized Educational Program (see IEP)
Individualized Family Service Plan, 100
Informal assessment, 81-93
Informal observation, in evaluation of behavior, 178-179

Intelligence, 63, 64
Interest inventories, 208-209
Interval scales, 22
Interviews, 90-91
Inventories, 91-92, 208-209
Item analysis, 29

L
Linguistic background, influence on assessment results, 55
Litigation, influence on assessment, 60
Lora vs Board of Education of City of New York, 52-53

M
Mathematics, scope of, 149-150
Maturationist theories, 95
Mean, 24
Measurement scales, 21-23
Median, 24
Mental retardation, 63
Mode, 24
Modifying assessment techniques, 92
Morphemes, 160
Motivation, influence of, 59
Multidisciplinary team meeting, 44-46

N
National Council on Measurement in Education, 19, 50
Near-point vision, 197
Nominal scales, 21
Normal curve, 23-24
Normal distribution, comparative chart, 27
Norm-referenced assessment, 6-7, 8

O
Ordinal scales, 21

P
Parameters, 30
Parent permission, for assessment, 40-41
Percentiles, 26-28
Perceptual abilities, 195, 198
Perceptual-motor skills, 198
Phonology, 160
Planned reassessment, 48
Population, 30
Practice effect, 58
Pragmatics, 160

Prereferral intervention, 38
PL 94-142, 4, 11, 13, 16-17, 45, 46, 51, 53,
    63, 96
PL 95-207, 205
PL 99-457, 96, 97, 98-99

Q
Qualifications, of assessment personnel,
    57
Quantitative language, 150
Quartiles, 28-29
Questionnaires, 91

R
Ratio scales, 23
Reading assessment, 137-138
Reading, definition of, 137
Reassessment, 48
Referral for assessment, 39-40
Release of assessment data, 51
Reliability, 34
Reporting assessment results, 229-231

S
Sampling, 30
Screening procedures,
    general, 40
    in early childhood, 106-107
Semantics, 160
Sequence sample, 85
Significance (of a statistic), 30-31
Speech, definition of, 159
Social skills, 211-212
Sociocultural factors, 54-57
Sociolinguistic development, 56
Standard deviation, 25-26
Standard error of the difference, 35-36
Standard error of measurement, 35
Standard scores, 26
Standards for Educational and
    Psychological Testing, 19
Stanines, 29
Statistical significance, 30-31
Summative assessment, 6
Syntax, 160
Systematic observation, 84-85

T
Talent, 219-221
Task analysis, 89
Test anxiety, 58

Tests, definition of, 19-20
Trait sample, 86
Transition assessment, 225
Transition, education for, 205-206

V
Validity, 33-34
    concurrent, 34
    construct, 34
    content, 33
    predictive, 33-34
Variability, measures of, 25-29
Visual abilities, assessment of, 196-198
Vocational aptitude, 206

W
Work sample analysis, 90
Work samples, 213-214
    informal assessment of, 215-217